GREAT QUOTATIONS
OF THE
TWENTIETH CENTURY

RICHARD BEWES

CHRISTIAN FOCUS

ISBN 1 85792 536 X

Published in 1999 by
Christian Focus Publications,
Geanies House, Fearn, Ross-shire,
IV20 1TW, Great Britain.

Cover design by Owen Daily

GREAT QUOTATIONS
OF THE
TWENTIETH CENTURY

Contents

Foreword

What on earth have Marilyn Monroe, Mahatma Gandhi, Billy Graham, Bob Geldof, and eight other notables of the 20th century got in common? Answer: they all uttered memorable epigrams which Richard Bewes has picked up and explored in this remarkable book.

He has a profound knowledge of Scripture, a close understanding of the contemporary world, and an uncanny knack of finding points of contact between the two.

Richard Bewes and I have been friends, neighbours and colleagues for many years. So I know that *Great Quotations* is an expression of his personal integrity. I warmly recommend it to anybody who wants to probe the basic issues of life. It is well conceived, well researched and well written. Readers will find in it, as I have done, a rich blend of insight, sanity, wisdom and humour, with Jesus Christ himself always at the centre.

JOHN STOTT
September 1999

Introduction

It was my colleague Richard Trist of Melbourne who suggested the idea for this book, and I am grateful for his encouragement. Naturally there are many books of famous quotations. The idea within these pages was that of selecting a twentieth century quotation that as many people as possible would recognise, and then – without doing an injustice to the source – comment as a Christian and Bible student upon it.

We are privileged to be alive at this time of transition from one millennium to another. The exercise of looking back a little should help us to prepare for what the future will bring us. And history helps. As my saintly mother said to me long ago in a letter, 'You simply cannot be educated unless you know some history.'

I dedicate this book to the two world public figures, man and woman, whom I consider to be the twentieth century's greatest inspirers of all – Billy and Ruth Graham of Montreat, North Carolina.

RICHARD BEWES
All Souls Church,
Langham Place,
London

1

**'Yes, lady, God himself
could not sink this ship'**

(Southampton, April 10th, 1912)

The Rev. J. Stuart Holden, thirty-eight years of age, faced a problem as he woke at his London vicarage on Tuesday, April 9th, 1912. *To sail or not to sail?* A celebrated preacher in his own Anglican church of St. Paul's Portman Square, he was in wide demand as a speaker at events such as the famed Keswick Convention in the North of England. His speaking trips had taken him across the Atlantic no less than thirty-five times, and he was about to embark on a thirty-sixth.

He was alone in the house. Unexpectedly his wife had been taken into hospital, and was facing an operation. Once more, Stuart gazed at the ticket that was staring up at him. It read:

Rev. J. Stuart Holden

WHITE STAR LINE

YOUR ATTENTION IS SPECIALLY DRAWN TO THE CONDITIONS OF TRANSPORTATION IN THE ENCLOSED CONTRACT. THE COMPANY'S LIABILITY FOR BAGGAGE IS STRICTLY LIMITED, BUT PASSENGERS CAN PROTECT THEMSELVES BY INSURANCE.

First Class Passenger Ticket per Steamship 'Titanic'

SAILING FROM 10/4/1912

There was no question about it, reflected Stuart. With his wife in hospital he would have to cancel his passage and forgo the maiden voyage of the biggest, most glamorous ship ever built. With a sigh he picked up the telephone.

Days later he was reading his own obituary in the press! Guided by the passengers' list, the newspapers had included Stuart Holden's name as among those drowned in the greatest of all sea disasters, the sinking of *The Titanic,* only four days out from Southampton. For the rest of his Christian ministry, Stuart Holden kept his unused ticket framed in his study, as a reminder of his debt to Providence. His church of St. Paul's Portman Square, later known as St. Paul's Robert Adam Street, was to become sister to our own church of All Souls, Langham Place, within a single united parish.

Yes, lady, God himself could not sink this ship.....
It is ironic that these words from one of the deck hands should have been spoken to a Christian missionary, Sylvia Caldwell who, with her husband Albert, was travelling Second Class, having returned from Thailand where the couple had been teaching at the Bangkok Christian College. With their baby boy Albert – who would be wrapped in a blanket on the fateful night of April 15th – they lived to tell the tale, and so provide the world with one of the memorable quotes of the twentieth century.

The stunning tragedy of *The Titanic* signalled an end to the age of unbroken optimism in the Western world, and put up a marker. It posed the question, 'What things can we be sure of in this fragile cockleshell of our existence?' It pressed the issue, 'What things really *matter,* when the stairs under your feet on the grand staircase don't feel quite right, when the deck is beginning to slope at an angle – but not yet to the extent that you could draw attention to it without seeming a little, well, *tactless*?'

The Titanic imprinted itself upon the collective memory

of our whole family – if for no other reason than that my mother at the age of nine, together with her four sisters and her brother, stood at Sea View on the Isle of Wight, watching and waving as the giant liner, eleven stories high and a sixth of a mile long came gliding past them, never to be seen again. They never forgot that first and last sight.

I know all the stories and the quotes backwards.

From the bridge – *'What do you see?'* – *'Iceberg right ahead!'* The calm acknowledgement – *'Thank you!'* The flimsy reassurances – *'There's talk of an iceberg, Ma'am.'* The banalities – *'There is your beautiful nightdress gone.'*

The lifeboats and deckchairs; the fate of Lady Astor's jewels (and fifteen hundred missing persons); the band on deck playing ragtime, and then *Nearer My God to Thee* as the great ship began its two-mile slide down – *The Titanic* was to become a universal symbol of the twentieth century's loss of confidence in safe, copper-bottomed values and institutions, and in our human capacity to govern our destinies.

When the crystal chandeliers are hanging at a tilt, when they're winching down the lifeboats – but only enough for half the passengers – what *matters* at that moment more than anything else in the world? What counts as a valuable to be salvaged? Plenty of incidents in the early hours of April 15th illustrated the age-old principle expressed in the challenge of Christ: **What good is it for a man to gain the whole world, yet forfeit his soul? Or what can a man give in exchange for his soul?** (Mark 8:36,37).

A crisis, whether on *The Titanic* or not, is enough to highlight the issue, and turn our distorted human values on their heads. A chemist from Toronto, Major Arthur Peuchen, paused in his first-class cabin as he wondered what to take with him from the stricken liner. Eventually he left behind a tin box containing $200,000 in bonds and $100,000 in preferred stock – and stepped out onto the freezing deck clutching just three oranges.

There's Second Class passenger Stuart Collett, a young theological student, leaving everything behind except the Bible he had promised his brother he would always carry until they met again. Like Peuchen, he survived.

Everything is topsy-turvy in a crisis. Your sense of time gets skewed, for one thing. It becomes stretched – from the moment of the unwelcome phone call at 6.00 am onwards. Later in the day you think it's 4.00 pm and are amazed to discover that it's only 11 o'clock in the morning. Reactions vary too, as they did on *The Titanic.* 'At 12.15 it was hard to know whether to joke or be serious – whether to chop down a door and be a hero, or chop it down and get arrested.'[1]

'Man, are you saved?' asked the Glasgow preacher, John Harper, of a fellow Scot as they both struggled in the sub-zero water, holding onto pieces of wreck.

'No, I am not,' came the reply.

'Believe on the Lord Jesus Christ and you will be saved!' urged Harper.

The waves took the preacher away, but a little later he was washed back alongside his companion.

'Are you saved now?' he persisted.

'No, I cannot honestly say that I am.'

Once more Harper repeated the Scripture sentence,

---

1. Walter Lord, *A Night to Remember,* Corgi Books.

'Believe on the Lord Jesus Christ, and you will be saved'. Then, losing his hold, he sank.

As the young Scot later told a meeting in Hamilton, Canada, 'And there, alone in the night, and with two miles of water under me, I believed. *I am John Harper's last convert.*'

The 'John Harper Memorial Church' can be visited in Glasgow today; there is also a memorial at the Moody Church in Chicago, in commemoration of an outstanding ambassador of the Christian Gospel.

What good is it for a man to gain the whole world, yet forfeit his soul? Or what can a man give in exchange for his soul? As Jesus spoke these words to the crowd around him, he was drawing a contrast between two things. Not, as we might suppose, between the present and the future. He was not asking what good it would be for someone to gain the present and lose the future. Certainly, the person who gains the fleeting present and loses the eternal future has made a bad bargain, but that is not the contrast implied here. Actually the New Testament never teaches that if we lose our soul we shall even gain the fleeting present. Certainly we would lose the future, but Christ never suggested for a moment that we would gain even the present by making it the focus of our ambitions.

At the same time, the people who save their life for all eternity don't lose the *present!* On the basis of Jesus' teaching, the eternal future is gained, but they also gain the best in this *present* life too. Such is the teaching of the Scriptures.

But just supposing that I, as a Christian, was wrong,

and that my materialist critic was right? That there was no spiritual dimension, no God, no Christ, no soul that needed saving, no settling up at the end. *Just supposing?*

In such a case I must still maintain that I end up with the advantage. I put this once to a London cab driver as he took me to a wedding.

'I feel so sorry for people like you,' he had announced over his shoulder. 'There you are with your Bibles and your churches, and looking forward to some comfort and reward at the end of all your effort – only to get there and find that there was nothing there at all!' He began to shake with laughter.

I laughed too. But then I turned the tables on my unbelieving chauffeur.

'But just supposing you are right and that I'm deluded,' I countered. 'Even then I end up ahead of you! Here I am, convinced – in my delusion – that life isn't the product of chance; believing – in my delusion – that I'm here for a purpose and that a man called Jesus has overcome evil and death and has forgiven me my sins and given me eternal life and an underlying confidence! *And then,* if you as a materialist are right, I finally die and go out like a light – and don't even have the disappointment of knowing that I was deluded!

'But what about *you?*' I continued. 'If I'm right and *you* are wrong, without question you're the loser! There you are, living off your own batteries, trying to make sense of this short life, staving off ill health as best you can and keeping as cheerful as possible, until your energies fade and you die. And then you are in for the most appalling shock – when you will be confronted by the very person you've ignored all your life, and are made to realise that everything you lived for ended in waste and total loss. Just supposing such things can be enough to turn someone's thinking around.' We parted friends, as I got off the taxi for the wedding.

We don't have to stay in a *just suppose* mind-set, however. There is enough solid data in the life, deeds, teaching and claims of Jesus Christ to have created the biggest family of faith that the world has ever seen. It is to be found on every continent; in every country, from Iceland to Antarctica, from Fiji in the Pacific to the Greenwich Meridian Line in London. It is, actually, the only truly *world* faith that there has ever been. Every day some 100,000 new believers are added. Every week some sixteen or seventeen hundred new congregations come into being, that were not in existence previously. All told, there are around two billion people who, in one way or another, come at least nominally under the banner of Jesus Christ. In addition there must be many more secret believers and underground fellowships in countries where Christian belief and practice are firmly banned.

It takes the prospect of martyrdom, or a crisis like *The Titanic,* to bring the issue of life and eternity – and of our human response to Christ's claims – into clear focus. But, emphatically, it is not the future and the present that are in contrast. According to the teaching of Christ in Mark 8:36,37, the contrast is between *the World* and *the Soul.*

The World! The tangible, material world and all it contains; wealth, success, power, gadgets, pleasure, educational advancement, business promotion, reputation – everything, in fact, that appeals to the senses; the things we eat, see, do, possess and experience.

There is nothing intrinsically wrong in those things by

themselves, unless – by riveting our main attention upon *them,* we lose sight of what Jesus says outweighs everything else, namely, *the soul.* The soul! The real, irreplaceable *You* that thinks, plans, decides, wills, weeps, dreams and worships. Which is the more important – the world or the soul? It's quite clear that the greatest Teacher of all time regards the *soul* – our basic person and character – the true and unique personality that each of us comprise – as of far more worth than any accumulation of material gain or fleeting sensual experiences.

Wealth meant so little on that freezing April night in the Atlantic. Much might have been made, at other times, of wealthy John Jacob Astor, and Mrs. Astor's lost jewellery; or of Mrs. Widener's pearls; or of the Ryerson family on board *The Titanic,* with their sixteen trunks all floating in the ship's hold; of the valets, nurses, governesses and paid companions – all there to make life easier for someone. But not on that night! There is nothing like the prospect of a ship going down within the hour to concentrate the mind on what is really important.

True, you could still have had quite a good time, and even a little fun, in that short hour, if you chose to ignore the impending disaster. You could break off a piece of iceberg for your highball, or turn up the ragtime, louder....faster....

'Everyone who is in Third Class, you can now go into the First Class section!'

'Drinks? Yeah, they're free from now on!'

'You want to play football in the First Class dining room? Go right ahead; it's okay about the chandeliers!'

But in an hour the ship will be at the bottom of the ocean.

There's something about treating the world as a pleasure cruise that is basically unsatisfying to the human spirit. To side with the *consumers* of society, rather than with the *contributors;* to have joined the good-timers, and to end one's days with a collection of memories only; nothing done of any lasting worth – and with a moral character about the size of a pea-pod – *we were not born for that.*

Many enthusiastic photographers have had the galling experience of taking a series of pictures, and then of attempting to squeeze one more exposure from the allotted thirty-six. And then to try for yet one more – only to realise as the 'film' continues to wind on – that there was no film in the camera at all! All you have had is a series of existential experiences as you have pressed the trigger for picture after picture – and at the end, *nothing to show for it.* This can happen to the irreplaceable apparatus of a person's life. Everything depends upon the value system, upon the response made in life to Christ's good news, upon the character that was in evidence when the moment of truth comes at the end, because character is the only thing you take out with you.

It was with wistfulness that Charles Darwin, the great scientist of the nineteenth century, wrote to an acquaintance, J.D. Hooker, on June 17th, 1868. It appears that in earlier life Darwin had had some connection with the Christian faith, but these ties had become ever looser with the passing years. The letter included this admission:

I am glad you were at *The Messiah.* It is the one thing I should like to hear again. But I dare say I should find my soul too dried up to appreciate it as in olden days. For it is a horrid bore, to feel as I constantly do, that I am a withered leaf, for everything, except science.

Dried up....a horrid bore. Surely we are more valuable than that! The soul....the unique being that every person is – why are we valuable in ourselves?

The Christian answer is twofold. We are valuable first by right of Creation and secondly by right of Redemption. We were *made* in the image of God, then – subsequent to our rebellion against the Creator – we were *bought* by the love of God through the Cross of Jesus Christ. *Who are we?* There are life-changing answers to that question!

The Titanic was a terrible disaster that left its stamp upon the whole of the momentous twentieth century. If it made any kind of a positive impact upon our race, it did, perhaps, help great numbers of men and women to *think:*

If the best piece of technology we had ever come up with is so fragile, what are we all about? What are we here for? What is the matter with us? Where are the things that can last? How can I as an individual survive and live on?

Let's not wait for our own personal crisis to hit before finding answers! Those who survived the ordeal of April 15th, 1912 never forgot it – the muffled thuds, the crashing of those five grand pianos, the tinkle of breaking glass and then the final roar as everything broke loose; the crockery, the fittings, 30,000 eggs, the crystal chandeliers, and myriads of abandoned valuables.

Don't wait for your own crisis. It is the Cross, supremely, that faces us with the definitive crisis and decision of our lives, that challenges us to respond to the Christ who died to win us forgiveness and eternal life. The stark events of our rocking, reeling world come as a reminder of his sobering message: **A man's life, a woman's life, does not consist in the abundance of things that they possess.**

The only thing we are going to take out at the end of our lives is our character. What will have happened to it by then? It is stories of people like Sylvia Caldwell, Stuart Holden and John Harper which can help us to find the answer.

2

'I have in my hand a piece of paper'

(British Prime Minister, Neville Chamberlain, 1938)

'At 2.30 we were again attacked by two submarines; both of them are supposed to be chasing us now. I actually saw the torpedo miss us by inches (the captain said about 10 feet only) – a great red thing splashing through the water. As we watched it, fascinated and horrified, we saw that it had indeed missed us but was aiming straight at a big grey boat behind us in the convoy. Our boat, The Malda, hooted violently, and to our joy and amazement we saw the big grey boat swerve to the side, and the torpedo just miss its bows. Shortly afterwards we just missed a torpedo on our other side.

A few moments later, a violent explosion told us that one of the boats in our convoy was torpedoed – a big oil tanker to our right – with her side ripped right out. She listed right over in the water, and the last we saw of her was a thick cloud of smoke. A destroyer went to her aid and the crew got into their boats safely. We have altered course and are going out west to the Atlantic in the hopes of eluding the submarines.

We are in another, safer, cabin tonight, near the top deck, and everyone is sleeping in their clothes with life-belts at hand. I have packed the rucksack with the kids' shoes and overcoats, and all are wearing identification discs. The men passengers, under Cecil, have organised a special "look-out" watch for submarines all night and all day.

"Kept by the power of God" – that's been my special thought all day – and now I'm going to sleep. Heaps of love darlings; God keep you going too.

Your loving Sylvia'

My mother's letter – written from the Atlantic during World War II – still makes my spine tingle as I read it. I was one of the 'kids', aged four, and 'Cecil' was my missionary father, booked onto the British India Line ship *The Malda*, for another term of missionary service in my country of birth, Kenya, as war broke out. The hazardous journey in the zig-zagging convoy of forty ships left an impression on our family that has stayed with us for life. Hitler was the trouble centre for everything. Only when the voyage was over did we children find the courage to run around, wearing little 'Hitler' masks that we had devised. The associations of that sinister name have remained with me always.

With hindsight it is all too easy to look back and wonder with amazement how civilised governments at that time could contemplate any kind of a deal with a man who came to be recognised by millions as the pariah of the twentieth century. It was British Prime Minister, Neville Chamberlain who, at the time of the 1938 Munich meeting with Hitler and the Italian leader Mussolini, accepted Hitler's word at its face value and achieved a peace accord. It was obtained by part of Czechoslovakia being handed over to the ever-grasping Adolf Hitler. The quote attributed to Chamberlain at that time is, *I trust Adolf Hitler.*

Chamberlain arrived back in London, holding what eventually transpired to be a worthless piece of paper. His return from Munich was hailed with rapture and relief by the crowd that greeted him off the plane. *'I have in my hand a piece of paper!'*, cried Chamberlain as he held up the agreement before the press cameras:

We, the German Führer and Chancellor and the British Prime Minister, have had a further meeting today and are agreed in recognising that the question of Anglo-German relations is of the first importance for the two countries and for Europe.

We regard the agreement signed last night and the Anglo-German Naval Agreement as symbolic of the desire of our two peoples never to go to war with one another again.

We are resolved that the method of consultation shall be the method adopted to deal with any other questions that may concern our two countries; and we are determined to continue our efforts to remove possible sources of difference, and thus to contribute to assure the peace of Europe.

(Signed) *Hitler*
Neville Chamberlain

The euphoria was immense. But before we think too hardly of Neville Chamberlain – a thoroughly honourable man – or of those who applauded him, it is as well to ask how later critics would themselves have reacted to the news of a peace agreement, had they been living in 1938. Might they also have joined in the cheering, or at the very least expressed a sigh of relief – while perhaps sparing a prayer for Czechoslovakia, the victim of the deal?

History has provided us with the advantage of seeing in retrospect what Winston Churchill saw all too clearly at the time, expressed in his own press statement: '*The belief that security can be obtained by throwing a small state to the wolves is a fatal delusion.*' Within three years Churchill had become Britain's wartime Prime Minister.

'To prophesy,' runs the ancient Chinese proverb, 'is extremely difficult – especially in regard to the future.' The twentieth century has borne this out with a vengeance, in the numerous unforeseen crises, conflicts, atrocities and disasters, in which a single misjudgment could catapult whole nations into a nightmare without an obvious end – and, in addition, consign innocent optimists into the future ash-heaps of history's heroic failures.

Back in 1938 and 1939, we would not have wished it on anybody, least of all on the German people themselves, to be partnered with Adolf Hitler in a deathly dance of deception! The banal sentiments of the pathetic Munich document are palpable now for their contentlessness – no one today would have any difficulty in estimating the moral value of a scrap of paper signed by Hitler.

Where did the 'piece of paper' end up? How long did a copy of it stay in Chamberlain's desk drawer? Did he look at it from time to time? What have we to learn from that typed scrap of paper, and Chamberlain's innocent trust?

It is, perhaps, a major lesson of all history, and of life upon a fallen world – that human sin and the presence of evil have to be taken seriously. Repeatedly their power is underestimated by the inadequate and self-deceiving world-views that swirl around our civilisation. Over the centuries there have been philosophers, politicians and reformers alike, who have aspired to believe in human nature and to improve it. But as Bernard Levin once declared in *The Times* (August 16th, 1986), 'Those who plan to sit around until it happens to all mankind had better bring a cushion and a very long book.'

A classic example of stern resolve in the face of weak vacillation is found in Elijah, Israel's outstanding prophet of the ninth century BC. Ahab was the pliable king, and Jezebel his foreign-born Phoenician wife was the subtle influence behind the throne, driving her husband into compromise with the one power that could threaten the peace of the nation. The Canaanites, with their alien worship, were now accommodated within the royal court itself, through 450 of the false prophets of Baal, together with another 400 prophets of Asherah, the mother-goddess of the Canaanite belief-system.

Ahab is all for the quiet life, and is content to ride along with the dangerous arrangement. It is Elijah who stands obstinately against the blasphemous liaison, and provokes the irritation of his king:

> When he saw Elijah, Ahab said to him, 'Is that you, you troubler of Israel?'
>
> 'I have not made trouble for Israel,' Elijah replied. 'But you and your father's family have. You have abandoned the LORD's commands and have followed the Baals. Now summon the people from all over Israel to meet me on Mount Carmel. And bring the 450 prophets of Baal and the 400 prophets of Asherah, who eat at Jezebel's table' (1 Kings 18:17-19).

The man of principle is insistent; this wavering of God's people between two alternative theologies has got to stop, for Israel's sake, for the truth's sake, for the sake of God's name and integrity. The time for compromise is over, with Elijah's challenge, '*How long will you waver between two opinions?*'

It is the age-long tension that has been with us from the beginning. We can see it as the issue of:

Principle against expedience

It started with Eve, back in Genesis chapter 3. A little flattery from the Devil, and she's won over.

'He's very nice,' she says to Adam. 'I've been having quite a chat with him. He says if only we follow his advice, we can be like God. *I trust Satan.*'

As Billy Graham once wrote, 'Satan's purpose was not to make Eve as ungodly as possible, but to make her as god-like as possible, without God.'[1]

So it is, in the case of Ahab, with his easy-going gullibility and his hope of gaining the best of two worlds. Sure, he would like to worship the true and only God of Israel – but to fit in Baal and Asherah as well. And, with his wife beside him, why – it would help the marriage too! Perhaps, he reasons, there can be more than one 'truth', and some principles are terribly uncomfortable to live with. We don't have to be so strait-laced. *'I....I trust Jezebel!'*

It was a perennial deathtrap for Israel. A century later, Hosea the prophet protests that his people are *like a dove, easily deceived and senseless, now calling to Egypt, now turning to Assyria* (Hosea 7:11). They were engaging, as he saw it, against God's will, in useless peace pacts that only blunted Israel's distinctive witness to the nations. *I trust Egypt.*

Principle against expedience. As against that, there is the example of Jesus. In the baking wilderness of temptation, the Devil is pulling out trick after trick:

Jesus, you're weak! Have you really *come to save the world? Don't you realise the world is* mine?....

---

1. Billy Graham, *Approaching Hoofbeats,* Word Books, 1983, p. 105.

> *Look here, I'll make you an offer; we'll be partners.*
> *You can change the world. Armies and navies, roads*
> *and ships, banks and businesses; ALL YOURS....in*
> *exchange for one little bow to me?*
>   But Jesus is firm: *Satan, your power is very great.*
> *But I haven't come to join you. I've come to beat you*
> *....There'll be no short cuts, no cheap tricks, no*
> *stunts....*[2]

The final crisis approaches with the death of Jesus. His close disciple, Simon Peter, had tried to discourage him from taking the road to Jerusalem and danger, but Jesus would have none of it. Can we imagine him saying, 'Oh, very well, if you say so; *I trust you, Peter*?' From the start, he was consistent in his attitude:

> Jesus would not entrust himself to them, for he knew all men (John 2: 24).

Back in the story of 1 Kings, Elijah is under no illusions. There before him are a people of ditherers. Perhaps some would have claimed that theirs was a broad-minded and strong approach to religious outlook – a fusing together of the God of Israel with Baal and Asherah. How tolerant and open-minded! How mean and narrow of Elijah!

But no – their 'broadmindedness' was what James describes in his New Testament letter as 'double-mindedness ....unstable in all its ways'. Frankly, the appeal of such 'toleration' is no more than that of Hinduism with its coalition of gods. With such a worldview, you can believe anything you like. The appropriate question to a traditional Hindu – or a modern New-Ager for that matter – is not

---

2. Andrew Knowles, *The Way Out,* Collins, 1977, pp. 27, 28.

'What do you believe?' but rather *'What do you deny?'*

The ideological contest, staged by Elijah on Mount Carmel some twenty-eight centuries ago, was a battle for the preservation of God's given revelation of himself as the only God. It was a collision of truth against synthesis, as God's prophet ordered two rival altars to be prepared with a sacrifice. The test was terrifying and unequivocal. It was agreed that prayers would be offered by Elijah and his Canaanite opponents, and *the God who answered* would, from then on, be respected and worshipped as the only God. The consuming by fire of one of the sacrifices would alone constitute a valid 'answer'!

Elijah is indomitable. *'Asherah?'* he exclaims, 'this non-existent fertility queen? *Baal* – this supposed nature god of fire? Then let's meet fire with fire!'

And the contest is on. King Ahab's eyes are popping, for this is an issue that is very personal to him. It is one of *Principle against Expedience.* Once identify this as the crux of the problem – and it is not all that far removed from Chamberlain's accommodation of Adolf Hitler. But there is a second issue to be recognised:

Engagement against Appeasement

The word e*ngagement* is chosen with care, because, in any confrontation – whether political or ideological – *engagement* can take a variety of forms. It does not have to be limited to the raw power of military force. Indeed, when God's people historically have relied upon arms to achieve their objective as a church – as in the days of the Crusades against the Turks – the inevitable result has been an immediate loss of moral and spiritual power.

Israel, for its part, was for ever placing its reliance upon foreign military deals that invariably ended in failure. This is not to make a rigid argument for pacifism in the case of Britain in 1939. The main issue lies in a question: Are we simply to cave in when faced by a power that is unacceptable to our own belief-system? The answer must be that in one way or another such a power is to be engaged, resisted and, if possible, overthrown – and supremely with the weapon of Truth. Strength of conviction and cool resolution play the key role when false ideologies are on the rampage.

Alien world-views are not to be appeased, but opposed.
To go back to 1938, with hindsight it can be recognised that the British government seemed to be underestimating what it was up against in the Hitler regime. Neville Chamberlain told the House of Commons that he thought he had established *'some degree of personal influence over Herr Hitler'*, and that he was *'satisfied that Herr Hitler would not go back on his word once he had given it'*.

It is tempting to place all the blame on Chamberlain. There were plenty of others willing, like him, to believe the best and to hope that the tensions would be peaceably resolved. It would have been the same in Elijah's day. There would have been those who would have preferred not to see Jezebel's packing of the royal court with false prophets:

'You know these Baal-worshippers; they aren't all that different from us; they're really quite decent people. Some of them are among my best friends.'

'We must try to get *close* to these prophets of Asherah; we must try to *understand* them.'

But to all this, Elijah would have retorted, 'I understand

them very well! We're not going to accommodate this idolatry. Come along! Set up the altars. The God who answers by fire – *he* is God. Agreed?'

Faced by this human bulldozer, the Israelites complied, and the sacrifices were prepared. *No compromise.* When for some years I ran a newspaper question and answer column, I recall one fascinating question from West Africa. It ran as follows: *We are told to pray for our enemies; so would it not be right to love our enemy the devil and to pray for his conversion?* My answer had to be in terms of the Scriptures being a book of salvation and belief for *humans* and not for angels, and that there was to be no dialoguing with the Devil, whose fate is in any case already sealed.

No compromise! No parleying when confronted by outright evil and error. Not for a moment does Elijah waver. He exemplifies a policy of engagement, not appeasement, and in this he lays down a marker for future generations of believing people, buffeted and bullied into joining hands with alien beliefs. When this has happened in the church, the result is disarray, a drop in membership and a massive loss of spiritual power, for God makes fools out of those who negotiate with idolatry and error.

But a third issue presents itself:

The Prophetic against the Hysteric

Sometimes the line that separates these two categories seems paper-thin, but it's there all right. It is perfectly highlighted in Elijah's encounter with the false prophets:

At noon, Elijah began to taunt them. 'Shout louder!' he said. 'Surely he is a god! Perhaps he is deep in thought, or busy, or travelling. Maybe he is sleeping and must be awakened.' So they shouted louder and slashed themselves with swords and spears, as was their custom, until their blood flowed (1 Kings 18: 27,28).

With the hysterics it's all push and shove, noise and chanting – and very human-based. That can never be God's way. As Sören Kierkegaard once put it: *Ten thousand lips, shouting the same thing, makes the statement fraudulent, even if it happens to be true.*

Something of that frenzied atmosphere prevailed on the day when Jesus Christ rode into Jerusalem on the first Palm Sunday, only days before his death. Much of the clamour was unthinking hysteria, surrounding a mistaken view of Messiahship: *He's here at last....the Conquering Hero ....Freedom at last from the Roman yoke....Peace in our time!* But, according to prophecy, that never was to be the style of the world's true Messiah. 'He will not shout or cry out, or raise his voice in the streets' (Isa. 42:2).

The prophetic against the hysteric; the prophet Elijah may be the fiery 'troubler of Israel' – but he stays cool; and very confident. He is confident partly because of a fourth issue that is at stake in this dramatic showdown:

Prayer against Inertia

The gulf between the true prophet and the false is huge. Elijah stands for prayer; the false leaders attempt magic. *What is the difference?*

In magic, humans are attempting to exert *control* – to bend unseen forces to become their servant and bring about their desired will. *They* are in the driving seat. Even though religious words and emblems may be used, *they are trying to make it happen,* and in so doing they are plugging in below.

With prayer it is the other way round completely. Essentially, it is *God* who is in the driving seat. In no way is he there as our servant; we are *his* servants, co-operating with his set purposes by prayer – which is his chosen way of involving us in the bringing about of his will. Through the means of prayer he is saying, 'As my servants, *you* pray; *I* will work!' Elijah's prayer shows all too clearly who is in charge and who is the servant!

> At the time of sacrifice, the prophet Elijah stepped forward and prayed: 'O LORD, God of Abraham, Isaac and Israel, let it be known today that you are God in Israel and that I am your servant and have done all these things at your command. Answer me, O LORD, answer me, so these people will know that you, O LORD, are God, and that you are turning their hearts back again.' Then the fire of the LORD fell....(1 Kings 18:36-38).

When many people look around at their city, at their country – at the world as it is at this moment – they wonder whether the whole human race is out of control. Is there anything that can be done by anybody, beyond being armchair TV spectators, while whole societies become dismembered before their eyes?

But we don't have to lapse into a passive inertia. Prayer is the most powerful activity we will ever engage in. As Toyohiko Kagawa of Japan once declared, *The world is opened by prayer.* In prayer we may exert as much influence in some distant country as if we were there in person. Elijah turns to God, the only God, the God who *answers,* and the prayer is used to unlock the situation of apathy and compromise that had so gripped the nation....and the fire falls.

One is enough – in a business, a family, a student campus, or in a cabinet of political ministers. Actually, in Elijah's case there were more than one; in the following chapter the prophet collapses in reaction after the strain and triumph of Carmel; and he imagines that he is the only faithful believer around. It is then that he is reminded that there were actually 7,000 others who had stayed faithful; *silent,* perhaps, but they were there. It only took one person of conviction and initiative to bring them out of their lethargy and to stop wavering.

On the political front it was Winston Churchill who did that for Britain in the dark days of World War II; who encouraged the waverers and 'provided the roar' of resolution and confidence for the free world. Who were the other leaders who expressed for millions of people a rallying cry for freedom and truth during the century just passed? Among them must be named Billy Graham who, even by his mid-thirties, had spoken to more people face to face than any orator, secular or religious, in all history. He is joined by Alexander Solzhenitsyn, Nelson Mandela, J.F. Kennedy and Martin Luther King.

The new century is beginning with a blank sheet of paper. Whose names will be paramount, for *good* – standing for Principle as against Expedience, Engagement as against Appeasement, the Prophetic as against the Hysteric, and Prayer as against Inertia? With the prayer of faith we may believe that they will surface.

One name alone will dominate, and it will be Christ's Name. Numerous attempts will be made to suppress it, but they will fail.

The great eighteenth century Swiss theologian, Johannes Von Muller, wrote some 17,000 pages of history – but summed them all up with his significant statement:

> Christ is the key to the history of the world....I marvel not at miracles; a far greater miracle has been reserved for our times, the spectacle of the connection of all human events in the establishment and preservation of the doctrines of Christ.

The key to the twenty-first century lies in that piece of analysis. I shall be happy, if I can summon the strength to enter the new millennium sharing a sentiment that will be common to some two billion people: *I trust....Jesus Christ.*

3

'Power grows out of
the barrel of a gun'

(Chairman Mao Tse Tung,
November 6th, 1938)

Did you know that when Alfred Nobel of Sweden introduced dynamite to the world in 1866, he called it *Security Powder*! The idea behind his invention was to promote peace and stability across the world.

'I hope,' he once wrote, 'to discover a weapon so terrible that it would make war eternally impossible.' It is sobering to reflect that the profits from Nobel's inventions were dedicated to what became known as the Nobel Peace Prize.

If Alfred Nobel had understood the Biblical doctrine of the Fall a little better, he would have been under no illusions! From the bow and arrow onwards, however dangerous newly-invented weapons might be to human life, people and entire nations have had no hesitation about using them – not for 'security', but to promote violence and war. By 1970 a single American nuclear submarine possessed the capacity to destroy 160 Russian cities simultaneously. Despite the deterrent of 'Mutually Assured Destruction' between East and West, the arms race continued its incredible acceleration.

Here was a conflict of Capitalism against Communism; it was an ideological contest. But are convictions and thought forms to be overcome by force of arms? Professor Bob Goudzwaard of Amsterdam thinks not:

A little reflection shows that ideologies can be fought only with spiritual weapons. A military attack calls for a military defense, but an advancing ideology requires a spiritual defense. It is therefore a mistake, and a fruit of ideological thinking, to exacerbate existing military tensions in the world for the sake of fighting an ideology. Then deploying every military means is fully legitimated by the desire to battle *a demon*....

Against that demon, we permit ourselves the most hideous means of destruction. But have we not fallen prey to an ideology equally as totalitarian as communism?[1]

This was the fallacy lying behind the Crusades of eight and nine hundred years ago. It spells out the ultimate death-knell facing every *jihad* or holy war between religious groups today. You are simply not going to capture the mind-sets and loyalties of great numbers of people by force. It is amazing that no totalitarian regime or authoritarian religious body has learnt this yet. One by one, each ends up in the dustbowl of extinct belief-systems and vanished empires.

For this reason the quotation from Mao Tse Tung that heads this chapter was archaic even as it was being written. Born the son of a peasant farmer, Mao rose to become the first chairman of the Chinese People's Republic in 1949. Earlier he had urged, 'Every Communist must grasp the truth, **"Political power grows out of the barrel of a gun"**.' Mao expands thus:

Experience in the class struggle in the era of imperi-alism teaches us that it is only by the power of the gun that the working class and the labouring masses can defeat the armed bourgeoisie and landlords; in this sense we may say that only with guns can the whole world be transformed.[2]

---

1. Bob Goudzwaard, *Idols of our Time,* Inter-Varsity Press, 1981, p.74.
2. *Problems of War and Strategy,* 1938, p.224.

It remains to be seen how far into the twenty-first century this Maoist teaching can keep running! From the Babylonian, Greek and Roman empires through to present-day tyrannies, we have come to recognise that every apparatus of state dedicated to keeping a people docile and obedient to a doctrinaire system has a limited lifespan. *These monoliths cannot last.* There is something about the human spirit that knows when it is being crushed down, and eventually finds the will to resist.

As against these oppressors, there is another kingdom that has been steadily growing for thousands of years. It boasts no armies or navies; it runs no banks or businesses; it is not confined to any one country or area of the globe. It is universal and it is permanent. *It is the Kingdom of God*, the rule of the one and only God, through Jesus Christ the chosen King, in the lives of his subjects everywhere, hundreds of millions of them. By grace I am a member of this kingdom. Are you yet?

Power grows out of the barrel of a gun. The lie takes a long time dying!

Such a statement must always reckon with the kingdom which will outlast all others. To read the prophecy given to John, writing as an exiled apostle of Jesus Christ, is to discover that there is an alternative interpretation of 'power' and its true source:

And I will give power to my two witnesses, and they will prophesy for 1,260 days, clothed in sackcloth. These are the two olive trees and the two lampstands that stand before the Lord of the earth. If anyone tries to harm them, fire comes from their mouths and devours their enemies. This is how anyone who wants

to harm them must die. These men have power to shut
up the sky so that it will not rain during the time they
are prophesying; and they have power to turn the
waters into blood and to strike the earth with every
kind of plague as often as they want (Rev. 11:3-6).

We will come on later to the identity of the 'two witnesses'.
But for the present, here is John the beloved evangelist –
himself the victim of first-century Roman violence – iso-
lated on Patmos, a small island off what is now the Turkish
coast. It is there that he receives the dramatic apocalyptic
vision from Christ, risen, ascended and glorified. It is the
vision that rounds off the Scriptures in a burst of inspired
prophecy. The book of Revelation has comforted believers in
Jesus Christ from the time of the imperial dictator, Titus
Flavius Domitian, through to today's rampaging funda-
mentalisms of all brands, political and religious. There have
always been such oppressors – razing villages to the ground,
setting places of worship alight and driving citizens from
their homes by the tens of thousands.

In this prophecy, awesome and riveting, John has set
out for his readers, first, seven 'letters' from Christ in glory
to certain selected churches, bringing them messages
containing comfort, praise, rebuke and challenge. The vision
switches in chapters 4 and 5 to the throne of God and the
Lamb of God – the ultimate centre and explanation of all
our life on earth. This is followed by the seven seals and
then the seven trumpets – a spectacular panoramic spread
of the patterns in history that may be expected both by the
church and by a rebel world under judgment (the plagues,
the wars, the calamities and persecutions) and through them
all, the preservation and advance of the church.

Here in our passage, we are in between the sixth and seventh trumpets, with these chapters 10 and 11 coming as a kind of interlude of reassurance for the people of God. In chapter 10, John receives a 'scroll' of commissioning from the angelic messenger. In chapter 11, we are presented with an unfolding of expectations in the face of a world that refuses to repent at the warning judgments of history – turning its wrath and power on the church. But then comes the surprise!

And I will give power to my two witnesses.....These men have power to shut up the sky....to turn the waters into blood.

Divine 'power' of this kind is surely the only kind worth having. The passage in Revelation bears a strong link with the Old Testament prophet Zechariah and chapter 4 – where God's message is given to the prophet after a period of national disaster, faced now by the urgent task of Jewish reconstruction. How was God's servant to succeed? Zechariah 4:6 spells out the principle: **'Not by might, nor by power, but by my Spirit,' says the LORD Almighty.**

Here are principles that carry down through all history, for those who have eyes to see them, and a willingness to be teachable.

Ideas are sharper than swords. Think of Moses and the deliverance of the Israelites from Egyptian might; or of Gideon and his 300 men – the 'few' against the many – or of David the unknown herdboy against the Philistine giant, Goliath. I am not making out a case for pacifism here, but rather contending that the world is changed not by the war machine so much as by the power of an idea.

Spirit is superior to flesh. I can think of Corrie Ten Boom of Holland, whose shining faith during World War II carried her through intense adversity. 'Love is larger than the walls that shut it in,' she later confided. I think too of the Ugandan evangelist-bishop, Festo Kivengere. Hounded out of his own diocese during Idi Amin's terror campaign of the mid-1970s, Festo was asked by a reporter in New York what he would do if he was sitting in a chair opposite the dictator, and had a gun at his side. 'I would hand the gun to President Amin,' replied the bishop, 'and say to him, "This is not my weapon. I think it must be yours. My weapon is love".'

Good is stronger than evil. There is a permanence about goodness that evil can never share. Good and evil are not parallel and equal forces running side by side in eternal conflict; there is no dualism in Christian thinking. God and goodness belong to eternity, whereas evil has entered as an interruption, and will be brought to a definite end at the close of the age when Christ returns to consummate the victory won over evil at the Cross. When the kingdom of darkness is finally destroyed, there will be no comeback! Goodness and love will reign supreme for ever.

These are the convictions that have given the church its confidence as it has witnessed and suffered across the ages. As the sixteenth century French scholar Theodore Beza once commented to his king, 'Sire, it belongs to the Church of Christ, for which I speak, to receive blows rather than to deal them; but your Majesty will remember that it is an anvil which has worn out many hammers.' The twentieth century, more than any preceding era, has been marked by the persecution and killing of Christian believers by the million, in numerous countries – but the church continues inexorably to grow, despite its appearance of weakness. How to explain its resilience, its *power*?

Back to the 'two witnesses' and to Revelation chapter

11. Here we see four facets of the church that are typical from earliest times down to the present day:

The squeezing of the church

In Revelation 11:1-2, the evangelist is told to go and 'measure' – or *sanctify* – the temple of God, distinguishing carefully between its sanctuary and its outer courts. The language is borrowed from Ezekiel 42:20. Those within the sanctuary are numbered; they are the *insiders,* and they are safe. They are God's own people. But the outer courts are vulnerable; they are for the peripheral, the careless, the nominal believers. Oppression sets in as the unbelieving world, represented by 'the Gentiles', takes over this area and proceeds to trample down the holy city for forty-two months.

The real church is safe. This does not mean that there are no casualties and martyrdoms; there are. But Christ's own people remain intact throughout this period of adversity. This is what we are to expect throughout our Christian era. We were promised no less from our founder – oppression, but throughout, his own divine and permanent security:

In this world you will have trouble. But take heart! I have overcome the world (John 16:33).

But hand in hand with this portrayal of the church, and simultaneous with it, is a second historical facet:

The spreading of the church

Revelation 11:3-6 introduces the enigmatic 'two witnesses'. The clue to their identity lies in their actions – they have power to shut up the sky and to turn waters into blood (v.6). Why, of course! One is Elijah, who pronounced drought upon the land that would last for three and a half years (forty-two months); and the other must be Moses, who pronounced a series of plagues upon Egypt – including the turning of the waters of the Nile into blood. *Elijah,* the most prominent of all the Old Testament prophets, and *Moses,* the great lawgiver of the Old Testament people of God.

The law and the prophets. *These* are the two witnesses, symbolising the powerful mission and outreach of the church at times of great oppression. Here are clear tokens of authority, reinforced by mention of the two olive trees and lampstands of verse 4. The olive trees and lampstands refer back to the Old Testament, to Zechariah 4:11-14, where they are identified as *missionary* representatives – 'These are the two who are anointed to serve the Lord of all the earth.' Perhaps there is an intended allusion here to the product of the olive tree, oil being a symbol of the Holy Spirit, and also used in anointing for special service.

This passage, then, of the two witnesses portrays a period of great *ascendancy and power* for God's people – lasting for....how long? 1,260 days. Why....that is identical in time to the forty-two months of the *oppression* mentioned in the previous verse. It is precisely equivalent to the *three and a half years* of Elijah's stopping of the rain!

> Elijah was a man just like us. He prayed earnestly
> that it would not rain, and it did not rain on the land
> for three and a half years (James 5:17).

It comes together now. Elijah's period out in the wilderness
was one of intense opposition for the people of God, but it
was also a time of unparalleled influence and power. *This
three and a half year period for Elijah is taken in the book
of Revelation to symbolise the **advance through adversity**
of our entire Christian era*. When we pray we may expect
results, however great the pressures; when we proclaim
the good news of Christ in the power and energy of the
Holy Spirit, we may look for things to happen! Down to
our present day we can say that we are in the testing but
powerful period of the 'two witnesses'! Ever since Christ's
first coming, we have experienced fierce opposition, but it
has been matched by the spreading of the church.

A third facet:

The silencing of the church

The evangelist portrays a grim episode in which it appears
that the enemies of the church have finally won the battle:

> Now when they have finished their testimony, the
> beast that comes up from the Abyss will attack them,
> and overpower and kill them. Their bodies will lie in
> the street of the great city, which is figuratively called
> Sodom and Egypt, where also their Lord was cruci-
> fied. For three and a half days men from every peo-
> ple, tribe, language and nation will gaze on their
> bodies and refuse them burial. The inhabitants of the
> earth will gloat over them and will celebrate by send-

ing each other gifts, because these two prophets had tormented those who live on earth (Rev. 11: 7-10).

Is this futuristic? The answer is Yes and No. No, because we have frequently witnessed in history this phenomenon of the church's apparent destruction, much to the joy of its enemies. Why, the Roman emperor Diocletian even had a special medal struck in the third century AD to celebrate the demise of the church! Little did he know that the day would come when the church would stand over the grave of the empire he represented.

But yes, this passage indeed possesses a futuristic element in the rise and apparent victory of 'the beast' – the persecutor of the church who is portrayed in Revelation 13 as rising against the church at the end-times.

The pattern of the prophecy reveals that when the period of Christian witness has been completed, there will be a short period (only three and a half days, as compared with the three and a half years of verse 3) – during which the church's voice will appear to have been silenced. Wickedness (Sodom and Egypt) will seem to have triumphed conclusively. No longer will people's consciences be troubled by the two witnesses; the celebrations will begin. The church is dead! God is dead! But then comes the turning of the tables:

The rising of the church

The defeat of the church is short-lived. It is heaven that has the last word, as God acts on behalf of his own, in stupendous and vindicating power:

> But after the three and a half days a breath of life from God entered them, and they stood on their feet, and terror struck those who saw them. Then they heard a loud voice from heaven saying to them, 'Come up here.' And they went up to heaven in a cloud, while their enemies looked on (Rev. 11:11,12).

Again and again the book of Revelation reminds its readers of the victory theme – victory over evil, won initially at the Cross of Jesus Christ, and then sealed eternally with his triumphant Return. It is the theme of the winning goal – filmed on the video repeatedly from different camera positions. At the end of time, events will force even the bitterest of Christ's enemies to concede, however grudgingly, his power and victory.

It is said that the cat has nine lives. The church has infinitely more! Squeezed and hemmed in across the centuries, it possesses nonetheless a power and influence in the lives of millions of people. Threatened with extinction on numerous occasions, it continues to rise again.

Power grows out of the barrel of a gun.

The history of the human race, coupled with the testimony of Christ's community and the voice of God's book, come back with their own riposte; *Terribly sorry, it ain't true.*

4

'I have a dream'

(Martin Luther King, August 28th, 1963)

History is just about the most thrilling subject in the world....but it took me a long time to fall in love with it. Perhaps I was unlucky with my teachers at school. Whatever the period – King Alfred, the Battle of Agincourt, Cromwell or the Boston Tea Party – my mentors could be guaranteed to strip from the action all imagination, colour and movement, and reduce the adventure of our civilisation to a weary, grey calendar of yawning tedium. But there is no mistaking the real thing.

'History is made by imagination,' wrote the historian T.R. Glover. 'No man creates till his own imagination is touched, and till he touches the imagination of his fellows.'

Such a man was the Rev. Martin Luther King.

There were 210,000 people waiting for the black Civil Rights leader that Sunday morning by the Lincoln Memorial. It was exactly a hundred years after Abraham Lincoln's momentous announcement of emancipation for every slave in America, and the speaker had chosen his moment well. 'We have come to our nation's capital,' he cried, *to cash a check*!'

It was also significant that the steps of the Lincoln Memorial, from which Luther King spoke, had been the site selected some years earlier by Eleanor Roosevelt, for the performance of songs by a black singer whom she was supporting. Her action then had been in protest against the refusal of her protégé's performance by the nearby Opera House. This was on account of the singer's colour.

Imagination, drama and fever-pitch resolution were converging, then, on a day in history – August 28th, 1963 – as the vast audience watched the magic settle on their spokesman. He was only thirty-four, born in Atlanta, Georgia, the son of a Baptist pastor. Already he had reached national prominence as leader of the Alabama bus boycott. Now, at the end of the march he had led on Washington, he was ready with his speech. He had finished preparing it at four o'clock that morning.

> I have a dream that my four little children will one day live in a nation where they will not be judged by the color of their skin, but by the content of their character.
> I have a dream today.
> I have a dream that one day the state of Alabama, whose governor's lips are presently dripping with the words of interposition and nullification, will be transformed into a situation where little black boys and black girls will be able to join hands with little white boys and white girls and walk together as sisters and brothers.
> I have a dream today.

*I have a dream....*It was, by wide acclaim, the political speech of the twentieth century; a speech that will endure for always. In it, King outlawed violence as a pathway to civil rights, inspiring his listeners instead to 'rise to the majestic heights of meeting physical force with soul force'.

Within months, Martin Luther King was magazine *Time's* 'Man of the Year', and in 1964 he was awarded the Nobel Peace Prize. Civil Rights Acts were carried through Congress in 1964 and 1965. And on Thursday, April 4th 1968, King was assassinated. The whole civilised world seemed to shake with his passing.

I have a dream. It is this kind of visionary feel for history, for the big landmarks, that draws its inspiration from the gigantic worldview of the Bible. Martin Luther King's speech drew generously from its thought-forms and language:

> I have a dream that one day every valley shall be exalted, every hill and mountain shall be made low, the rough places will be made plains, and the crooked places will be made straight, and the glory of the Lord shall be revealed, and all flesh shall see it together.

Such language, with its vision of healing and unity between peoples and of ultimate universal accord, is the language of Isaiah and the prophets; it is the language of eschatology and the last things; it is language that expresses a belief in the sweep and destiny of all history. It is the way of interpreting life and the future *that inspires action in the present.*

The visitor to London, England, should pause at the capital's centre, Piccadilly Circus, where the statue of Eros was erected in commemoration of the great Christian philanthropist, Ashley Cooper, the seventh Earl of Shaftesbury. Known 200 years ago as 'The Poor Man's Earl', he worked tirelessly in Parliament and through the institutions to bring about better conditions for workers, for children and the disadvantaged. Always it was his confidence that the future belonged to Christ and the church that fired his public service:

> I do not think that in the last forty years I have lived one conscious hour that was not influenced by the thought of our Lord's return.

It is the old principle of a person's view of the *final* Day giving depth and meaning to the actions of *every* day. If you have an inadequate grasp of the future, be sure that the present will not make much sense at all! The toil and frustrations facing all campaigners for civil and religious liberty will exact such a toll, that the enterprise would run into the ground, but for the final vision that inspires all lasting reforms. This vision finds expression in the last chapter of the Bible:

> Then the angel showed me the river of the water of life, as clear as crystal, flowing from the throne of God and of the Lamb down the middle of the great street of the city. On each side of the river stood the tree of life, bearing twelve crops of fruit, yielding its fruit every month. And the leaves of the tree are for the healing of the nations.
>
> No longer will there be any curse. The throne of God and of the Lamb will be in the city, and his servants will serve him. They will see his face, and his name will be on their foreheads. There will be no more night. They will not need the light of a lamp or the light of the sun, for the Lord God will give them light. And they will reign for ever and ever (Rev. 22:1-5).

The healing of the nations....In this, the concluding prophecy of a great kaleidoscope of visions, the apostle John writes from his enforced exile on the island of Patmos. With luminous clarity he visualises the ultimate scene that awaits him and the whole of Christ's believing community on earth. It is of a garden city – and its very images speak of beauty and purity, of refreshment, worship, health and control; of universal understanding and *unity* – the very qualities yearned for in that historic meeting with Martin Luther King in 1963.

It was around AD 95 when John's prophecy was received. No President Kennedy or Johnston, then, but the 44-year-old Roman emperor Domitian, who a year later would be assassinated. By force he governed a vast domain that was served by some 60 million slaves, who faced no living possibility of emancipation. The Christian church within the Roman empire was for the most part composed of slaves. It is with this readership in mind, together with the harassed church of all the ages, that John shares his dream-like vision – and not just of what *can* be (as in Luther King's speech), but of what *will* be!

The final vision! As the reader comes to these last pages of the Bible, there is a sensation of walking into a cinema at the precise moment when the feature film is just ending. Only five minutes have to elapse before the next showing begins. You can have the experience, then, of seeing both ends of the same film rather close together!

That is my own impression of Revelation 21 and 22. It is as though I have taken up my Bible, and bent the back of it *around,* to make the last page meet the first! In a remarkable and divinely-inspired way the Bible – over the long sixteen centuries during which it was written – concludes with such astonishing unity of thought, that the end can be said to have met the beginning again. It could never have been contrived like this.

John's battered, squeezed and enslaved readers were, by this dream and vision, lifted out of themselves and given, in these glowing chapters, a unified rationale for living and overcoming. Here was a credible worldview that would enable them, in and through the church, to outlive and outlast the Roman galleys, the enforced labour, the power-mad Caesars and the ten major persecutions that would be launched against them in their first three centuries of witness.

The end meets the beginning. The entire Bible story holds together in a unity. Life and existence – in Christ and his church – *do* make sense, even when you possess neither citizenship nor voting rights. It is this conviction that has marked all the world's great reformers – Florence Nightingale, Ashley Cooper, William Wilberforce, Luther King and Nelson Mandela. It is a confidence in the big picture; that – despite all our earthly confusions – the end meets the beginning in a cohesive whole. Life on this world *does* hold together – first in what I call:

The two creations

Again we must emphasise that the unity between the Bible's beginning and end could never have been planned. Here is the first sentence in the Old Testament:

In the beginning God created the heavens and the earth (Gen. 1:1).

Compare this with the apostle John:

Then I saw a *new* heaven and a *new* earth, for the first heaven and the first earth had passed away (Rev. 21:1).

It is, then, as we come to the final vision that we can perceive how the end has met the beginning, with reference to the two Creations, the old and the new. And it is this expectation of the new that puts fresh heart into those who fight against the evils of the old order. Jesus referred to *'the renewal of all things, when the Son of Man sits on his glorious throne'* (Matthew 19:28). The phrase 'renewal of all things' is translated from a single Greek word, *palingeneseia* – literally, *the new Genesis.* As the commentators put it, 'the first chapter of the Bible describes God *making* the world; the last chapter shows him *remaking* it.'

Again, we can observe the reference, back in Genesis 2, to the tree of life and the tree of the knowledge of good and evil (v.9). Verse 10 tells us of a river, watering the garden and flowing from Eden. By the time we get to Revelation 22, it is just one tree (v.2) – but what a tree! It stands, we learn, 'on each side of the river', providing a never-ending supply for all who are given access – with its very leaves giving healing to the nations.

As for the river, it flows, crystal-pure (v.1) – but now, not out of Eden, but from the divine throne, occupied jointly by God and the Lamb. The underlying emphasis is of purity, of plenty – and perhaps especially of *unity.* It is *one* tree, not two; and *one* river, no longer divided, as in Genesis.

Foundational to the vision is the prophecy of Ezekiel 47:12, in which a river is pictured, flowing out of God's temple, spanned with trees. This is clearly fulfilled in Revelation's final scene. *Is this YOUR projected final scene?* How would you describe your own view of the end times? The channelling of your energies, your ethics and value-system, all that you stand and live for, are vitally affected by your concept of the future.

In his book on England, covering the years 1870-1914, the radical historian R.C.K. Ensor commented that no one will understand nineteenth century England if they fail to understand its Evangelical influence – particularly as exercised by the reforming group based at Holy Trinity Church, Clapham. They were known as The Clapham Sect:

> If one asks how nineteenth century English merchants earned the reputation of being the most honest in the world (a very real factor in the prominence of English trade), the answer is: Because hell and heaven seemed as certain to them as tomorrow's sunrise and the Last Judgment as real as the week's balance sheet.[1]

Ensor goes on to write that the other side of this moral accountancy was the belief that this life is only important as a preparation for the next, for Evangelicalism made 'other-worldliness' an everyday conviction and inspired a highly civilised people to put duty before all else.

The knowledge that the old creation is to be transformed into the new is enough to rejuvenate every generation that feels tired and weighed down by this present, dying world. The end will meet the beginning again, as we see in the two creations. But in John's final curtain call I discern something else:

The two Testaments

And the leaves of the tree are for the healing of the nations. From the start, God had all the nations in view. He said as much to Abraham, in the initial establishing of the divinely contracted covenant:

---

1. R.C.K. Ensor, *England, 1870-1914*, 1936, p.137.

> And all peoples on earth will be blessed through you
> ....I have made you a father of many nations (Gen.
> 12:3; 17:5).

Israel, to be sure, was to be the lamp-standard to the nations, but ultimately it is Jesus, in the new covenant and the gospel, who – as the sacrificial Lamb of God – completes God's mission to the nations, at the Cross. It is for this reason that 'the Lamb' features so prominently at the Bible's close. It is because of him – the figure who spans both the Old and New Testaments – that Eden comes to be restored, and sin abolished entirely: *No longer will there be any curse* (Rev. 22:3).

In this wonderful last chapter, the evangelist is saying, *I have a dream.* It is a vision which will 'soon' be implemented. The tree is back! The curse is gone! Men and women are back in communion in the garden city of God! The end has met the beginning again, in the two Testaments, old and new. We bend the last page of the Bible back to meet the first – and Moses and John grasp hands across the centuries. They are combined now in the *one* united testimony to the truth of the Bible.

But now for a third facet:

The two humanities

And his servants will serve him. They will see his face, and his name will be on their foreheads....They will reign for ever and ever (Rev. 22:3-5).

Here is a wonderful combination of ideas within a single paragraph. God's servants in the new order will 'serve' him. But they will also 'reign' for ever and ever. The word *serve* is that used for a bondman, a slave. And yet there is a difference. Here, in the future perfected order, is not a service of oppression, but of *royalty*. God's redeemed people will be King Slaves, Queen Slaves! We may think of it as a future 'dream' – but the members of God's kingdom should be anticipating such service *now,* in the fellowship of the Christian church.

It is this that lies behind Martin Luther King's inspired leadership:

> This is our hope. This is the faith with which I return to the South. With this faith we will be able to hew out of the mountain of despair a stone of hope. With this faith we will be able to transform the jangling discords of our nation into a beautiful symphony of brotherhood.

King's words carry echoes of the harmony described by the apostle Paul – the reconciliation of the outsiders with the insiders. It is more than a vision or dream. It is because of the Cross of Christ that Paul can proclaim reconciliation as an historic achievement:

> He came and preached peace to you who were far away and peace to those who were near. For through him we both have access to the Father by one Spirit (Eph. 2:17, 18).

It is possible that Martin Luther King, as a preacher himself, had the words of Galatians 3: 28 in mind, as he spoke of alienated communities joining hands: 'There is neither Jew nor Greek, slave nor free, male nor female, for you are all one in Christ Jesus.'

The healing of the nations is symbolised by that tree of life in Revelation 22. The New Testament declares it as a present reality – reducing all our cultural or idiosyncratic differences to little more than blips. Christ is the great unifier of humanity. When Richard Chartres, Bishop of London, visited us in July 1999 at our London church of All Souls, he described the congregation as 'one great United Nations!'

Sometimes the cry goes up: 'Why can't we reconcile all the traditions and cultures within a single universal religion, and so have the best of everything in one system?' The answer is that *it has already been done, in a single person.* 'For God was pleased....through him (Christ) to reconcile to himself all things, whether things on earth or things in heaven, by making peace through his blood, shed on the cross' (Col. 1:19,20).

This is already a reality in our world. Certainly, it is far from perfect. It is all too easy for believers to stray back into a world where the dividing walls go up again. We should insist within our fellowships, worldwide, that the barriers are kept down, and that such unity between divided humanity must be firmly practised in a grand rehearsal of the new order. It is not that ethnic or cultural diversities are done away with by Christ; it is that we are united by something *bigger*. The day of Pentecost was definitive in this respect, as the Gospel was preached and the listeners understood, even in their own languages, the wonderful works of God. It was a projection of what was to be!

Babel is reversed
The curse is lifted
Eden is restored
The tree is returned
The gates are open

By the time of the end, the tree is standing for open access and welcome. No longer is it guarded by the angels of Genesis, with their flaming swords flashing back and forth. The way is open.

But to whom is it open? It is spelt out for us in terms of glowing hope:

> Blessed are those who wash their robes, that they may have the right to the tree of life and may go through the gates into the city (Rev. 22: 14).

Their robes.... What are these 'robes' that need to be purified? Why, they are the things you clothe yourself with – the real you that is comprised of attitudes, habits, outlook....the entire system of values acquired over a lifetime. In short, *your robe is your character.*

And how or where is it to be 'washed'? The answer has been given earlier:

> These are they who have come out of the great tribulation; they have washed their robes and made them white in the blood of the Lamb (Rev. 7: 14).

I have a dream....

Civilisation owes a salute to those men and women who have entertained a vision on behalf of their fellows, and then have bent their energies to fulfilling the dream. In our Christian understanding, it is – in its best interpretation – a *connected* dream. It is connected to a man called Jesus, who died in humiliating agony on what the Bible calls a *Xulon,* a 'wood'.

But the tree of life here in Revelation 22 is termed by

the same word. It, too, is a *Xulon.* Here then is a fourth theme of John's final picture:

The two trees

There are two trees, and one opens the way to the other. Here is the apostle Peter:

> He himself bore our sins in his body on the tree, so that we might die to sins and live for righteousness; by his wounds you have been healed (1 Pet. 2: 24).

The tree of the Cross opens the way to the tree of life. We can look backwards to the Cross, and forwards to the tree of life, whose leaves are for the healing of the nations, your healing! Hold onto that message. It makes the difference to everything. The garden city....the tree of life....the throne of God – are you heading that way?

The signposts are clear in John's vision – of the two creations (the old and the new), the two Testaments (Moses touching hands with John), the two humanities (the outsiders reconciled with the insiders), and the two trees, one leading to the other.

'I have a dream.' Do we? It is vital that we do, for it is the vision of what must be that colours all present energies and plans, and puts shape and substance into them. Without a sense of future and direction, life can only strip us of what the old hymn called the *solid joys and lasting treasure that none but Zion's children know.*

5

**'I've been on a calendar,
but never on time'**

(Marilyn Monroe, 1950)

Despite being something of a last-minuter, I managed to keep my weekly question-and-answer newspaper column going for a full fifteen years. The trick was to disbelieve the editor when he asked for my copy by the Wednesday. I reasoned that every true editor keeps a day or two in hand. At one point he was so alarmed by the fineness of my safety margin that he invited me to send him in a 'spare' column, to be used only in dire emergencies. It was a fine idea, but I blew the precious spare, first time off! We didn't try that one again.

Over the issue of tight deadlines, I have a small affinity with Marilyn Monroe; her reputation was a byword in this regard. It was after her appearance on a calendar in 1950 – for which she was paid $50 – that the twentieth century goddess of film and fashion was asked whether she had ever been in *Time* magazine. She gave her ambiguously memorable reply, '*I've been on a calendar, but never on Time.*'

There were only a very few individuals of the twentieth century who were universally identified by their first name alone – Elvis....Diana....possibly Monica – and ahead of them in sheer staying power, *Marilyn.* Even in recent times her image has featured on advertisements in the London Underground, for such selling points as air-conditioning units (with caption, *Some like it cool*), and low-cost flights to Ireland.

Perhaps the most famous twentieth century icon of all, Marilyn was everywhere, but nowhere. She never knew for sure who her real father was. A possible candidate was C. Stanley Gifford, a man who offered Marilyn's mother financial help, but refused to have anything to do with the baby.

Thus the baby had no daddy of her own. She was born on June 1st, 1926, and the name on her birth certificate was 'Norma Jean Baker'. Her mother Gladys married twice, but neither man was the father of Norma Jean. When Gladys was finally committed to a mental institution, Norma Jean had to spend her infancy and childhood in a series of foster homes in Los Angeles, belonging nowhere, and perpetually uncertain of her own true identity.

She married James Edward Dougherty at sixteen; later she married the great baseball star Joe Di Maggio, and later still Arthur Miller. Although her girlish dream of getting into movies materialised and she was catapulted into world fame as Marilyn Monroe, stability and permanence were to elude her all her short life. She died from an overdose of barbiturates in August 1962 at the age of thirty-six.

It's too easy to place world celebrities into neat categories after their departure; to accept the pronouncements of TV studio experts or to swallow wild rumours and conspiracy theories bounced around the Internet. Marilyn – as no one before or after her – became a commodity of the twentieth century, and for this reason care has to be taken over any real attempt to define her life, lest the identity of this beautiful, fragile person is simply buried as a sex symbol, only to be exhumed at intervals convenient to consumer and image-making forces.

If her life, and the century she represented, could possibly be interpreted by a piece of Scripture, the Old Testament book of Ecclesiastes is relevant in its portrayal of the meaninglessness that has characterised the last hundred years. This remarkable book gives profile to the 'vanity' of life, once God is removed from view.

'Meaningless! Meaningless!' says the Teacher. 'Utterly
meaningless! Everything is meaningless' (Eccl. 1:2).

The book of Ecclesiastes could have been written for the
twentieth century, in its exposition of the empty life.
Certainly the Christian Gospel has taken a firm hold upon
our civilisation – but you have only to take a walk along
Oxford Street, the Champs Elysée, Kenyatta Avenue or
Sunset Boulevard, to see what the twentieth century did to
people as yet untouched by the faith of Christ. Marilyn
speaks to us in exactly the same terms as 'the Teacher'.

Every baby needs a da-da-Daddy, she sang, back in the
'fifties. She sang of the traveller *on the River of No Return*
– swept on, as she put it, *for ever to be lost in the stormy
sea.*

Compare Marilyn's lyrics with those of Ecclesiastes:

Marilyn:

You're always wishing and wanting for....
Something;
When you get what you want,
You don't want what you get....
After you get what you want,
You don't want what you wanted at all.

Ecclesiastes 2:10,11

I denied myself nothing my eyes desired;
I refused my heart no pleasure.
My heart took delight in all my work....
Yet when I surveyed all that
my hands had done

> *and what I had toiled to achieve,*
> *everything was meaningless,*
> *a chasing after the wind;*
> *nothing was gained under the sun.*

The book of Ecclesiastes derives, as its opening sentence declares, from the 'son of David, king of Jerusalem'. Solomon reigned for forty fabulous years in the tenth century BC. His words present us with an inspired critique of life that has become secularised and devoid of faith in God.

Readers have reacted in various ways to the book. Some have romanticised its third chapter and turned it into songs: *For everything there is a season, and a time for every purpose under heaven.* The superficial interpretation would be, 'How attractive; we must write a song on this theme....*a time to be born, and a time to die; a time to plant, and a time to uproot....*

Indeed we would like to think that there was a pattern to nature and to life; *a time to weep, and a time to laugh*; it feels like a rhythm of security. However, if we are a little more perceptive we can discern that the philosopher, or Teacher, as Solomon styles himself, is portraying a different, a deliberately cynical view of things.

> *The race is not to the swift*
> *or the battle to the strong,*
> *nor does food come to the wise*
> *or wealth to the brilliant*
> *or favour to the learned;*
> *but time and chance*
> *happen to them all* (9:11).

By means of this cynical approach, the Teacher is prodding and pushing his contemporaries into *thinking*. He is goading readers of every age into asking questions. For when people begin to ask questions, there is hope for them!

*A time to be born and a time to die....*and behind this catalogue of seasons and activities is the lurking question, 'Are we being made to dance to a tune?' As Marilyn Monroe once perceptively put it, 'Hollywood is a place where they'll pay you a thousand dollars for a kiss, and fifty cents for your soul.'

In Ecclesiastes, the Teacher is using cynicism to wake people up! He follows the materialist and the cynic along the lines of their own reasoning. He's pushing his readers along their own logical pathways; he bends himself delib-erately in their direction – towards emptiness and despair.

Michael Hews, in the Scripture Union *Viewpoint* magazine (No. 38), has written in similar vein of the hollow 'freedoms' pursued by so many:

> *Free! To sleep, rise, eat, work, eat,*
> *work, watch, sleep, rise;*
> *Free to grow older, older,*
> *Free to retire.*
> *Free to weed our gardens,*
> *Free to grow older still*
> *– and shakily water our window-boxes.*
> *Free to die – and get our names in the*
> *local papers for just one more time.*
> *Free to live, to die, to be forgotten;*
> *We who have lived all of our lives*
> *in the slavery of the fear of death,*
> *and the fear of life without meaning.*

A closer look at the book of Ecclesiastes enables the reader to identify several cameos of the empty life in its opening chapters:

Chapter 1: Identity eroded by the ceaseless cycle

Life is perceived, first of all, as the frustration of travelling endlessly in circles. You are travelling, but getting nowhere:

> Generations come and generations go, but the earth remains for ever. The sun rises and the sun sets, and hurries back to where it rises. The wind blows to the south and turns to the north; round and round it goes....What has been will be again, what has been done will be done again; there is nothing new under the sun.... (Eccl. 1:4-6, 9).

The celebrated American playwright, Tennessee Williams, summed up the mood of his generation vividly: *What else are we offered? The never-broken procession of little events that assure us that we and strangers about us are still going on? Where? Why? And the perch that we hold is unstable!*

Many are assailed by the question: In one hundred years' time, what evidence will there be that I ever existed?

> There is no remembrance of men of old, and even those who are yet to come will not be remembered by those who follow (Eccl. 1:11).

Identity eroded. Marilyn Monroe was the public face of millions of people who have never been able to answer the question of their own personhood. Who am I? What am I? But there is a second cameo here:

Chapter 2: Energy wasted by the aimless life

Solomon, the king who had the world at his feet and could satisfy every passing whim, is in his element throughout chapter 2. He has a try at everything: *The pleasure trip* (v.3) 'I tried cheering myself with wine.... *The business deal* (vv.4-8) ' I undertook great projects....I built houses....I planted vineyards, I made gardens and parks....I bought male and female slaves....I amassed silver and gold for myself....*The study course* (vv. 12-14) 'Then I turned my thoughts to consider wisdom....'

In all this, what is missing? *It is the lack of any obvious centre and any significant relationships.* Before she went to New York, Marilyn Monroe admitted, 'I never had any friends, only conquests. I didn't have the time to find real friends. I was always being looked at; I had no chance to look.'

Not that Marilyn was without the capacity for affection. The indication from her two failed pregnancies and one miscarriage is that she loved children and longed to have had them. There is no solid evidence for the stories of numerous abortions that pursued her. Nevertheless the crucial question remains to face everyone looking for fulfilment – whether Solomon, Marilyn Monroe or the children of the new century ahead of us: *Where is the centre, the focus point?*

The Teacher is teasing and tantalising the reader with the elusive goal of success. When the summit has already been gained, what then? '*What more can the king's successor do than what has already been done?*' As Dean Inge of St. Paul's Cathedral in London put it many years ago, 'Nothing fails like success.' Further back still,

Theophan the Recluse declared, 'Most people are like a shaving of wood which is curled round its central emptiness.'

Identity eroded; energy wasted. But the Teacher has a third cameo waiting for us in chapter 3:

Chapter 3: Eternity blocked by the full agenda

The much-romanticised *A time to be born and a time to die* passage isn't romantic so much as robotic. Chapter 3, in contrast to the first chapter, presents life without God not as a ceaseless cycle but rather as a backwards and forwards affair. A too-full life carries us by tides, currents and seasons that take us with them – whether we wish it or not. We may deceive ourselves that we are in charge of our destinies, but no; we're at the beck and call of the crammed filofax, the ever-ringing mobile phone, the stream of e-mails. We're part of the dance routine of twenty-first century back-packers. In the words of that cliché of utter banality that could have been uttered by the Teacher himself, we've *been there, done that, got the tee-shirt.* And none of it amounts to anything that can be taken into eternity, because the big thing – our life with God – has been blocked from view.

It is only after the litany, in chapter 3, of tearing down and building, scattering stones and gathering them, searching and giving up, that the gentlest of hints is given as the Teacher reveals his true colours in verse 11: *He has also set eternity in the hearts of men.*

Why is it that this vital dimension remains hidden to so many? It is because all the available files have been filled up, and none of them is marked *'God',* or *'Building my*

Character', or even *'Establishing my relationship to the Universe'*.

Marilyn Monroe somehow personified the restless insecurity of the twentieth century. 'I've tried to change my ways,' she said, referring to her scatty lifestyle, 'but the things that make me late are too strong and too pleasing.'

Her life surely continues to speak to thoughtful people. Is it possible to be everywhere, yet nowhere? The answer seems to be Yes. To be known and celebrated by millions of people, yet to be lost in terms of personal identity and lasting fulfilment? The Teacher of Ecclesiastes confirms from his own experience – as someone who had everything – that it is all too possible.

To have identity eroded by the ceaseless cycle is to have *no direction!* To have energy wasted by the aimless life is to have *no centre!* To have eternity blocked by the full agenda is to have *no home!*

The road taken by Ecclesiastes is one of cold, hard logic. Have a look at your presuppositions! Follow them to their natural conclusion, and ask yourself how satisfied you are with your present worldview, and how well does it fit with your deepest instincts about life?

Os Guinness has written, 'There is always a tension between what people *say* they are, and *who* they are.'[1] He instances Issa, the Japanese poet of the eighteenth and nineteenth centuries. All five of his children died before he was thirty, and then his wife died as well. After one of these deaths he went to his master of Zen, and asked for an explanation of such suffering.

His tutor replied, 'Just as the sun rises and the dew evaporates, so on the wheel of suffering sorrow is transient;

1. Os Guinness, *The Dust of Death,* Inter-Varsity Press, 1973, p. 223.

life is transient; *man* is transient.' That was Issa's religious answer, and, on returning home, he wrote a poem – which he found himself unable to finish. It began:

> *The world is dew....*
> *The world is dew....*
> *And yet....And yet....*

The poem was never finished. The 'and yet' explained the basic dilemma. For Issa, the orthodox Zen believer, life was nothing more than a drop of dew, soon to evaporate. But for Issa the father and husband, crushed by bereavement, agonised by grief, the sheer logic of his feelings and emotions told him that life must be more significant than *that!*

Just to think along these lines is enough to alter one's whole view of life. *He has set eternity in the hearts of men.* 'Is it possible, then, that I have been conned into believing a binful of lies? Is it not time for my intellect to catch up with my deepest human instincts about love and life; the creation, and the future, and God?'

It need not take much! For the intellectual C.S. Lewis, the actual change of worldview was a matter of minutes only:

I know very well when, but hardly how, the final step was taken. I was driven to Whipsnade one sunny morning. When we set out I did not believe that Jesus Christ is the Son of God, and when we reached the zoo I did. Yet I had not exactly spent the journey in thought. Nor in great emotion. 'Emotional' is perhaps the last word we can apply to some of the most important events. It was more like when a man, after long sleep, still lying motionless in bed, becomes aware that he is now awake.[2]

Ten minutes quiet may be enough. Away from the clangour, the lights, the distractions of high living that so cluttered the life of tragic Marilyn Monroe, Ecclesiastes can be our tutor, prodding us with our own logic, insistently and patiently: *Yes, in your spirit you are just about dead. But you can change now, to a new world of thought and belief, where love, and forgiveness, and sacrifice and prayer begin to operate. Trust the lesson of the Teacher. All along you are being prompted to know God and his Son Jesus Christ, who loves you and has died for you. It is not too late. You are not on the River of No Return.*

---

2. C.S. Lewis, *Surprised by Joy,* Collins, 1955, p. 189.

6

'If you can meet with
Triumph and Disaster
And treat those two Imposters
just the same'

('If' – Rudyard Kipling, 1910)

Randolph Lycett of Australia was persevering valiantly on Wimbledon's Centre Court. It was 1921 and he was playing Zenzo Shimidsu of Japan in the quarter finals. The match was played on one of the hottest days in memory, and Lycett felt obliged to revive himself with gin every time the players changed ends.

John Olliff of *The Daily Telegraph* later reported: 'The fifth set provided perhaps the most extraordinary spectacle ever seen at Wimbledon. It was a long set of twenty games, and in the middle of it, it became apparent that Lycett was on his last legs. He could not go on drinking any more gin, because the combination of the gin and the heat of the sun was making him feel extremely muzzy. On the other hand, he was in desperate need of some further stimulant. He then did the most courageous and unprecedented thing in the history of Wimbledon. He ordered a bottle of champagne to be brought out on to the Centre Court for him.

'It was placed on the umpire's chair for him, and he consumed the last drop of it as the umpire called the score, "Shimidsu leads by nine games to eight in the final set". By now Lycett was beginning to stagger about the court. At one time the spectators were sympathising with him, at another they were angry, and at another moment they were laughing. They did not know which to do when he fell and dropped his racket, and then, on hands and knees, crawled round in search of it. To every one's relief Shimidsu won 6-3, 9-11, 3-6, 6-2, 10-8, and so Lycett was forgiven for his indiscretion.'

What days they were! Lycett lived to fight again another day, and reached the final the following year. Those were

1. John Olliff, *The Romance of Wimbledon,* Hutchinson, 1949, p. 53.

the days of the true amateur, when people played tennis solely for the love of the sport. It was at that time that the words of the quotation heading this chapter were engraved over the portals of Wimbledon's Centre Court:

> *If you can meet with Triumph and Disaster*
> *And treat those two Imposters just the same*

Rudyard Kipling's famous poem was entitled simply *If* – but it could just as fittingly have been called *The Art of Frustration*, for it is a eulogy to the enduring spirit that persists, like Randolph Lycett, in the face of every trial and disaster. The last round, the final straight, the fifth set! Translate that into every arena of living, whether political, domestic or commercial – and you are into the philosophy – no, the *theology* – of Perseverance, in an imperfect and fallen world.

It is to do with the tension of finding yourself poised between Triumph and Disaster; stranded between A and B; having begun, but not yet having finished. It is the tension of living – and waiting – during the 'In-Between' times, those boring, dull periods of life when you are longing for the breakthrough which refuses to come. Our civilization is full of exponents of the principle. Let us select the Christian apostle, Paul of Tarsus, as our example. Here he is, writing to that infant church in Philippi, the first foothold of the gospel in all Europe:

I have learned to be content whatever the circumstances. I know what it is to be in need, and I know what it is to have plenty. I have learned the secret of being content in any and every situation, whether

well fed or hungry, whether living in plenty or in
want. I can do everything through him who gives
me strength (Phil. 4:11-13).

Content (v. 11) is a key word. In the Greek it is *autarkeia*.
It is an entirely non-religious, 'secular' word. In ancient
literature it was used by the Stoics of old – with whom
Paul was familiar. The Stoics were a school of Greek
philosophers founded by a man called Zeno, 308 years
before Jesus was born. Their central plank of belief was
that virtue was the highest good, and that all passions and
desires should be rigidly subdued to the great priorities of
discipline, endurance, control and fortitude. We sometimes
use the phrase, 'Stoic courage', to describe someone of
outstanding durability.

The ideas of the Stoics had persisted to the time of the
New Testament and the apostle Paul. 'Autarkeia' means
sufficiency, self-sufficiency, competence, self-mastery. The
Greek lexicon describes 'autarkeia' as 'the state of one who
supports himself without aid from others'. And that, of
course, was a favourite characteristic hailed by the Stoics.

However, once we come to the New Testament, the
apostle Paul seems to inject the word with an entirely new
quality of meaning. It takes on a 'God' dimension that
wasn't there before. When writing to his readers at Corinth,
he makes his financial appeal on behalf of the poor at
Jerusalem, and then promises, 'And *God* is able to make
all grace abound to you, so that in all things at all times,
having *all that you need* (autarkeian), you will abound in
every good work' (2 Cor. 9:8). Again, when writing to
Timothy his colleague, Paul states, 'But *godliness* with
contentment (autarkeias) is great gain (1 Tim. 6:6).

It only remains for Philippians 4:11, instanced above, to complete the trio of references to 'autarkeia' in the New Testament – and we can see what the apostle has done. The word has altered its meaning, almost imperceptibly, but significantly. No longer is it made to mean *self*-mastery. In each of the three uses, the context indicates a *God*-centredness that has been built in. It is only because of Christ that Paul can say of his own experience that he has learned to be *content*.

So it is 'autarkeia' – this God-centred capacity to *manage,* to *endure,* to be *content* with every circumstance – that puts substance and meaning into daily living. 'Autarkeia' is what imparts significance to people of every walk of life, whether they are computer programmers, students, cab drivers or telephone operators. Or indeed Christian ministers such as Paul.

I have learned to be content whatever the circumstances.

These words were not given from an armchair or lecture podium but from a prison cell – by a man who on his very first venture into Europe finds himself, in Philippi, accused unjustly, beaten and put in the stocks. Now here he is, writing to those same people in Philippi, and once again in prison!

Kipling, then, is right on target. These lines from his poem illustrate the principles in view:

> If you can keep your head when all about you
> Are losing theirs and blaming it on you,
> If you can wait and not be tired by waiting,
> If you can bear to hear the truth you've spoken
> Twisted by knaves to make a trap for fools,
> And so hold on when there is nothing in you

Except the Will which says to them 'Hold on!'
Yours is the Earth and everything that's in it,
And – which is more – you'll be a Man, my son!

It happens to people every day; the creative producer in
the studio whose best productions are hacked to bits by an
editor and end up in small pieces on the cutting room
floor....the athlete hampered by an unforeseen injury....the
church minister whose fresh ideas for the running of the
church are tossed out of the window by an unfeeling
council. Ultimately, it is the truly goal-orientated operators
– with the long-term view – who can learn to step back
and view their reverses against the backdrop of the wider
scene.

Back to tennis. Take Boris Becker, victim of an upset
win at Wimbledon. 'What went wrong?' he was asked in
the television interview afterwards. The blue eyes opened
wide in surprise: '*Wrong?* Nothing has gone wrong.
Nobody has died! I lost at tennis, right?'

Tennis again: Here is John Bromwich of Sydney,
Australia. In between tennis practice he does his milk
round; he's a real amateur. Much loved by the crowds. But
now it's July 1948, and he's reached the final of Wimbledon
against Bob Falkenberg of USA – and he's standing at
match point! Up goes a weak shot from Falkenberg who is
way out of court; all John has to do is gently *pat* the ball
over the net. Instead he excitedly slams it – and it goes out.
Falkenberg goes on to win. The crowd is in tears. End of
Bromwich? Well, hardly – he always has his milk round
to go back to! *That was his job.* And the crowds never
stopped loving this particular Aussie.

Take Borotra. Yes, tennis again! Borotra was the French

champion of the twenties. He got so popular he had to get his faithful chauffeur Albert to sign his autographs for him. The present-day Centre Court at Wimbledon was built to accommodate the extra crowds who turned out to see the Bounding Basque. An amateur always however, he was philosophical about both winning and losing; he was actually a businessman in his daily life. My only meeting with him was when he was ninety; he turned up at the memorial service for commentator Dan Maskell – held in our church of All Souls.

'It's an honour to meet you at last,' I exclaimed over a cup of tea afterwards. 'You *made* Wimbledon'.

'Ah, non!' he smiled back. 'Wimbledon – it made *me*!' He paused, gallantly, to kiss the hand of a lady admirer.

This is the point. When your triumph is snatched away, when your energies are fading and your props are removed, *who are you?* Look again at Paul – how would you summarise this giant of the church? A brilliant evangelist? The greatest debater of the age? Lecturer in three languages? The informed traveller of the Mediterranean basin? The most influential theologian of the last 2,000 years? The enemies of the Christian faith could see the threat represented by this man.

Very well, *bang him into jail.* Neutralise his abilities! Take away his books. Chain him to a guard and shut him up tight! Paul is nothing now.

And so it might have been but for Paul's sense of completeness in Christ alone, and the flexibility of outlook that could learn to convert a prison cell into a broadcasting studio. True, they've got the preacher captive – but Paul now has his own captive audience, courtesy of the Roman Caesar! The letter from prison slips out to inform his friends:

> Now I want you to know, brothers, that what has happened to me has really served to advance the gospel. As a result, it has become clear throughout the whole palace guard and to everyone else that I am in chains for Christ. Because of my chains, most of the brothers in the Lord have been encouraged to speak the word of God more courageously and fearlessly (Phil. 1:12-14).

Perhaps it was with a smile of irony that Paul was able to add this salutation to the end of his letter: 'All the saints send you greetings, *especially those who belong to Caesar's household.*' It was the gentlest of hints that the imperial arrest of a Christian was the surest way of starting a church at the very seat of power!

Once believers in Christ become integrated with the Christian framework of thinking that was Paul's, we have a starting point far ahead of the rest. We should be able, through this 'contentment' within the will of Christ, to handle the most complex and trying of circumstances, like a juggler with fifteen balls in the air.

A great bundle of tensions confronts the beginner, and one of the secrets of progress is to see adversity as part of normal Christian living, and to learn to live with it. This is basic to the New Testament, wrote Hugh Silvester:

> In practice when suffering comes, the Christian (if he is anything like me) says, 'Why me? Why should this happen? Am I not a child of God?' He regards suffering as an interruption, an unwelcome interlude. When it is over he can get on once more with living a 'fruitful' Christian life. Not so; suffering *is* the

Christian life. 'Since therefore Christ suffered in the flesh, arm yourselves with the same thought.'[2]

If we can understand that difficulties are a necessary part of Christian discipleship, we shall never have to face the perpetual disillusionment confronting people of other worldviews, for example, the traditional Marxists. The Marxists always believed in a kind of Utopian ideal, attainable here on this earth. *They were always going to be disappointed.* It is inevitable that such ideologies will eventually cave in and leave their supporters stranded.

We in the church have never thought in terms of a perfectible society *in this life.* We are certainly called to aim high; indeed, to aim for perfection – the very top! In moral terms, we are called by God to be 'perfect', as he is. Did we expect anything else – that our Leader, the purest being that has ever walked on earth, would ask us, please, to try and sin a little *less?* No, to settle for anything short of 100 per cent makes us already 'backsliders'! We are, then, to make the standard of Christ himself our aim, nothing less – but knowing meanwhile that it is not going to be achieved this side of the grave. *We can live with this tension, once we understand it.*

We can also learn to live with the same adversities and hostilities of the unredeemed world that confronted Paul and his companions – and even make them work to the advantage of God and his kingdom. This is 'the art of frustration' – to come to terms with these things and turn them to advantage. It is a learned art – when frustrations can be transformed into an internal dynamo of creativity and service!

---

2. Hugh Silvester, *Arguing with God,* Inter-Varsity Press, 1966, p.117.

We knew a missionary called Ken Ogden. He used his skills as a carpenter and builder to good effect in one of the developing countries. At one point he had shown his local pupils how to build a church. They did it together. They were just about to embark on the final lesson of making the seating, when the blow fell. The totalitarian government of the day found fault with Ken and ordered him out of the country at twenty-four hours notice.

What would you have done? Run round to the bank, and try to extricate what funds you could? Scraped up your most precious belongings, and frantically gathered all together for a hasty exit? Ken did none of that. Those last hours he spent with his pupils, and made *one seat* for the new church. 'There!' he said, when it was done. 'There's your model. Now I'm going, but you finish the rest.' He left them, not only with the prototype for a church seat, but also with a standard of how an integrated Christian behaves under pressure. It was the lesson of *autarkeia*.

'*I have learned the secret*,' wrote Paul. When did he learn it, and how? Was it an instantaneous thing, when the vision and call of Christ was given on the Damascus Road? Certainly it began there. What kept Paul in those times of shipwreck, mob violence and imprisonment? When man after man let him down and left him without support? Why, it was the fact that he was an apostle; he knew that he had been sent! In the last analysis it is *only* those with a sense of call who are still in the field when everything has gone wrong.

But in another way the lesson is only learnt over a lifetime, through hardship, pain and disappointment. The twentieth century, as in no century since the first three, highlighted the resilience of Christian faith where the church was tested by fire – in war zones, tyrannies and killing fields. A Rwandan bishop – after many brushes with death in the mid 1990s – described how, in one locality, many of his people had been killed. Some, who had managed to escape the massacre, had gathered with him. It was Sunday, at around midday.

'From the top of the hill,' he said, 'we could see hundreds of people coming, armed with various weapons. They stopped at a distance from us. We had been praying for two days and teaching people how to receive Jesus Christ, to repent of their sins and to prepare for heaven. Three people came and told me, "Bishop, we come to tell you that people are coming to kill you."

'The words that came into my mind were from 2 Kings, when Elisha, the servant of God, was surrounded by an army of angels, bigger than that of the enemies who were coming to destroy him. I told these people, "You go and tell them that this hill is surrounded by many angels. If these angels allow you, then you will come and destroy us. But if they don't allow you, nobody will approach us. So we are ready. Go and tell them that we are ready. We are not afraid."

'We waited. Thirty minutes later, they just stopped a hundred metres short of the hill where we were. Then we saw them going away, and I was aware that it was the angels who had restrained the army which was surrounding this hill' *(Church Mission Society News*, April 1995*)*.

Triumph or Disaster? They had been ready for either. And then, which is the harder – the immediate crisis or the slow ordeal? The death squad or the grinding prison sentence? Steve Biko or Nelson Mandela? Again, the apostle Paul was ready for either. Perhaps the hardest was waiting in prison and not knowing. Waiting is always hard!

The greater part of our lives is taken up with *waiting* for the next thing to happen. Waiting for news of the expected baby....for the examination results to come through....for the long-distance flight arrival at JFK....for the next vacation....for promotion....for the reports of the medical test....for the elusive answer to prayer – it's hard to wait! *But it is what we do with the waiting times of life that determines the kind of people we are going to become.*

If you can wait, and not be tired by waiting....

We incline to think that it is the high, soaring moments of achievement that are significant, but it is not so. It is all too possible to spend a decade wishing your life away! It's what you do with those boring, frustrating 'in-between' periods that makes the difference between effectiveness and superficiality. We have to believe, as Paul did, that God himself is at work when apparently nothing is happening! 'My Father is always at his work to this very day,' said Jesus, 'and I, too, am working' (John 5:17). God is just as alive, just as personally involved and active five minutes *before* the awaited breakthrough – when the answer to prayer still seems a million miles away – as he is five minutes *after.*

Autarkeia. All this is tightly tied into theology. The Christian is essentially, deep down, an *in-between person.* We work and witness as people living between the first appearance of Jesus Christ – in his earthly ministry – and his return at the end of the age. It is a period full of tensions for the Christian church. There is advance across all five continents, and the final Triumph is assured, but along the way there will be frustrations, setbacks, persecutions, martyrdoms – and the nonstop attrition of the world, the flesh and the Devil!

Learn this lesson of biblical, godly sufficiency, and keep in the learners' lane – developing a framework that will hold when everything around us seems to fall apart. That way we shall fulfil the goal of the whole of our lives, which is to grow in Christlikeness. We are in the fellowship of the In-Betweens! At times it feels like Triumph *now*. Often it looks like Disaster. The trick is to do a Kipling and treat *both* as perhaps Randolph Lycett did, in his Centre Court epic with Shimidsu. But this time without the gin.

7

'That's one small step for
a man, one giant leap
for mankind'

(Astronaut, Neil Armstrong,
July 21st, 1969)

Bishop Trevor Huddleston, famed for his human rights record during South Africa's apartheid days, was telling of his experiences at the time of the moon landing in July 1969 – and I was in the room.

'I was standing in the typical African bush of Tanzania that very day,' he recalled, 'and I was listening intently to a little radio I had with me, as Neil Armstrong's voice crackled dramatically through space: *One small step for a man, one giant leap for mankind.*

'Just by my side was a small inquisitive African boy. "Who is that speaking?" he asked, "what is he saying, and where is he speaking *from*?"

'For the life of me,' continued Huddleston, 'I could not find the language to explain the drama of what was taking place just then. I simply gave him what I later realised was the most brilliant reply I could ever have given. "Ni muntu", I explained briefly. *It is a man.*'

In those four words lies the explanation behind the age-long voyage of discovery embarked upon by the human race – from the first flint axe right through to the space rocket; through the agrarian, industrial and micro-processor revolutions up to the present day.

It is a man.

Naturally it is to the Bible that we must turn for the only satisfying answer to the question of our own identity as a race. *Who* are we – *what* are we – that we should be capable of such exploits? Just to look at the advances that have taken place in the twentieth century! Assuming the average human lifetime to last for some sixty-two years, Alvin Toffler highlighted the point some years ago:

Only in the last seventy lifetimes, has it been possible to communicate effectively from one lifetime to another, as writing made possible to do. Only during the last six lifetimes did masses of people ever see a printed word. Only during the last four has it been possible to measure time with any precision. Only in the last two has anyone anywhere used an electric motor. And the overwhelming majority of all the material goods that we use in daily life today have been developed within the present lifetime.[1]

We can expect the pace to quicken further. But this will not be because modern innovators are any cleverer than, say, Aristarchus of Samos, who around 270 BC, anticipated Copernicus by 1800 years in his conviction that the earth was not flat, but a sphere travelling around the sun. In our basic human make-up, we have not essentially changed. Anthropologists have traditionally used such categories as *homo erectus* and *homo sapiens* in their study of our past. But I believe that it was John Stott who first coined the term *Homo Divinus* in his basic definition of a human being; someone who is characterised by the original stamp of the image of God, and therefore capable of worship, prayer and fellowship with the Creator. The surrounding creation is our environment, and it is our home!

Then God said, 'Let us make man in our image, in our likeness, and let them rule over the fish of the sea and the birds of the air, over the livestock, over all the earth, and over all the creatures that move along the ground.'

---

1. Alvin Toffler, *Future Shock,* Bantam, 1970, p.14.

So God created man in his own image, in the image of God he created him; male and female he created them.

God blessed them and said to them, 'Be fruitful and increase in number; fill the earth and subdue it' (Gen. 1: 26-28).

Is this easy to believe, situated, as we are, on a planet that is only an astronomical atom among our surrounding, whirling constellations? In our sun alone, there is room for one and a quarter million earths such as ours. And the sun itself is only one star among a great group of such stars. On beyond the Milky Way, in immeasurable distances, are yet other systems such as that of Andromeda, with its countless suns.

And yet the stars are very thinly scattered in the universe. To bring the scale down a bit, supposing a star were just the size of a pinhead, and were placed here on earth – it would be between twenty and thirty miles from its nearest neighbour. Is it easy to believe that all this was purpose-designed as our home?

Stephen Hawking of Cambridge University describes the earth in these terms:

...a medium-sized planet, orbiting round an average star in the outer suburbs of an ordinary spiral galaxy, which is itself only one of about a million million galaxies in the observable universe. Yet the strong anthropic principle would claim that this whole, vast construction exists simply for our sake. This is very hard to believe.[2]

---

2. Stephen Hawking, *A Brief History of Time,* Bantam Press, 1988, p.120

It is more than hard to believe; it is impossible – without an authoritative *witness* that can stand astride and outside all of our history and scientific probings, a witness that can stand the test of time. We have this in the biblical record. For it is the Bible that gives us our proper perspective, and corrects the flaw in Stephen Hawking's worldview, for all his brilliance. What is noteworthy is what was *left out* of Hawking's statement.

First, there is the factor of *God*-centredness, not man-centredness, in our fantastic universe. Secondly, Hawking fails to take into account the possibility that creation could be the home, not just of the human *species* as such, but of a race of God-like beings! That is our stature and calling. And thirdly, we must never forget that the whole of creation centres in....*a Man,* who is described in the Scriptures as the image of the invisible God, the heir of all creation, in whom everything holds together, and for whom it all consists. He is Jesus Christ, fully God and fully human. He is the prototype human being, and it is only in relationship to him, the Lord of all creation, that our residence in the immensity of this cosmic home begins to lose its absurdity. Here then is an account of our origin and home – that can satisfy a tribe in a developing country, or a business person in a hotel room, reading the Gideon Bible.

Ni Muntu....it is a Man! James Irwin, one of the American moon astronauts, worshipped and spoke at our London church on one occasion. He gave us a framed photograph of the moon landing. Under the picture he had added a caption in his own hand. It reads, *God walking on the earth is more important than man walking on the moon.*

Irwin's point was important. It may be that journeys

can be made to the moon, to Mars even, or Neptune. But what is the whole thing *for?* The revelation – and it has to be a revelation from God for us to grasp it at all – is that there is a Creator, and that he is concerned personally about this world and its inhabitants. This realisation unlocks so many philosophical puzzles.

In opposition to atheism, the Bible proclaims *God.* In opposition to polytheism and the belief in many gods, the Scriptures emphasise *one* God. In opposition to Pantheism, which identifies God with nature, the Bible declares the *separateness* of God from his creation. In opposition to materialism, we learn of the *spirituality* of God and of the human race. In opposition to Deism – the concept of a world wound up like a watch and then left alone by an absentee God – the Bible declares that God the creator is also God the *sustainer,* and furthermore that he is God the *intervener* in our affairs and our history.

It is God in Christ, then, and not just an amazing world as such, that provides the true background and proper identity to *Homo Divinus.* Before the two opening chapters of Genesis are over, the reader is beginning to get some answers. As a Chinese man once exclaimed, 'Whoever made this book made *me!*'

This is the message of the grand overture to all the Scriptures – that behind all that we can see, know, sense and are, is the God of all creativity, the originator of the universe. Of course we are not here faced with an account as a journalist would have presented it. No person was present to see the creation of the world in any case. It is the emphasis that is so important.

Science places much emphasis on the stages following the original Big Bang – the formation of the continents, oceans, vegetation and the animal kingdom – as taking place over many millions of years. So vast are the statistics that our own apparently short history is reduced in significance to virtually vanishing point. But the Bible reverses that proportion and turns it completely around:

'The forming of the continents? Those tortuous procedures, those millions of years that are said to have gone into the creation of the first jellies and crustaceans, and the forming of the mosses, the trees – and the dinosaurs? *A week's work, that's all.* We'll give that bit a page. *Correction –* we'll give it two pages! And then the real bit, *your* story; the bit that those experts of yours dismiss as a single page? Why, we'll need well over a thousand pages before we're through!'

In the face of the countless galaxies and the billions of years that shrink us, we would feel completely lost but for this divine word that puts the balance right and gives us orientation and *size.* And responsibility!

Let them rule over the fish of the sea and the birds of the air....over all the creatures....(Gen. 1: 26).

*Rule....*not exploit! The human responsibility is to be one of care and custodianship over the world of nature. Our concern is to extend beyond the earth itself, and into the heavens and the cosmos as well – hence the areas of astronomy and space exploration. We have only to refer to the New Testament letter to the Romans for this wider involvement to be apparent:

The creation waits in eager expectation for the sons of God to be revealed. For the creation was subjected to frustration, not by its own choice, but by the will of the one who subjected it, in hope that the creation itself will be liberated from its bondage to decay and brought into the glorious freedom of the children of God (Rom. 8:19-21).

It is evident that the destiny of the human race is strangely locked into that of all the created order; both are waiting for the future 'liberation' – for the redemption of our bodies (Rom. 8:23), but also for the new heaven and the new earth that Scripture promises. So space exploration? If carried out responsibly, yes. It is part of our domain.

We are cast in the role of God's estate managers. We are separated from the animal kingdom and are placed over it and all the created order – not by dint of brute force, but as trustees who are to govern, husband and protect the earth's resources, to name and categorise the animals; thus there is the beginning of zoology and science.

We are in the image of God; that tells us of our high calling – but also of our limitation. We are *images* of God, but only images. We are not God himself; we exist only by derivation, unlike Christ who is the exact replica of God (Col. 1:15). For this reason the New Age teaching will one day fall flat on its face. You can, after all, persuade tired business executives in New Age seminars that they have a god inside them and that there is nothing that they cannot achieve. But it will not be long before it becomes all too obvious that they have been sold a lie; they are failing to meet their deadlines, failing to satisfy their spouses, suffering from duodenal ulcers and ingrowing toenails – manifestly they are *not* God!

Only one thing was stated *not* to be good, in those first

two chapters of Genesis, and that was that the man was alone. So Genesis chapter 2 gives us the Magna Carta of sexuality and marriage, and the summons to community. We were made for each other, side by side, male and female – with the *differences* between the sexes being, as one writer has put it, 'the single most important fact of human society'. After all, it would be unthinkable to say, 'In Oxford Street, *a human being* asked me the way to Trafalgar Square!'

Again, who are we? The Bible's definition of Genesis 1:27 places us on a far higher level than the secular humanist, or indeed a few clerics on the extreme edge of the church's life. The Rev Don Cupitt, who frequently graced British television screens in the 1980s, no longer believed in an objective God. But it also appeared that he scarcely believed in himself:

> My self is a mere temporary aggregation of processes....My own desires are part of the flux of forces in nature.[3]

I only wonder what suitable format could be found for the communication of such sentiments. The pastoral interview? The pulpit? The Sunday School? The deathbed?

No, we are *Homo Divinus* – raised to our status by the God of creativity, of personality and of responsibility. Chapter 2 of Genesis places the man in his garden, somewhere near where the rivers Tigris and Euphrates flow close together. Perhaps our human race had its beginnings a few miles west of Baghdad? The point is that already in the Bible story, place names are being featured; it is not just a fairy tale. Here are the beginnings, not only of science and zoology, but the taking seriously of geography too.

---

3. Scott Cowdell, *Atheist Priest?*, SCM Press, 1991, p. 62.

The truth is, we were not intended to forage for ourselves out in the jungle or the desert; we were to be in the place, the garden, the *home* appointed by God. Our responsibility was to keep the garden, to look after it and to observe its laws.

And the tree of the knowledge of good and evil? The implication is that Adam would not have known what good and evil were, unless he transgressed. The choice facing him, then, was not between good and evil, but between God and himself. We may ask, Should we have been made with this capacity to choose against God? But if fellowship with God is to mean anything at all, there has to exist the possibility of refusal. Otherwise we are no more than robots, reduced to the level of machine programming.

The Fall takes place, and it is real. Did it take place in heaven – with Satan – *before* it happened on earth – with the guilty pair? The right answer is that it is conceived as *one* fall, not two. It is advisable to avoid applying standards of modern chronology to God's account of the Fall.

Although the image of God upon us is defaced by the Fall, it is not obliterated. Again and again we are able to see flashes of the heights that men and women can attain, irrespective of whether they are religious. In times of crisis, or faced by the challenges of nature, we have it in us to rise to the occasion, as noble King man, as regal Queen woman!

An example took place some years ago when an airliner crashed into the Potomac River. Scenes from the disaster were flashed on TV screens everywhere. One of the most vivid incidents recorded was of a man on the bank throwing off his jacket and plunging into the river to rescue a young woman victim of the crash, who was drowning. His name was Lenny Skutnik. Ignoring the rescue services, the helicopters and the television crews, he reached the girl, got her to the bank, and then melted quietly away into the crowd. Only later did his identity become known. In that moment of rescue we saw King Man as he ought to be, the apex of God's creation.

Was such an event entirely predictable? Was Lenny Skutnik *not* responsible for his actions; was it all attributable to his genetic make-up? The glib theorists can sound plausible enough in a lecture room or TV studio. They become totally irrelevant in the great moments of human crisis, surging emotion or supreme creativity. We are people, not machines. It is within our capacity, even as sinful rebels, to love, to sacrifice and dedicate, because of who we are.

It is the Michelangelos of this world, the Nelson Mandelas, the Florence Nightingales and Joni Earecksons who explode the theory that we are no more than blobs of protoplasm wrapped around an appetite. Our ultimate model, however, is not to be found among these inspirers. Nor are we turning to Plato, Aristotle or Isaac Newton.

One model alone is enough. He is permanent and he is universal. We should let this description of Christ burn into our mind-set:

> He who descended is the very one who ascended higher than all the heavens, *in order to fill the whole universe* (Eph. 4: 10).

The whole universe centres around a human being! Of course there are those who carry out earnest research into the possible existence of other forms of life in the universe, little green men and all – but we could save them the bother if they only knew. God is a human being, and we who are made in his likeness, though we have fallen from our original stature, are called back by the gospel of the Cross and Resurrection, to aspire to know him, the prototype human, Jesus Christ. Only as we commit ourselves to him will all of our existence begin to make sense and take on significance. For what is to be found at the centre of the universe?

It is a Man. And not only so, but *with* him there at the centre, is his redeemed church! The *church* at the centre of the universe? I can hear the emperor Domitian laughing in the first century AD – 'The *church?* What's that?' Later on it's Stalin – 'The *church?* How many armoured divisions have they?'

But we go along with the apostle Paul. He takes as already established this indissoluble link between Jesus and his friends. Christ's destiny is our destiny!

> The first man was of the dust of the earth, the second man from heaven. As was the earthly man, so are those who are of the earth; and as is the man from heaven, so also are those who are of heaven. And just as we have borne the likeness of the earthly man, so shall we bear the likeness of the man from heaven (1 Cor. 15:47-49).

It is one small step that is required, not at the foot of a lunar module, but at the foot of a Roman cross. *It is the only place where God will meet us.* Here lies the difference between staying as an earthly human being, unforgiven and without a future hope, and making the giant leap to a place at the side of the man from heaven, Christ, Master of the universe. To come to know him, follow him and become progressively like him is literally the space adventure of a lifetime.

8

'The moment the slave resolves that he will no longer be a slave, his fetters fall'

(Mahatma Gandhi, 1949)

Liz and I stood above the valley, gazing down in awe at the Pont du Gard, the sensational Roman aqueduct near Nimes in Southern France. Built by slave labour before the time of Christ, there it stood, column upon mighty column in perfect preservation. It is so massive that its base is used as a busy motor thoroughfare to this day. We found ourselves compelled to return a few days later for a second visit.

The fact that so many of the celebrated monuments of the world are associated with slavery and oppression should send a pang through the thoughtful visitor. The pyramids of Egypt are a prime example. The Taj Mahal in India is said to be the most beautiful building in the world; but its beauty is marred by the ugly truth that when its hundreds of workers had completed their task, they all had their eyes put out, so that they would never build anything as beautiful again. In Rome it is entirely appropriate that the Coliseum is now officially designated a memorial to the Christian martyrs who met their deaths there.

When we look back at the twentieth century, Mohandas Karamchand Gandhi is widely hailed as one of the great champions of the oppressed. Born in 1869, he was renowned for his prolonged fight against racial legislation in South Africa, and then in India for his civil disobedience campaigns in the struggle for home rule. *Mahatma* ('Great Soul') Gandhi became venerated across India for his self-discipline, for his commitment to non-violence and his championing of the underclass; not least the 'Untouchables' of the caste system – whom he renamed *Harijans* ('Children of God'). How could people know freedom from slavery – politically, socially, or internally within themselves? This was a theme running through his life:

The moment the slave resolves that he will no longer be a slave, his fetters fall. He frees himself, and shows the way to others. Freedom and slavery are mental states.[1]

Gandhi's sentiments can be paralleled with those of a black American slave, Frederick Douglass, a century earlier. Writing in 1845, he described how, the moment his master's mistress had introduced him to reading and writing, the seed of self-conscious thought was sown in his life. From that point on, it was impossible mentally to go back:

> I have observed this in my experience of slavery, that whenever my condition was improved, instead of its increasing my contentment, it only increased my desire to be free, and set me to thinking of plans to gain my freedom. I have found that, to make a contented slave, it is necessary to make a thought-less one.[2]

This has always been true. Hence the determination of all authoritarian regimes, without exception, to keep the education of their slave class at the lowest possible level. Anything to stave off that dangerous moment of self-consciousness, when an entire people, even, may come alive and defy the ruling powers, and start to live as they were born to live. But how is that moment arrived at? Here undoubtedly lay an area of frustration for Gandhi. *'He frees himself,'* is his phrase. Similarly with Douglass – *'My desire to be free.'*

---

1. *Non-Violence in Peace and War,* 1949, Vol. 2.
2. *Narrative of the life of Frederick Douglass, an American Slave,* The Norton Anthology of American Literature [5th edition], Vol. 1, W.W. Norton & Co., 1998, pp. 2044-5.

The vital question is, How? India became independent in 1947 ('the noblest act of the British nation'), but Gandhi's dream of a country united in peace and freedom was never fulfilled. So much that he campaigned against – poverty, cultural strife and the caste system – remained impenetrable to his influence. Half a million deaths from civil war, and the shock separation of Pakistan from India, were part of the darkening clouds surrounding the Mahatma before his death at the hands of a Hindu fanatic on January 30th, 1948.

Gandhi's single-minded contribution to India's independence firmly established him as one of the great leaders of the twentieth century. But India was never able to shake herself loose from the inner turmoils inherited from her cultural past. *How then is it done* – freeing an entire people from the 'fetters', of whatever kind, that hold it down? The issue has confronted protagonists for freedom and national unity from Moses onwards.

A classic example centres on the prophet Ezekiel in the middle of the sixth century BC. He had been caught up in the tragedy that had overwhelmed Israel and Judah, in three successive deportations of the Jewish people by the Babylonian king, Nebuchadnezzar. Ezekiel had found himself, together with thousands of his fellow-citizens, forcibly exiled to an area about fifty miles south of modern Baghdad. It was slave labour there, in a heat of over 100^0F. Five hundred miles away, the holy city of Jerusalem was now a scene of complete destruction. It was the worst thing that had ever happened to God's chosen people.

It was when they were ten years into their ordeal that Ezekiel, the Jews' remarkable seer, received one of those luminous prophetic visions that characterised his long career – the Valley of the Dry Bones! Here was an opportunity for a people with a slave mentality to become 'thoughtful', and to gain at least an inner spiritual freedom. Here was a revelation that would inspire Ezekiel and generations of leaders after him, faced by people stuck in a captive, no change situation. The vision holds a key of priceless value for every civilisation:

> The hand of the LORD was upon me, and he brought me out by the Spirit of the LORD and set me in the middle of a valley; it was full of bones. He led me to and fro among them, and I saw a great many bones on the floor of the valley, bones that were very dry. He asked me, 'Son of man, can these bones live?' (Ezek. 37:1-3).

Ezekiel stood above the valley, gazing down in awe at the scene below. Was the vision coloured, perhaps, by Ezekiel's own memory of thousands of corpses, resulting from Nebuchadnezzar's conquest? The picture is stark and grim. This is where slavery to Babylon has brought you! Dry bones; irreversible catastrophe. Israel will never rise again. *Stop thinking.*

A hopeless case

If the captives had entertained any hopes of a reprieve when they had first arrived in Babylonia, those hopes would by now have been sunk without trace in the marshy swamps that surrounded the Euphrates. The mentality had become dull, memories of past glories had dried up; spiritual hardening of the arteries had set in, and devotion, prayer and worship had become arid, dead things.

It can happen to a nation, it can happen to a church, it

can happen to spiritual leaders and it can happen to you. It is possible to become *accustomed* to a narrow, earthbound existence, and even to find a certain security in such captivity. When this takes place in a community, language becomes gross and coarse, awe disappears, the sky becomes closed off and worship is a bore. No amount of public exhortations will wake up a people when death has set in. You can make resolutions, advertise on hoardings, write in the radical press and free up the rules of admission! Nothing will change.

Here, in Ezekiel's people, was a nation that had been singled by God out of all history, to bring his light and rule to the world! But something in the corporate spirit had died. It looked like a no-hope diagnosis: 'Son of man, these bones are the whole house of Israel' (v. 11). And the crunch question comes, *Son of man, can these bones live?*

The logical answer would seem to be 'No'. There is little chance of a slave 'resolving that he will no longer be a slave', once the mentality has been stifled, the spirit killed, and opportunity crushed in ruins 500 miles away. As it is, Ezekiel gives a diplomatic answer: 'O Sovereign LORD, you alone know.' It is then that the prophet is given his task:

> Then he said to me, 'Prophesy to these bones and say to them, "Dry bones, hear the word of the LORD! This is what the Sovereign LORD says to these bones: I will make breath enter you, and you will come to life. I will attach tendons to you and make flesh come upon you and cover you with skin; I will put breath in you, and you will come to life. Then you will know that I am the LORD" ' (Ezek. 37:4-6).

Have you ever heard of the Wesleyan revival? Of the awakenings in America under Jonathan Edwards and Charles Finney? Of the Welsh, the East African, the Korean revivals of faith? It is passages such as Ezekiel 37 that repeatedly inspire belief that the blood and fire of the Christian Gospel are as powerful today as in the first century of the Christian mission. But never did a mission field or congregation look such a hopeless case as Ezekiel's!

A useless task

The dead, dry bones of Ezekiel's vision are completely stripped, and scattered over the valley. Yes, death is complete. However, the power of the word of God is such that even a universe can be preached into being! It follows then that lifeless, dead bones – bleached and dried in the relentless sun of Babylonia – can be prophesied into life again. And so the prophet is given his mandate. It looks absurd:
Preach to the bones!

'Er....yes, right. To the bones? Over there? Um....it won't do any good, Lord. You see, we haven't had any temple worship for the last decade. It's hopeless....and after all, the Christian group at my campus has died on its feet, Lord....It's no good trying to reach my particular group of colleagues; they're as hard as nails....Don't ask me to try and win *my* family for Jesus Christ – might as well try and communicate to a bunch of dried-up Egyptian mummies! .... *You see, Lord, we're now living in a post-temple era.*'

'Never mind all that,' comes the command. 'Preach to them anyway.'

And then, as Ezekiel complies, a stirring begins; there's a rattling and a shaking in response to the words of the prophet. It's a miracle. He sees the hip bone connecting to the thigh bone, and the thigh bone connecting to the knee bone – as they hear the word of the Lord!

In his vision, Ezekiel watches it happen – but all through history *we* have watched it happen too.

Come, for example, to the crunch day for Europe – August 24th, 410 AD. The end has come for Rome and for all Christendom. Yes, it all happens on a single day. There are simply too many Barbarians around for civilised society to contain any longer. Alaric, leader of the Visigoth hordes, is at the very gates of a city that for so long has stood for the stability and unity of all Europe. Then the unbelievable happens. Rome is sacked, *Rome!* Word gets around. It's all over. Despite the emperor Constantine's earlier conversion and subsequent establishing of Christianity as the State religion in 324 AD, everything solid has come apart. Rome is sacked.... dead bones everywhere. Christianity has failed. If only we'd stuck with the pagan gods all along!

Over in Carthage, a middle-aged man of fifty-six chose to disagree with this diagnosis, as the shocking news reached him. He was Augustine, Bishop of Hippo. Rome – was it worth preserving anyway? Surely, he reasoned with his Christian friends, every earthly city falls eventually. Christianity had never been interested in preserving *Rome!* We have always been citizens of another and eternal City.

Augustine began to write, as he rallied the Christian believers of shattered Europe. *It is not all over.* He compared Rome's destruction with that of Sodom, and encouraged his friends to focus instead on the Bible's vision of the City of God:

There will be an end to every earthly kingdom. You are surprised that the world is losing its grip and full of passing tribulations. Do not hold onto the old man, the world; do not refuse to regain your youth in Christ, who says to you: 'The world is passing away, the world is short of breath. Do not fear, thy youth shall be renewed as an eagle.'[3]

The City of God was a monumental work of twenty-two volumes. It took Augustine fifteen years to write. Its impact was colossal. It helped to remake a single community for all of Europe, centred at base level upon the objective truth of Scripture. Without Jesus Christ, Europe would not have been – *and never will be* – anything more than a collection of competing Barbarian tribes! The combination of Augustine and his contemporary, Jerome – whose life work was the Vulgate version of the Bible – produced for Europe a single, great culture which was to endure for the next thousand years.

The scattered bones can be reconstituted a unity, and given flesh and breath! *It has been done before; it can be done again.*

Could not Gandhi have done something of this kind for India? The answer, reluctantly, is 'No'. Gandhi, for all of his fascination with Jesus (his favourite hymn was *When I survey the wondrous Cross*), never could come to the conviction of a single, all-encompassing and integrating Truth, that followers of Christ ascribe to him alone. Gandhi was a Hindu, and in his view every tradition had its own differing and complementary 'truth'. He was unable to cope with the idea that *one* great teaching could possibly be true

3. Augustine, *De Civitate Dei, 412-427 AD.*

in itself. His worldview was comprised of 'all that I know to be best in Islam, Christianity, Buddhism and Zoroastrianism'.

There can never be unity along that road. Gandhi's solution for India of uniting Muslims and Hindus met with total failure.

How can one unite a society and rid it of the elements that keep it in mental slavery? Ezekiel was to share the great secret with the world, in his vision of the valley of the dry bones. It is done by the word of God and the Spirit of God. Nothing else will bring integration to a community.

> '**Prophesy to these bones** and say to them 'Dry bones, hear the word of the LORD....Then he said to me, '**Prophesy to the breath**....and say to it, 'This is what the Sovereign LORD says: Come from the four winds, O breath, and breathe into these slain, that they may live' (Ezek. 37:4, 9).

There were then – and are – two necessary parts to the operation; the communication of God's *Word*, and the animation of God's breath, or *Spirit*. This is reminiscent of the book of Genesis, where God *speaks* – and the initial act of our creation takes place – and *breathes* – and man becomes a living being.

Preach to the bones....and address yourself to the Spirit. It is as the twin activities of preaching and prayer are engaged that the miracle takes place in Ezekiel's valley. As though a divine wand has been waved over them, the entire, disintegrated confusion of dead skeletons becomes a living, vibrant army of animated people. A hopeless case? A useless task? History would say 'No'!

An impossible dream

It certainly looks impossible – restoration from the death of slavery in a foreign land to a rejuvenated army with a message for the whole world!

> Therefore prophesy and say to them: 'This is what the Sovereign LORD says: O my people, I am going to open your graves and bring you up from them; I will bring you back to the land of Israel....I will put my Spirit in you and you will live, and I will settle you in your own land (Ezek. 37:12-14).

This indeed took place. As in the case of Rome's overthrow, Babylon fell on a single day, October 16th, 539 BC, under the leadership of Darius, co-regent of Cyrus of the Medes and Persians. Cyrus himself entered the city seventeen days later, amid scenes of jubilation, and shortly afterwards proclaimed the decree that let the slaves return to their own land. It has been said that Judah went into exile as a nation, and returned to her land as a church.

But the fulfilment of Bible prophecy always goes beyond the immediate circumstances of the original utterance. We have to see a secondary fulfilment of Ezekiel's vision in the New Testament people of the gospel, set free from the bonds of sin and death by the preaching of Jesus and his death upon the cross. Then there is a still further fulfilment of the prophecy – in the far-off reaches of the End Times – with the rejuvenation of our tired, dying world in the new heaven and the new earth that all history is pointing us towards. If you believe that, then you have a cohesive worldview which is going to affect everything that you touch!

It is not an impossible dream. The bones can and will live! At times doubts will raise themselves. In the middle ages, Europe seemed to have lost its way spiritually, with salvation obscured under a welter of error and superstitious practices. But then, as Erasmus observed in a letter of 1519, *The world is waking out of a long, deep sleep.* The great Reformation of Luther and Calvin followed – which Erasmus had helped to usher in by his massive scholarship – and once again the yoke of spiritual slavery under a corrupt system was lifted on a vast scale. Four hundred years later my own life and that of millions of others are profoundly affected by that Reformation – an open Bible, a clear view of salvation, and an unshackled spirit. Later still after the Reformation came a further release of the human spirit in the Wesleyan revival:

> My chains fell off, my heart was free,
> I rose, went forth and followed thee!

No amount of sociological campaigning, or inter-faith manoeuvring, can bring about such a radical liberation. It is here that we sense the wistfulness of Mahatma Gandhi, and the extraordinary lengths to which he went in his spiritual search:

> What I want to achieve – what I have been striving and pining to achieve these thirty years – is self-realization, to see God face to face, to attain *Moksha* (spiritual deliverance).... I have not yet found Him, but I am seeking after Him.... For it is an unbroken fortune to me that I am still so far from Him.... I have not seen Him, neither have I known Him.[4]

---

4. *An Autobiography,* J. Cape, 1949, p. 252.

It is Jesus who gave the vital clue to all human searching, when he declared to doubting Thomas, 'If you really knew me, you would know my Father as well. From now on, *you do know him and have seen him*' (John 14: 7).

This possibility is open to all who recognise in Christ the way, the truth and the life; that universally and exclusively, he is the only way to the Father (John 14: 6). A child can come this way. And so can a slave of the Roman empire.

The Christian slaves of the first century are a model for us all! A great proportion of the Gentile church was initially composed of such slaves – the very people who built the Pont du Gard aqueduct. But what was their status as Christian slaves? How should they now behave? Present a petition to Caesar? Organise a sit-in, a protest march, a people's revolution? Attempt to throw off their Roman fetters in a violent uprising? But that would have been to reduce their leader Jesus Christ to the level of a mere Spartacus or Che Guevara.

In the event, they were inspired to do something more revolutionary still. Within the Christian fellowship they began to treat the social classifications *as though they didn't exist at all.* Christians, such as the Roman slave-owner Philemon, found themselves challenged by a new code, as in the test case of a returned runaway slave, one Onesimus. The apostle Paul's letter to Philemon was like a time bomb, awaiting its future moment of detonation through Christian reformers such as Wilberforce and Shaftesbury. For the time being, the recommended action over Onesimus the slave was very simple:

> Perhaps the reason he was separated from you for a little while was that you might have him back for good – no longer as a slave, but better than a slave, as a dear brother. He is very dear to me but even dearer to you, both as a man and as a brother in the Lord (Philemon 15, 16).

The days of official legislation against slavery in civilised countries still lay far ahead. What do you do in the meantime? The apostle Paul was clear in his advice to Philemon: *Just do it in your own household – live like a Christian!*

That, after all, is the best laboratory for a test-case. Not the law courts so much as your own living room – 'the church that meets in your home,' writes Paul (Philemon 2). The Christian meeting at Philemon's place was about to experience a small revolution. As the fellowship and prayer time ended, no longer would Onesimus the slave then be allowed to enter the room, carrying the pizzas, only to depart again. He was now to be one of the circle, taking his part in the mutual support and the sharing of prayer requests. Paul is very clear:

> You are all sons of God through faith in Christ Jesus ....There is neither Jew nor Greek, slave nor free, male nor female, for you are all one in Christ Jesus (Gal. 3:26-28).

In that first century the slaves were just about the only available working models of this principle. If you were looking for an attractive lifestyle to emulate, Paul would have pointed you to the slaves of Crete, whom he expected to 'make the teaching about God our Saviour *attractive*' (Titus 2: 10). If a slave can do it, then anyone can do it!

And that is how social revolutions are achieved; simply by enough people living as Christians – taught by the Word of God, and inspired by the Spirit of God. It is actually happening in practice all over the world, and in some of the hardest arenas ever known – in Southern Sudan, in central Asia, in Indonesia and China.

Wherever we are we must practise this ourselves. Even if you are only one in six billion, there is always something that calls out to be done. Pornography on the Internet may worry us – but we are to see to it that pornography has no entry point within our own homes. We may fret over the decline in the institution of marriage; then the standards of Christ must rule in our own private lives. We may lament the tight-fistedness of governments in dealing with world debt – but are we tight-fisted ourselves?

The world may well stagger in confusion and disillusionment in the opening years of the third millennium. It certainly did after the 1,000 AD mark was passed. The Word and the Spirit of Ezekiel's vision provide the lesson for us: the Bible and Prayer. *How dull that sounds!* But do it anyway, and you will find to your amazement that you are part of the fulfilment of Ezekiel's vision – a living member of *a vast army*. And dull it won't be.

9

'I'd like to be a Queen in people's hearts'

(Diana, Princess of Wales, November 20th, 1995)

It was early in the morning when the telephone shrilled beside me. I was sitting at my desk in our London home, thinking about the Sunday that lay ahead of us at All Souls Church. I picked up the receiver. It was my Australian colleague, Richard Trist.

'Richard?' he started.

'O, hullo, Richard. How are you doing?'

'Fine, thanks. But I was wondering whether we ought to do anything different to the morning services in view of the news.'

'News? I haven't heard anything.' I began to feel shaky.

'It's Princess Di. I'm afraid she's been killed.'

There are only a very few of the great public crises in which everyone can remember precisely where they were and what they were doing when the news story broke for them. I was on the doorstep of my parents' home in Tonbridge, on the evening of Thursday, November 23rd 1963, when the door opened and my mother came out, distraught. 'Have you heard about Kennedy?'

'No. Mum. What's happened?'

'He's been assassinated.'

Now it was Diana. I staggered for some minutes. Then it came to me; there wasn't a moment to lose. *Church this morning.* Steadily, Richard Trist and I went over the checklist. Our preaching colleague Rico Tice must alter his sermon. Our director of music, Noël Tredinnick, must change the music; in the event he omitted the first hymn and played a lament instead. Church Council member Alison Grieve would have to be rung about the prayers – had she heard the news yet? Then I must give out a careful announcement, for the benefit of those who would arrive at church not having heard of the stunning events. Everything would be coloured by what had happened in the Alma tunnel in the early hours of that fateful Sunday. Days later I was asked to write a page for the *Sunday Express*. Before long I was to be interviewed on an American TV programme – simply because we were in London and had ready access to the crowds, the atmosphere in the underground trains and on the streets. And, of course, in the church.

There's nothing like a very public death to shake the world, to make millions catch their breath and think long and hard about the 'Candle in the Wind' that represents every person's short, flickering life. **'I'd like to be a Queen in people's hearts, but I don't see myself being Queen of this country,'** Princess Di had told BBC interviewer Martin Bashir fifteen months earlier. Now she was gone – and the remembered remark was reflected in the many 'heart' emblems that featured in thousands of messages and flowers that descended upon Buckingham Palace and Kensington Palace. The most celebrated woman on earth had died in a Paris underpass, and the reverberations went worldwide. Indeed for weeks afterwards, I took extra care over my driving. If I was in an underpass, my thoughts would immediately switch to the events in the Alma tunnel. Crossing the road, I would be more alert than usual. Everyone had been made more aware of their own frailty.

But all the shakings of history, warns the Bible, are only curtain-raisers to the universal shaking that will take place at the end of the world – when the only thing to survive Christ's return and the great day of judgment will be what the Scripture describes as *the kingdom that cannot be shaken:*

See to it that you do not refuse him who speaks. If
they did not escape when they refused him who
warned them on earth, how much less will we, if we
turn away from him who warns us from heaven? At
that time his voice shook the earth, but now he has
promised, 'Once more I will shake not only the earth
but also the heavens'....

Therefore, since we are receiving a kingdom that
cannot be shaken, let us be thankful, and so worship
God acceptably with reverence and awe, for 'our God
is a consuming fire' (Heb. 12:25-26, 28-29).

The biblical writer is saying that the earth has had its times
of shaking. Far ahead of the time of Christ, those people of
Israel felt *their* world shaking around them – as God's
giving to them of the ten commandments forged them into
a nation....as the divine Covenantal contract was hammered
out in smoke and rumblings at the sacred mountain of
Sinai....as the Jebusites, Amorites and Perizzites tumbled
one after another into the dust around them....in the
adventure of the great trek towards the Promised Land.

The battles! The crises! The judgments! And, in our
own time, the unexpected twists and turns of a climactic
twentieth century that have shaken our media-driven world,
as none other. But – warn the Scriptures – these are only
the prelude to the final crisis! They are given to point men
and women to the only entity that will survive *everything*
– the 'kingdom that cannot be shaken', whose members
are declared to be *the first-born, whose names are written
in heaven* (Heb. 12:23).

There is something personally significant about getting
your name onto a roll or register, or – as millions did in

September 1997 – into one of the books of condolence that were opened for Princess Diana all over the world. The act gives permanent recognition to something that you have done or decided; you are now established in the annals. *It has become official.*

However our writer to the Hebrews declares that only one register matters eternally, when the final convulsions of history end with Christ's return and the supremacy of the unshakeable kingdom. To have your name 'written in heaven' stamps you into the annals of eternity; you are in what Revelation chapter 20 calls *the book of life.*

This connects with the death of Diana, Princess of Wales. For the tragedy of the Alma tunnel aroused a number of very deep-seated instincts in people. Of course we must firmly set aside the hype – even religious hype, of the 'prophecy' brand that immediately jumped in and predicted a nationwide Revival of faith within weeks. Plenty of mad legends were flying around; the Internet was thick with conspiracy theories. I refer rather to what the Daily Mail columnist Paul Johnson pleaded for. **'Give us a spiritual dimension. For Diana's sake, tell us that life has a purpose, and give us an idea of what that purpose is.'**

There were, perhaps, four great human instincts that lay behind the worldwide outpouring of grief and the reverent crowds that lined London's streets. Four widespread yearnings – and coupled with them we may recognise how the message of God in Jesus Christ *meets* people at the precise point of these felt desires:

The desire to atone

How could matters be put *right* with someone who was now irrevocably removed from all chance of reparation to her for damage inflicted? Diana was perceived at her death as a woman of beauty, fragility and compassion, who had apparently died in the process of escaping from the very predatory cameras that were feeding the public's appetite.

Michael Ignatieff, writing in *Prospect* magazine, commented, 'Sorrow is more intense when compounded of guilt, and ours was a guilty sorrow. We all had a hand in making the myths which killed her.'

Part of the guilt-ridding exercise was the hunt for a scapegoat. The *paparazzi?* The chauffeur? The Ritz Hotel? The House of Fayed? Who would take the chief burden of blame? And behind the bringing of flowers and the creating of little shrines by the Palace was the sentiment, *We are sorry; we seek for absolution.*

But there was another element present too:

The desire to unite

In a strange way people felt that they 'knew' Princess Diana. Somehow, in all her insecurities, she seemed close to ordinary people, deprived and buffeted people; consequently her death carried with it a remarkable *power* – as an American friend of ours put it – 'to give us something to make us *unified.*' In that sense there was something valid in her TV reference to being a queen in people's hearts. Many felt her empathy with the ordinary people.

Hence the enormous crowds – and I could sense, as I stood in the Mall to see the coffin going by, the reverence, the quiet, the feeling of mutual consideration and 'oneness' – of a kind reportedly not experienced in Britain since the testing days of World War II.

'It can't last, of course,' I murmured to a minister

colleague, Paul Blackham, as we gazed at the quiet massed crowd outside Buckingham Palace. But it was a national phenomenon for about two weeks. Millions of people felt united by the power of a single person. There was great wistfulness. How could that mood be preserved ....recreated? And how does God meet us – in the deeply-felt desires, to atone and to unite?

The desire to identify

It was impossible to ignore Princess Diana during her short life. Clive James, in the *New Yorker* (September 1997), noted the astonishing impact she made on virtually all nationalities:

> Diana once flew to Japan, addressed 125 million people *in their own language,* and made the most stunning impact there since Hirohito had declared that the war was over....
>
> She wasn't just beautiful. She was like the sun coming up; coming up giggling.

It was virtually impossible for anyone to stand outside this death. It had come after a whole series of signals that events were not under control, despite the final glimpse of fleeting happiness. So it was that millions of people felt a compulsion to identify, to *register* that they were not uncaring. Jean Seaton, writing in a magazine, commented, 'I (and many others) *worried* about Diana, like a wayward younger sister. When the dresses looked good, we felt pleased. When she looked frumpy, we felt irritated. When she took infant Will to Australia, us new mothers nodded with approval.'

Thus, when the news of the tragedy became known, there was something in people across the entire world that compelled them to go somewhere, do something, *sign and register*. There is, deep within the human spirit, a desire to place one's mark, to belong and to identify.

The desire to survive

That is, to survive in *ourselves*. Instinctively, many were thinking, *If even the celebrated Diana, surrounded by wealth, a protected VIP in a bullet-proof car – with a bodyguard – can have her life cut off in seconds at thirty-six years of age, what of me? And what is it all for, anyway? If I, too, could die just like that, where's the meaning? How can a person such as myself survive the shakings of life? How can I extend my own existence?*

I received this letter from a member of the public, unknown to me:

> I remember me and my sisters were arguing during the funeral service whether Diana was in heaven.... I am desperate to go to heaven when *I* am dead, although I am frightened of death too....

This instinct to survive is absolutely basic to human beings, across all the centuries.

In point of fact, all four of the desires that I have outlined above are essentially part of being human; they are with us all the time. It takes a crisis or an event of high public profile to strip us down a little, to the real person that we essentially are – God-like beings made for eternity – but under judgment for our sins, and restless with half-felt, unspoken desires to be *right*. They are the desires to **atone** for our faults and to know that we are free of guilt; to **unite** around something – or preferably *someone* – big enough to fill out the meaning of life in a lasting way; to **identify**, register and respond to something massive enough to demand our allegiance; and fourthly to **survive**, beyond the brittleness of this life, and to preserve the little candle-flame....for ever!

On page after page of the Bible, we learn that God can meet us at every one of these four critical desires – supremely through his historical intervention in our world's affairs in the life, death, resurrection and triumph of Jesus Christ, who is none other than God in human form.

God in his book says, 'You want to atone for things said and done, and things not done too? To deal with all your guilt accumulated over many years – the guilt that you fear will one day find you caught out, unforgiven on the final day of reckoning when it's *your* turn?'

It is right to be concerned, for Hebrews chapter 12 reminds us that God is a consuming fire, and that there will be a judgment day, when everything unworthy will be shaken to pieces. But the same passage also tells us of Jesus, and of the 'sprinkled blood' of his death upon the cross, through which God has intercepted his own judgment upon us. In this way our guilt – of whatever kind – can be atoned for, as an act of divine and free love. The condition of this forgiveness is given in verse 23 – '*You **have come** to God, the judge of all men, to the spirits of righteous men made perfect.*' But, we may ask, How can guilty people ever expect to be 'made perfect'?

It starts on the day we come to Jesus Christ, once crucified for us, for our forgiveness; and it is completed on the day when we die; when, as forgiven sinners, we are admitted to be with God – not as a flickering candle-flame, but as God's living children who are to receive glorious resurrection *bodies*! The desire to atone for our sins is met by the atoning death of Jesus Christ. He has done it all.

And the desire to unite? To be unified around someone big enough to captivate the loyalties of great numbers of people from every culture and background? How I longed that the atmosphere of trust and togetherness experienced outside Buckingham Palace and Kensington Palace could have been maintained! The thought that Princess Diana might have been remembered as a Queen of people's hearts was a sentiment recalled and even embraced – but, as *Prospect* magazine commented only weeks after the funeral, *Already normality is returning.*

That was inevitable. But the unity theme can never be far away from the Christian church! I look around us in our own central London congregation, and I see – besides traditional Londoners – Australians, Koreans, Americans, Nigerians, Indians, Brazilians and scores of other nationalities.

There is only one factor that can possibly unite such a cosmopolitan crowd of people week after week, despite the many cultural differences. It is *Christ,* the man whose very public death in another historic city – that of Jerusalem – is *still* reverberating on, two thousand years later. It is he who unites us all, and not just on Sundays. In small groups we eat together, trust and support one another....and it is he who is the centre of the entire worldwide fellowship, putting the purpose and the meaning into our existence, within this widest and most all-embracing community of belief that there has ever been on earth. 'You have come,' enthuses our writer, 'to Mount Zion, to the heavenly Jerusalem, the city of the living God.' It is spoken of as already done, in and through a *person* who unites his followers permanently and eternally.

And the desire, thirdly, to identify? To register one's name when something tremendous is on? At the time of Diana's death, many put their names in those books of condolence. Thousands of tributes to the Princess went into the Internet, designated to last in perpetuity. But in this world, nothing actually is for ever; least of all a web page on the Internet.

On the final day, when even the heavens are shaken and rolled up like a scroll, nothing will remain, except the things that 'cannot be shaken'. The only thing remaining will be the rule and kingdom of God. The desire to register, identify and belong is very strong within us. That instinct can only find lasting fulfilment when an individual moves on from a vague, perhaps nominal, interest in Christ and his church, registers his response to the cross, signs up her commitment to the kingdom that cannot be shaken – and makes it personal. The name is then written in heaven; it goes into the book of life. *It has become official.*

And the fourth instinct – to survive as a person? The letter from my enquirer had asked, 'Is Diana in heaven?' Thankfully, it is not for us to pronounce as to who is and who is not specifically accepted by God, and particularly when we have no knowledge of a person at first hand. That is God's business. We can certainly say that no one at all will quarrel with God's verdict, when the book is opened and the ultimate truth about people's hearts becomes known.

At the same time, a person may know *for themselves*,

here and now in this life, that they are accepted by God! There is no need to wait until we die to discover our position. It is as I respond to all that Christ has done for me, in bearing my judgment at the cross in my place, as I repent of my sins and accept him as my resurrected Lord; it is at that point that the assurance of his promised forgiveness, his friendship and free gift of eternal life, is chalked into the book on my account. And my name is there. *It's official.*

There is help for people on every side; books, churches – and programmes. A very effective programme I know is one that we run at our own church. It is entitled *Christianity Explained.* A meal, an introduction, then discussion and a chance to find out more.

And then, wherever we go, there will be Christian people about, who can help by their witness and friendship. I think of one such friend, a Christian layman Steve Rowe, who gives much of his spare time to open air preaching in London. In Kensington High Street one day in the summer of 1996, by a strange coincidence, Princess Diana was a few yards from him, by St. Mary Abbotts Church. Steve felt bold enough to speak with her of his concern for her and the two princes, and asked her to receive a Christian pamphlet. It was entitled *Four Things God wants you to Know.* In no way was he rebuffed – quite the opposite. The princess accepted the pamphlet, and they parted amicably.

'Imagine my amazement,' Steve told me, 'when three months later she was in the same area. Again we had an opportunity for a brief word. "Do you remember, Ma'am," I said, "that I gave you a little leaflet some weeks ago?" Then she told me, "I've still got it." And yes, she had read it.'

Make it official for yourself. This very day. Use, if you

will, this adaptation and expansion of the hymn, sung at both Diana's wedding and funeral – as an expression of your own prayerful decision to be part of the kingdom that cannot be shaken. It will still be there when everything else has gone.

I vow to you, my Saviour, all earthly things above,
Entire and whole and perfect, the service of my love;
The love that asks no questions, the love that stands the test,
That lays upon his altar the dearest and the best;
The love that never falters, the love that knows the price,
The love that stands indebted before your sacrifice.

And there's a royal country, I've heard of long ago,
It speaks of grace and heaven, a place that all may know;
We may not count her armies, we may not see her King;
Her emblem on a hilltop, the Cross of suffering,
And soul by soul and silently, her citizens increase,
Her ways are ways of gentleness and all her paths are peace.

O tell me of the Kingdom, that stands the test of time,
O lead me to its gateway, and speak the word sublime
That tells me I'm forgiven, my name is in the Book,
The Cross of Jesus holds me, as heav'nward I look;
Baptised into a living hope, I'll walk the path that's new;
And the prize of God in Jesus, for ever I'll pursue.

So light the fire within me, and let me fan the flame,
And fill me with the Spirit, that I may bear your Name;
In season and in hardship, to run my given race,
O keep me ever burning, until I see your face;
I vow to you, my Saviour, that where your feet have trod,
I'll serve and follow faithfully, my Master and my God!

(After Sir Cecil Spring-Rice, 1859-1918, revised and
expanded, R.T. Bewes, *Jubilate Hymns*)

10

'I'm going to ask you to get up out of your seat'

(Billy Graham, twentieth century evangelist to the world)

During the late 1880s, an evangelistic campaign was held by the renowned evangelist D.L. Moody in San Francisco. Just before it began, a professional photographer by the name of George B. Rieman offered to take Moody's photograph. He wanted to add the famous preacher to his collection of actors, politicians and other notables.

Moody declined the offer of a free sitting, saying that he had not come to San Francisco to have his photograph taken, but to save Rieman's soul. Rieman was beside himself with fury. But his curiosity had been aroused. On the very last day of the mission he attended the meeting, accompanied by his wife. After the sermon, an after-meeting was announced for enquirers. George Rieman turned to his wife: 'Well, we've been to the circus; let's go to the sideshow also.'

In the follow-up meeting, two Christian workers met with the couple, and by the end of the evening both had been led to faith in Christ. Rieman himself was to become an outstanding Christian preacher on the Pacific coast.[1]

What are the chances that two precious souls – besides a welcome new preacher – would have been lost to the kingdom of God, *if Moody had allowed his photograph to be taken?* But there was no risk of that. Moody was notorious for turning his back on photographers every time he saw them assembling their cumbersome equipment. He was altogether too focused on his calling as an evangelist to be seduced by diversions, adulation, or titled personages. Or, for that matter, by money. His main weakness was exhibited in a fondness for pork and beans. It has been said of Moody that he put one hand on Britain and the

1. John Pollock, *Moody without Sankey,* Christian Focus Publications, 1995, p. 230.

other on America – and lifted the two countries closer to heaven. Many millions of people came to a firsthand faith through this mighty preacher.

And what of his twentieth century successor, Billy Graham? We are, perhaps, a little too close to him in time for a complete assessment of his ministry as yet. But without any doubt Billy Graham is the only evangelist there has ever been, of whom it could be said that he placed a hand on all five of our continents, in a ministry that has touched the entire world, and countless millions of people. By the time I, as a teenager, had heard him at London's Harringay Arena back in 1954, he had already spoken, face to face, to more people than any orator – secular or religious – in all of history. And that is leaving aside radio, television and films. My father, who was on his council, spoke to him just before Harringay began: 'What would you like to have come out of this?' 'Well,' said Billy gravely, 'among other things, at least a thousand missionaries.' Eventually he was to realise all of that, and much more – and in addition, the spawning of numerous Christian enterprises, begun by people who had been touched at Harringay.

The same phenomenon would follow at Madison Square Gardens, Melbourne cricket ground, the Maracana Stadium and a host of other centres. *African Enterprise*, of which I first became UK Chairman in the 1970s, engages in evangelism and relief work in the great cities of Africa, and is truly African-led and African inspired. But it began in Madison Square Garden with a young white South African, Michael Cassidy, who was fired by the preaching of Billy Graham. Around the world it is virtually impossible to meet a gospel-centred family that has not, through one or other of its members, been influenced by this, the most effective of all the evangelists that the Christian church has ever had since New Testament days.

He kept it up, at Harringay Arena, night after night, for twelve weeks on end, as the campaign was repeatedly extended. Like Moody, Billy Graham was ruthlessly focused. Frequently a second meeting, and even a third, had to be hastily improvised in order to accommodate the crowds that kept coming. It was the only time in my life that I witnessed, repeatedly, the phenomenon of hymn-singing on the London underground, from one end of a train to the other – and all the way up the escalators. The most popular item by far was the theme song of the twelve weeks – *Blessed Assurance.*

It all culminated in an amazing final Saturday – when a capacity crowd, first of 60,000 people, assembled at White City stadium, followed *the same day* by a second meeting at Wembley – the home of English football. For once, the stadium authorities made an exception to their regulations, and allowed the crowd to spill out onto the football pitch; and so a record attendance of 120,000 was set for Wembley, which in the nature of the case could never be equalled. As I sat high up in the stands that day, little did I fathom that the time would come many years later, when I would be Billy's chairman for another great London mission, and would hold the umbrella over him in a packed, rain-soaked rally – once again at Wembley!

His trademark phrase, repeated in football stadiums all over the world, has etched itself into the memory of the countless numbers who, in the course of over fifty years of preaching, made their way to the front of the platform in response to Christ's call. It remains among the most celebrated quotations of the twentieth century:

I'm going to ask you to get up out of your seat

Here was the summons by a world ambassador of the gospel, issued in ringing tones and with urgent sincerity. My own allotted task, when we first went as a family to the Harringay meetings, was to keep a watchful eye on my saintly grandmother. After all, her deceased clergyman husband Tommy had, as a boy of fourteen, 'gone forward' under the preaching of D.L. Moody, back in 1882. Now as Billy's invitation was given, Evelyn Bewes' great desire was to demonstrate her ardent support and go forward with hundreds of others. My job was to hold her in check. We reasoned that once she got down there at the front we'd never see her again! I could feel her fidgeting beside me, as the choir began to sing *Just as I am.*

'No, Granny,' I would firmly whisper, 'this is for *others.* We have to *pray* for these people as they make their decision....no – *Granny*!'

It was among the most formative three months of my life. Night after night I would attend. Sometimes we would have guests with us. And all the time something was drumming inside me, *You are going to be doing this too – for the rest of your life.*

There is no higher calling than to be an ambassador of Christ's good news....and the wonder is, every believer is appointed to this office, regardless of whether we are public preachers or not. It is what the apostle Paul describes as 'the ministry of reconciliation'. It is something we share with all Christians, worldwide:

Since, then, we know what it is to fear the Lord, we try to persuade men.... For Christ's love compels us, because we are convinced that one died for all, and therefore all died. And he died for all, that those who live should no longer live for themselves but for him who died for them and was raised again....Therefore, if anyone is in Christ, he is a new creation; the old has gone, the new has come! All this is from God, who reconciled us to himself through Christ and gave us the ministry of reconciliation.... We are therefore Christ's ambassadors, as though God were making his appeal through us. We implore you on Christ's behalf: Be reconciled to God. God made him who had no sin to be sin for us, so that in him we might become the righteousness of God....(2 Cor. 5:11, 14, 15, 17, 18-21).

Fear...persuade...reconcile...ambassadors...appeal...implore. The passage is shot through with the pleading pathos and apostolic authenticity that has characterised such inspirers of the world as Richard Baxter of the seventeenth century: *I preached, as never sure to preach again, and as a dying man to dying men.*

Baxter's outlook may be contrasted with that of a cynical theologian I met at Durham University, during a mission I was leading. It transpired that he was an atheist. 'So why theology for you?' I asked. *'It amuses me,'* came the reply. As well as I was able, I warned him of his dire situation. He is quite likely to end up as a wicked old man. Once involve yourself in the Scriptures of God; once come under exposure to the realities of the blood and the nails of the Cross, and so face the stark alternative between forgiveness and judgment; once hear the urgent summons to faith – whether thundered or whispered by a servant of God – *and a person cannot remain the same.* We either become opened up and softened by the Gospel, or we become hardened to it. It's kill or cure; it's life or death, heaven or hell. Simply to be 'amused' is already to be under a cloud of judgment of one's own making.

Here, in this fifth chapter of 2 Corinthians, is a wonderful passage on the theme of what God has done in reconciling people to himself through the death of Christ – and how he involves his believing people in 'the ministry of reconciliation'. No one is too inexperienced for this, no one is too young, and no one is too old! An honoured missionary to Africa told us that on the day his retirement was due, the message that was waiting for him in his daily reading was, *Son, go work today in my vineyard.* We are to be in active service until we drop! There is a task out there, and it is urgent. **We are ambassadors for Christ.** There is a world of adventure in that description, and there is a lifetime of surprises beyond the many forbidding frontiers that we shall cross!

A cousin of mine, Robert De Berry, when ministering as a clergyman in Sheffield, England, felt impelled to pay a pastoral visit to a sex shop that was in his parish. Prepared by prayer and fully on guard, he entered the premises, equipped with nothing more impressive than his locally-produced parish magazine. He greeted the proprietor, had a few words with him and left the magazine on his counter. A few weeks later he repeated the visit. Little by little he built up an understanding with the sex shop proprietor, bringing nothing more than his parish magazine on each occasion. Eventually the proprietor came to a firm faith in Jesus Christ, wound up his business....and went to Africa as a missionary. *How are these things done?* Why, by the combination of certain elements that Christ looks for in each of his ambassadors:

An ambassador is compelled by both terror and love

Knowing therefore the terror of the Lord, we persuade men, writes Paul in verse 11 of our chapter (King James Version). The Greek word *phobos* (from which 'phobia' is derived) can mean anything from 'terror', through to 'fright', 'alarm', 'fear', 'reverence' and 'respect'. When it is used in the context of the actions of God in judgment, it invariably carries the stronger meaning, as it does here – for the previous sentence of the passage refers to 'the judgment seat of Christ'. Revelation 11:11 is a similar example.

It isn't simply, then, the terror of a servant of God entering a sex shop. It is that, of course – but it is more; in this instance it is the godly terror of responsibility before the Judge of all the earth. Earlier, Paul had written that the work of God's ministers 'will be shown for what it is, because the Day will bring it to light' (1 Cor. 3:13). We are sent as ambassadors of *Christ,* the universal Judge! In this awe-inspiring calling there should be a proper 'terror' of letting him down.

But Paul is also able to write that 'Christ's *love* compels us, because we are convinced that one died for all, and therefore all died' (v.14). The Cross, whose shadow falls right across the human race, is the greatest inspirer of love in action ever known.

In my father's battered photograph album is a faded sepia photograph that he took shortly after his arrival as a missionary in Africa in 1930, of an old, gaunt Englishman

with an unkempt beard and nondescript clothes, but fixing
the camera with a steely gaze. Underneath the picture was
Dad's written caption, *C.T. Studd.* The photograph told it
all. Charlie Studd, bred in luxury, and educated at Eton
and Cambridge, had been the sporting idol of England in
the early 1880s. Celebrated as a University and All-England
cricketer, the great W.G. Grace had described Studd as
'the most brilliant member of a well-known cricketing
family, and from 1881 to 1884 had few superiors as an all-
round player....His style of batting was free and correct,
and he scored largely and rapidly against the best bowlers
of his time'.

The change began with D.L. Moody's visits to Britain,
and the conversion of Studd's father. After his own
profession of faith, Charlie took members of the England
Test Team to hear Moody; and several told him later that
they had accepted Christ. Before long, massive meetings
for testimony and challenge were being held in Cambridge,
Oxford, London, Bristol, Newcastle, Manchester, Leeds,
Liverpool and Edinburgh....and the theme – a lost world
for whom Christ died. It was love, inspired by the Cross,
that lay behind this call for ambassadors of the gospel:

> If Jesus Christ be God, and died for me, then no
> sacrifice can be too great for me to make for Him.

So declared C.T. Studd. In his determination to serve Christ
abroad, he was joined by six prominent university friends.
The Boat Train pulled out of Victoria Station on February
5th, 1885, taking *The Cambridge Seven*, as they were
called, to Dover and Calais, Brindisi, Suez, Colombo and
China. The rest is history. Studd died in the Congo, a year

after the meeting with my father. A thousand African Christians saw him to his grave.[2]

Terror and love. They are both here in 2 Corinthians 5. They are necessary ingredients in the spirit of an ambassador prepared to go anywhere for Christ. But there is more:

An ambassador is invested with both authority and humility

'We are therefore Christ's ambassadors,' writes Paul, '*as though God were making his appeal through us*' (v.20). It is a sensational statement. When the representative of God is at work, there are to be no apologies, no weak qualifications, no back-trackings. At the same time there should be an accompanying, self-effacing grace, for 'We are not trying to commend *ourselves*,' says Paul (v.12).

A good historical example is seen in the remarkable missionary and outreach work of Kate Booth, oldest daughter of the founder of the Salvation Army. *La Maréchale,* she was called, after her exploits in Paris. One of her very first public meetings in England was as a girl of sixteen, facing a rowdy 1,500-strong audience. 'When all else fails,' her father William had said, 'put on Katie!' She quelled the crowd with the opening words of her song: *The mountains and the hills will all flee away, and you will need a hiding place that day; O may we be ready.* Then into her text: 'Let me die the death of the righteous, and let my last end be as his.' Those who responded to her witness that day were only the first of many thousands who would discover Christ during her next seventy-five

2. J.C. Pollock, *The Cambridge Seven*, IVP, 1955, pp. 105-108.

years as an ambassador of Christ.[3] She died just as Billy Graham's influence was beginning to touch Britain.

Authority and humility; boldness and grace. We are ambassadors, because we represent the sovereign Lord of the whole universe! But we are *only* ambassadors; we are not there for ourselves! Here now is a third combination of features that Jesus Christ looks for in his representatives:

An ambassador is appointed both to plead and to warn

'We try to persuade men....the ministry of reconciliation ....We implore you on Christ's behalf: Be reconciled to God....'

But Paul continues in his next chapter:

As God's fellow-workers we urge you not to receive God's grace in vain. For he says, 'In the time of my favour I heard you, and in the day of salvation I helped you.' I tell you, now is the time of God's favour, now is the day of salvation (2 Cor. 6:1, 2).

There is something in God's ambassador and evangelist that longs for individuals to engage with the gospel, as the moment of opportunity swings towards each person! When I was about fifteen, the time arrived for the taking of the school photograph. It only happened once in every five years; it was your one opportunity to obtain a pictorial record of your life, your time and your chums! There were 750 of us, arranged in a massive semi-circle, banked six high. In the middle was the intrepid photographer, with a motorised, swivelling camera.

'It's your one opportunity!' we were warned. 'As the

3. Carolyn Scott, *The Heavenly Witch*, Hamish Hamilton, 1981, p. 19.

lens comes opposite you, respond and be at your best; it'll never happen again – so no messing about!'

I still have the result; a photograph about a yard long; my total school career pictorially compressed into a single record. Occasionally I pull it out – so *that's* how the lens caught me!

Come to the Gospel account in the New Testament. Jesus is travelling through all of Galilee; he is God's lens of love and concern, *focusing* upon the needs of men and women, as he moves steadily from town to town. Those who have any awareness at all recognise that this is the time of opportunity; the moment is now and the tide is *in!*

Jesus reaches Capernaum. Interest is high. Here are four friends, desperate to take the opportunity for their disabled friend – but how to get him through the crowds to Jesus? The venue is jammed full of people....there's nothing for it – through the roof ! (Mark 2:1-12).

The focus swivels to a great crowd by the lake. Who will benefit from the opportunity? A woman! You can just see her as she manoeuvres her way through the mass of humanity, wriggling and squeezing.... just to touch his clothes! Perhaps he will help her....*he does* (Mark 5:25-34).

Now it's Jericho's turn. It's the Messiah's last visit; he will never come again. There is Zacchaeus, the diminutive tax collector, high up in a tree to get an unobtrusive view, as the Light of the World goes by....but then, *panic* – the gaze of Jesus has focused on the taxman! With those eyes on him – and the commanding voice: *I'm going to ask you to come down out of that tree; to receive me into your home* – it was now or never! Zacchaeus humbly obeys, and finds salvation (Luke 19:1-10).

So, moving on from Jericho....but wait! A blind man is

on the edge of the crowd. His cries stop Jesus in his tracks, on his way to achieve the salvation of the world. Everything stops as Bartimaeus grabs the opportunity, receives his sight – and then follows Jesus. It's goodbye to Jericho for ever.

Once to every generation comes the moment to decide! It is for the ambassador of the gospel to plead this message and to warn of the issues – in the sober knowledge that the favourable climate for the good news can switch as changeably as the weather. Shakespeare put it memorably:

> There is a tide in the affairs of men, which, taken at
> the flood, leads on to fortune; omitted, all the voyage
> of their life is bound in shallows and in miseries.
> *(Julius Caesar)*

Charles John Ellicott writes in the same vein: 'There is, so to speak, a *now,* running through the ages. For each church and nation, for each individual soul, there is a golden present, which may never again recur, and in which lie boundless opportunities for the future.'

I'm going to ask you to get up out of your seat

In one of Billy Graham's visits to Britain, a coach driver, on depositing his passengers at the stadium, was invited to come into the meeting. He declined the opportunity. Night after night the offer was repeated, but he preferred to stay in his coach and read the paper. The campaign ended, and the opportunity was over. Then the driver lost his job, and struggled to find his way again. Months later he emigrated to Australia, and was successful in obtaining a new post – once again in his familiar role as coach driver. He turned up to work the first day.

'So where am I off to?'

'Ah yes,' came the reply. 'There's a coach trip for you to a sports stadium. It's a Billy Graham meeting!' This time, when the passengers invited their driver in for the meeting, there was no hesitation. He went in with them – and went forward at the end to make his response.

It's like a lens of love and compulsion. You cannot guarantee, when it turns on *you* – summoning you to come to Christ, to change your ways, to make the comeback – that the opportunity will return. Your moment is *now*. And hence the sense of responsibility and urgency required in anyone who is an ambassador of Jesus Christ!

Once to every generation comes the moment to decide;
In the clash of truth with falsehood, all must choose and all must side.
On the rock of Christ's salvation stands or falls each mortal soul;
And the choice goes by for ever, sealed in God's eternal scroll!

Truth in every generation, fragile as a mountain flower,
Looks afresh for faithful guardians; who will speak in danger's hour?
When the enemy advances, flooding in with lies out-poured,
In the breach we'll fight together – raise a standard for the Lord!

Saints in every generation kept the flame of truth alive;
In the face of death, defying thrones they knew would not survive.
Heroes of the Cross of Jesus win with him in this our day,
By his blood and by their witness – come and follow in his way!

Christ in every generation; Greatest Name the world has known;
Teachers, thinkers, faiths and cultures find their goal in him alone.
His the truth and his the Kingdom, at his Cross our paths divide;
Once to every generation comes the moment to decide!

(R.T. Bewes, after J. Russell Lowell,
Jubilate Hymns and Hope Publishing Company)

11

'I did not have sex with that woman'

(President Bill Clinton, August 17th, 1998)

'Like to do a microphone test for us, Mr. President?'

It was August 11th, 1984, and Ronald Reagan was about to engage in one of his regular meetings with the American press. Obligingly he spoke the following words into the microphones in front of him:

> My fellow Americans, I am pleased to tell you I just signed legislation which outlaws Russia forever. The bombing begins in five minutes.

It was only a microphone test, but the words – recorded by a media opportunist – went all over the world. I was in Germany the week after the gaffe, and the quote was splashed across the front of the weeklies. Relations between the USA and Russia were under severe strain!

*Watch my lips....*President George Bush's three words ended up as one of the best-known quotations of the twentieth century. They landed him in terrible trouble.

It is an embarrassment to a great many American people that President Clinton's remark – in reply to widespread suggestions of a relationship with the White House staff trainee Monica Lewinsky – has become the most world-renowned and quoted sentence of any president to date:

> *I did not have sex with that woman*

It is a sadness also to friends of America, on this side of the Atlantic, where this book is being written. We take no delight in the scandal that broke over the president's head during the traumatic months of 1998, nor do we join in any of the ribaldry that surrounded it. Nor should we wish to dwell overlong on the details. But there may, perhaps, be some principles that thoughtful people can gain from Bill Clinton's moment of bombast.

Leadership has extra responsibility. This surely should be learnt from the beginning by all who are placed in any position of leadership – parents, teachers, clergy, lawyers and politicians. Even your most trivial remarks are going to be remembered long after you have forgotten that they were ever uttered!

I remember the inane comment of a British theologian. It related to a totally unfounded theory about the sexuality of our Lord. Six weeks later I was in Africa. His fatuous and idle musings had already reached the sixth form of a school in a dusty town of Tanzania. An obvious daily sentiment for any leader in the public eye ought to be, not 'Watch my lips', but *'Guard my lips'* (Psalm 141:3). Particularly when you are said to be the most powerful man around.

Truth has a price. Think of Pontius Pilate. 'I find no fault in this man,' he had said, on examining the case made against Jesus. Yet, when it came to the crisis of decision, he found that he could not pay the price of what he knew was the truth. Yet the responsibility could not be avoided. Sunday by Sunday, the credal statement of millions of worshippers – *He was crucified under Pontius Pilate* – have established Pilate's as the second best-known name in all history.

If you want to stand by truth, you are likely to have to pay for it. But, once you decide that you cannot afford the price, you will lie, perjure yourself, abuse your power and bring disgrace upon those who have trusted you. Back in the 1930s, before he ever became United States President, Harry Truman wrote, 'A man not honourable in his marital relations is not usually honourable in any other.'[1]

Nothing can be hidden. Especially has this been so in the goldfish bowl that is our world today – created by a ruthless media from the 1960s onwards. *It is all going to come out!* It is the height of naivety for a leader, in particular, to imagine that it could be anything different. Ultimately it is the Judgment of Christ that is the underlying principle governing our every idle word and action:

> There is nothing concealed that will not be disclosed, or hidden that will not be made known. What you have said in the dark will be heard in the daylight, and what you have whispered in the ear in the inner rooms will be proclaimed from the roofs (Luke 12:2, 3).

The low value placed on truth, in today's secular culture, means that plenty of people stand to profit from every scandal – the bigger the better. Fat contracts can be signed for the rights to the story. The errant TV clergyman can tearfully repent – preferably in the full glare of the cameras. Soon he can be 'restored' to his ministry, and then write a best-seller. A nation will learn that a disgraced politician has *the full confidence* of the government leadership, despite his unearthed sins (usually called by the press 'peccadillos'). If anything, his exposure is likely to result in a surge of popularity.

This is the style in which the twentieth century ended. *But it is also the style in which the first century began.* The wheel has very nearly gone full circle; we are back to Athens and Rome all over again. Today we are facing what is virtually a 'new' pre-Christian era. Despite the

---

1. David McCullough, *Truman*, Simon and Schuster, 1992, p. 186.

sensational growth of the Christian church in many parts of the world, there are hundreds of millions of people who are unaware that there should be any accepted standard for behaviour. Ethics are presented to them as totally fluctuating and relative in their value. The price tag on truth has been ripped away.

Sometimes it is clergy with an unbelieving attitude to Scripture who cause the damage. During the summer of 1999 I read two books on ethics, one by a layman – a professor of paediatrics at University College London; the other by one of our more extreme bishops. And who was the theologian of the two? It proved to be the layman, Professor John Wyatt. He came out so far ahead of the bishop as to permit no comparison. His book displayed a worldview based on Scripture that was able to take full account of the modern ethical issues that challenge us, and still come out at the end with an utterly cohesive and compelling value-system.[2]

And the cleric? He made it to the front page of *The Times* with his 'controversial' argument that 'it is better to leave God out of the moral debate and find good human reasons for supporting the system or approach we advocate....We are now poised on the brink of having the freedom to shape the very genes that previously shaped us.' Basically, the argument dates back to the secular humanists of the 1960s who insisted that ethics were perfectly possible without religion. As a matter of fact the argument really dates back to the Garden of Eden, where the man and the woman agreed on *deciding for ourselves* – which is the title of the bishop's last chapter.[3] As I write,

---

2. John Wyatt, *Matters of Life and Death*, Inter-Varsity Press, 1998.
3. Richard Holloway, *Godless Morality*, Canongate, 1999, p.151.

the bishop is still drawing a salary for promoting a view which, if taken to its logical end, would find the most useful part of the Bible to be the maps at the very back.

His arguments are not really new; they are old ghosts from the first century. Upon that century Christianity burst with a new morality that found its inspiration in Jesus, and met the old pagan order head-on. The above-mentioned bishop can write of today's young people who can *'have sexual intercourse with each other whenever they feel like it, the way they have a cup of coffee or a hamburger'*.[4] It is no different from the accepted morality of the first century, described by William Barclay:

> Chastity was the one completely new virtue which Christianity brought into the world. In the ancient world, sexual relationships before and outside marriage were the normal and accepted practice. The sexual appetite was regarded as a thing to be gratified, not to be controlled.[5]

The Roman empire was bad enough at that time, but Greek morals were worse still. Demosthenes of old had written, 'We keep prostitutes for pleasure, we keep mistresses for the day-to-day needs of the body; we keep wives for the begetting of children and for the faithful guardianship of our homes.' Later on Seneca was to write, 'Women were married to be divorced, and divorced to be married.'

Was it ever easy? The human sex instinct was bound to present us with some tensions, simply *because* it is so wonderful and so powerful; for it is the second strongest

---

4. Ibid, p. 60
5. William Barclay, *Daily Study Bible; Philippians,* St. Andrews Press, 1959, p.150.

instinct of all – the strongest being that for physical survival. Without the sex instinct, all human creativity, romance and our very continuance as a race would disappear.

The call for control on the part of the Christians was scoffed at by the second century Roman philosopher Celsus. He flatly disbelieved that Christianity could achieve a change in lifestyle. 'There,' commented the historian T.R. Glover, 'lay the great surprise. The Christians came with a message of the highest conceivable morality....They expected a response; they preached repentance and reformation; and people did respond, they repented and lived new lives.'[6]

A new scale of values had come. It wasn't the standard of Homer or Plato. It was the standard of Jesus:

> For you know what instructions we gave you by the authority of the Lord Jesus.
>
> It is God's will that you should be sanctified: that you should avoid sexual immorality; that each of you should learn to control his own body in a way that is holy and honourable, not in passionate lust like the heathen, who do not know God.... For God did not call us to be impure, but to live a holy life. Therefore, he who rejects this instruction does not reject man but God, who gives you his Holy Spirit (1 Thess. 4:2-5, 7,8).

This is as applicable and valid for the twentieth and twenty-first centuries as it was for the first. It is up to the followers of Christ, in the power and energy of the Spirit of God (verse 8), to offer an alternative and to set the pace!

---

6. T.R. Glover, *The Influence of Christ in the Ancient World,* Cambridge University Press, 1933, p.75.

An alternative framework

These Thessalonian believers of our passage were among the very first converts to the Christian faith in all Europe. In those early days of AD 49 or 50, when the apostle Paul had first come among them (see Acts 17: 1-9), they would have found the prevailing moral standards around them to be an immediate challenge. They needed as much to *unlearn* as to learn! The long-held assumptions of contemporary morality were about to be challenged, then undermined and finally replaced. And what *are* the fallacies that across the ages need to be corrected by the superior incoming ethic of Jesus? Here are just four:

Chastity is not truncation. The popular view is that if someone has not experienced sexual intimacy, then they are only half a person; they don't really *know* life. Paul denies this in verse 5 of our passage – that we are not to indulge in the passion of lust like the heathen *who do not know God.* Who are the ignorant ones? It is those with a casual attitude to sex, he insists, who don't know their way around. 'You *know*,' he emphasises in verse 2, as he refers to Christ's alternative way.

The problem today is not that secular society is emphasising sex too much; it is not emphasising it *enough,* or completely. It is society that is suffering from the truncation of sex. When I went into an Oxford Street store to buy candles for my wife's birthday cake, I discovered that many novelties were on sale – including manufactured replicas of human sex organs; detached and neatly packaged for sale. *Now that is truncation*, sex dehumanised and reduced. Take God out of the picture and we are left, as Malcolm Muggeridge once put it, 'with a choice of megalomania or erotomania, the clenched fist or the phallus, Nietzsche or Sade, Hitler or D.H. Lawrence'. No, chastity is not truncation.

Innocence is not ignorance. It is widely assumed that not to have experimented in sexual activity is to be ignorant and at a disadvantage. But there are enough people around who are living denials of this view. I think, for example, of Lorna Bowden out on the mission field where I grew up in Kenya. *Auntie Lorna* was a single lady of uncertain age. Whether she had ever had a boyfriend simply wasn't the kind of question you could possibly have put to her. We knew her as a woman of modesty and of apparent innocence in matters of this kind – and she certainly wasn't the poorer for it. She was a complete person. Certainly she was modest!

She was the only missionary for many miles around who had ever given injections. When, therefore, requested by a large, male missionary by the name of Harvey Cantrell to administer an injection in his backside, Auntie Lorna went pink.

'Oh Harvey, that's rather difficult, isn't it? O dear, I feel a bit....Harvey whatever are we going to do?'

'Don't worry a bit, Lorna,' came the reply. 'You stand one side of the door; I'll stand the other – and you can do it through the keyhole!'

History doesn't relate what happened. Yes, she was modest and innocent – and interesting. She could make a flourless, sugarless, butterless, eggless cake, entirely out of bananas. She was creative and *alive* – and infinitely more interesting to us children than the boring, boozy *White Mischief* type of Kenya colonial settlers of that time. To us, *they* were the ignorant ones!

Wants are not needs. It's a fallacy to say that every

individual has sexual 'needs', equivalent to the need for air, food and water. Richard Foster writes, 'No one has yet died from a lack of sexual intercourse. Many have lived full and satisfying lives without genital sex, including Jesus.'[7]

To understand this is helpful and liberating. The single person is not a half person. We should learn that the person who is living in a period of singleness, long or short, is the possessor of a charismatic gift. The apostle Paul describes the state of singleness as a *charisma* (1 Cor. 7:7.)

Permissiveness is not freedom. The strange thing is that as we have watched secularised society develop, it seems to have become a little 'greyer', more monotonous, less able to deliver. Young people are increasingly nervous as they witness the crashing failure that their elders are making of modern marriage:

> *My future career:* When I leave school I shall probably go to St. Paul's School, or the City of London, or King's College, Wimbledon. After that, I hope to go to the university. After that I will buy myself a house, a car, and furniture. I will probably get married, although at present I have doubts about it – because Mum spends half her time telling Dad off, for such things as buying the wrong beer, waking up the baby, and not keeping promises; and if this is the outcome of the weeding (sic), it isn't worth the salmon and a three storey cake (*Boy, 9 years of age, Twickenham, Middlesex*).

---

7. Richard Foster, *Money, Sex and Power,* Hodder & Stoughton, 1985, p.152.

It is up to modern Christians of the third millennium to emulate their spiritual ancestors of two thousand years ago, and prove the superiority of their alternative framework for living.

An alternative authority

When the apostle Paul wrote to the Thessalonian church, he would have been only too aware of its stormy beginnings, for he – as visiting evangelist – had been thrown out of the city. The chief complaint about the apostolic messengers was that they were saying 'that there is another king, one called Jesus' (Acts 17:7).

Another king – and an alternative authority for life and conduct – was being proposed. Paul is careful in his letter to remind his readers that the radical lifestyle he is setting out for them had been given 'by the authority of the Lord Jesus' (1 Thess. 4:2). It is possible that he had in mind Christ's endorsement, in Matthew 19:4, of the great creation principle set out for all time at the beginning:

> For this reason a man will leave his father and mother and be united to his wife, and the two will become one flesh (Gen. 2:24).

Our Lord adds his comment: 'Therefore what God has joined together, let man not separate.' In quoting Genesis 2:24, Jesus was setting out again the proper context for the ordering of intimate relationships between people – a one-man/one-woman, monogamous, publicly-recognised relationship for life. A precisely-defined and altogether new and different situation is implied by the man 'leaving' his parents and being 'united' to his (one) wife. This principle cuts across the concept of a couple sleeping together as a private arrangement. The *basis* of the relationship is to be understood publicly. 'No,' says Genesis 2:24, 'let it be clearly understood what is happening; an actual change is taking place, that is to be publicly recognised. Someone is leaving the parent-child bond, and is entering upon a husband-wife relationship. *It is a transaction.*'

Some may maintain that in sleeping together as a private arrangement, a couple are only testing their compatibility. While, naturally, it is right to exercise great care before embarking upon a lifetime commitment, the argument is a false one. Leaving aside the biblical restriction of sex to the marriage relationship alone, it needs to be understood that full adjustment between two people can take many months, even years. To rely upon sleeping together as a test of compatibility could be disastrous – to the point that an experimenting couple could actually *lose* each other, when they need not. Again, in the event of an experimenting couple breaking up, does the *next* partnership start on the same basis? You can reach the point when someone is doing it for the third, the fourth time. And having got into the way of it before marriage, is the habit going to be dropped so easily *after* marriage?

Here is an alternative authority. The *God* words occur with frequency in our passage – pleasing God (v.1)....It is God's will (v.3)....heathen who do not know God (v.5) ....the Lord is an avenger (v.6)....for God did not call us to be impure (v.7)....He who rejects this instruction does not reject man but God (v.8). The bishop who advocates a *Godless Morality* would have to put a clear line right through this passage. For it presents an alternative framework, an alternative authority, to every attempt at a human-based ethic.

An alternative confidence

It is a remarkable fact of history that those first-century believers won their way over the private lifestyle that God in Christ calls his people to observe. All the sentences in 1 Thessalonians 4 emphasise the *difference* that is to be expected among them. And the Father, Son and Holy Spirit all feature in the passage. God, the glorious Trinity is *for* us in the battle for purity! He has also given us, in the Christian fellowship, the 'love' of 'each other' (v. 9).

It is a wonderful encouragement. We are not out there on our own, as we face a new millennium, with all its pressures and temptations. How to break an illicit partnership or deal with some fantasy or fad? Coping with habits that are basically a part of growing up? One of the great answers is to be with people! This is where the church comes into its own. It's *people* who can help to blunt the loneliness of an obsession. A small group of trusted people around us for Bible study and fellowship is a tremendous protection. It is for this reason that balance and care must be exercised when judging the faults of someone as highly placed as a President of the United States. Who surrounds the President? Upon whom can he rely? Who gives him fellowship, in this loneliest of positions?

The Christian fellowship provides an obvious setting, within which the sexual impulse can be harnassed and channelled in natural and positive ways; where respect and affection between the sexes can be safely expressed – without the blithe assumption that a brotherly or sisterly kiss or squeeze must inevitably end in bed. Teaming together, praying together, eating and serving together, and going out together in mixed groups – here is a framework for a rounded, personal lifestyle. And, additionally, a platform for future marriages that will be strong, stabilising *and Christian.*

The divorce rate during the twentieth century is an indication of the urgency. In 1932, divorces in our own country numbered 700 during the course of a single year. By 1999 divorces were taking place at the rate of 480 *every day.* No marriage is without its dangers. Ruth Bell Graham once wrote in the light of her marriage to her evangelist husband, Billy:

> People have warned with great effectiveness about the 'dangerous forties'. And even about the dangerous eighth year of marriage. (I can't recall that anything of moment occurred during the eighth year of our marriage in 1951). But I am convinced that each year we are vulnerable....[8]

We do well to focus upon good models. The Grahams set an outstanding example, as did their predecessors in the nineteenth century, the evangelist D.L. Moody and his wife Emma. It was their niece, Louise, who said of them: *Aunt Emma and Uncle Dwight were so perfectly **one**, that no one could possibly tell which was **the** one!* [9]

Let us believe that the same courage and confidence that inspired the Christian church of the first century to defy the standards of an entire continent, will resurface in

---

8. Ruth Bell Graham, *Prodigals and those who love them,* Focus on the Family, 1991, p.102.
9. John Pollock, *Moody without Sankey,* Christian Focus, 1995, p.261.

the twenty-first century. It only takes a few, as Paul and his friends were to prove. Say to yourself, *I resolve that it is going to begin with **me**.*

12

'Is that it?'

(Rock musician Bob Geldof, July 13th, 1985)

In a rain-drenched and packed Wembley Stadium, the lightning had already hit one of the famous twin towers as Billy Graham ended a month of meetings in London. His subject had been the life resolve of the apostle Paul, *God forbid that I should glory, save in the Cross of our Lord Jesus Christ.* At the close, several thousand men and women crossed the pitch in response to the call of Christ, many of them holding their shoes in their hands as they splashed their way towards the platform. One of the evangelist's closing points had been taken from the best-selling book of the Irish rock singer Bob Geldof. As Billy delivered the punch-line, I recollected that my colleagues Pam Glover and Miranda Lewis had arranged to send the book to Dr. Graham from our church office, in response to a request from his hotel. The words boomed around Wembley with telling effect:

> Only a few years ago, in this same great stadium, 'Live Aid' – the biggest concert of all time – was staged by Bob Geldof and music makers from all over the world. When it was over, some young fans, at the foot of the platform, shouted up to the organisers: *'Is that it?'* And Bob Geldof wrote, as the final sentence in his book: 'It's something I keep asking myself.' The words became the title of his book – *'Is that it?'*
>
> Many of you, as you look at the emptiness of your own lives, are asking the same question: *Is that it? Is that all there is to life upon this world?* I'm here to bring you the thrilling announcement that there's more!

Even the cleverest people, from early days of our civilisation, have been asking the same question about the purpose of our lives here: *Is that it?* Aristotle's last prayer has come down to us from the fourth century BC:

> **I entered the world corruptly,**
> **I have lived in it anxiously,**
> **I quit it in perturbation.**

In our modern era, after the great triumph of sailing around the world in his boat *Gipsy Moth IV*, Sir Francis Chichester described his feelings when the celebrations were all over: 'I saw myself as a trickle of water draining away into a sandy beach, leading to a dead-end. Life itself seemed futile.'[1]

Is that it? Of all people on earth, it ought to be the believer who displays a confidence about the meaning of life, the direction of our human story – and the way in which it will all end! If we look at the people who shaped the collective thinking of our civilisation, we discover that – whatever the political or cultural confusions that swirled around them – they all had a God-centred worldview, and their thought-processes were based on the Bible. Irenaeus, Augustine, Erasmus, Luther and Tolstoy are all prime examples. If Bible concepts and idioms were to be outlawed from our society tomorrow, all the great music and literature that have formed our culture would become meaningless overnight. The works of William Shakespeare would be indecipherable.

It is engrained deeply in our thought-forms. And basic

---

1. Sir Francis Chichester, *Gipsy Moth Circles the World,* Hodder & Stoughton, 1967, p. 222.

Christian belief embraces a view of the universal and permanent kingdom of God as something that straddles every empire that has come and gone. It finds a remarkable focus in the inspired leadership of a Jew who lived twenty-six centuries ago – the prophet Daniel. Starting as a young, teenage captive in the alien Babylonian court of Nebuchadnezzar, Daniel was to rise to a stardom and an influence that still shines like a comet in our present era, as the second millennium gives way to the third. *Where is our story going? When is it going to end? How can people manage when chaos seems to rule, and when barbarians are occupying the seats of power?* Daniel had seen it all, as the fortunes of his people, the Jews, seemed to trickle away into the sandy wastes of a terrible seventy-year captivity in Babylon. **'Is that it?'** was the agonised cry of the ancient people of God.

The book of Daniel, from the very first chapter – when the Famous Four challenged the lifestyle of Nebuchadnezzar's heathen court – has a consistent theme: *How should God's people behave in an alien land?* It is a question we have always had to face throughout spiritual history, for all believers are 'strangers and pilgrims' in a world that has turned its back upon the rule of God. We find ourselves echoing the question of the captives in Psalm 137 – 'How can we sing the Lord's song in a foreign land?'

Like Daniel we are called, as citizens of heaven, to a life of **integrity**, whatever our surroundings. Daniel's friends face the fiery furnace; he himself is thrown into a den of lions – but through it all there is no inconsistency between Daniel's private and public behaviour. He shows the whole world how it's done! Furthermore, in the twelve riveting chapters that make up Daniel's prophecy, there is an insistent call to **stability**, as we watch the way in which a leader for God can outlive kingdom after tumbling kingdom. Dictator follows dictator, crisis follows crisis; and yet *'Daniel remained'* (Dan. 1:21).

There is also the theme of **humility** that weaves its way through the prophecy, as the reader is confronted by the key truth that 'the Most High rules in the kingdoms of men'. That was the message stamped upon chapter 2 and the dream of the great metal statue, representing the toppling kingdoms of this world. It was the great testimony that came out of the madness of king Nebuchadnezzar in chapter 4. It was the stark reality behind the terrifying 'writing on the wall' that heralded the collapse of Belshazzar's kingdom in a single night. It was the basis of Daniel's own vision of the evil beasts and the shining figure of the Son of Man in chapter 7. It was the reassuring background to chapter 8, with its vision of the apparently unstoppable he-goat of the Greek rise to power. It is God's hammer blow upon *the Abomination that causes Desolation* – the sinister personage who features so prominently in these chapters as a prefigure of the final Antichrist. All will be brought down, as the small stone of chapter 2 – uncut by human hand – smashes into the kingdoms of this world and reduces them to fragments, itself growing to the size of a mountain that fills the whole earth. It is a vision of the kingdom of God that will never be destroyed!

It is at the close of the prophecy, in chapter 12, that we can share a little of Daniel's telescopic view, as an angelic messenger brings 'the time of the end' into focus:

At that time Michael, the great prince who protects your people, will arise. There will be a time of distress

such as has not happened from the beginning of
nations until then. But at that time your people –
everyone whose name is found written in the book –
will be delivered. Multitudes who sleep in the dust
of the earth will awake: some to everlasting life,
others to shame and everlasting contempt. Those who
are wise will shine like the brightness of the heavens,
and those who lead many to righteousness, like the
stars for ever and ever. But you, Daniel, close up
and seal the words of the scroll until the time of the
end....(Dan. 12:1-4).

In this passage and the rest of chapter 12, some contrasts
are given, to sharpen the focus of all God's people as we
wait for 'the end'. They are there to energise us in the period
of endurance and waiting that confronts every generation
of believers.

The tribulation and the deliverance

'Michael' (v.1), that angelic figure – associated in
Revelation 12 with the victory of Christ over all evil – is
presented here as the great contestant on behalf of God's
people, during the time of their greatest trial. It is thought
by many Bible students that the New Testament letter to
the Hebrews, in its eleventh chapter, is referring back to
the terrible time of Greek ascendancy in the second century
BC – when the notorious Seleucid leader, Antiochus
Epiphanes, made war upon the Jews in his kingdom: *'They
were stoned; they were sawn in two; they were put to death
by the sword....'* (Heb. 11:37).

But these trials were the curtain-raiser for further and
even more terrible persecutions that were to be the story of

the church's life until the end of time. There is a certain running-together, a telescoping of events in Daniel's prophecy. Jesus did the same in his warning of the destruction of Jerusalem that lay ahead in AD 70. He described it in terms of 'great distress, unequalled from the beginning of the world until now and never to be equalled again'. But he linked the event with the trials that will be the prelude to the end of the world; trials so great that – as he put it – 'If those days had not been cut short, no-one would survive, but for the sake of the elect those days will be shortened' (Matt. 24:21,22).

Antiochus-like Antichrist figures will keep surfacing throughout history, usurping the place of God and oppressing his people. They will culminate in what the apostle Paul describes as the 'Man of Lawlessness', who will finally be overthrown at Christ's return and judgment (2 Thess. 2:1-12). It is perhaps understandable that at certain times in history, people are tempted to try and identify the Antichrist. But we are better advised to turn full attention upon *Christ*. He is our proper focal point.

We will never be without trials. At the same time Daniel emphasises the eternal security of those whose names are found written in 'the book'. As we saw in an earlier chapter, the 'two witnesses' will triumph. Followers of Christ have never ceased to be amazed at the continuance of the church, despite every indication that its light was about to be extinguished. *The tribulation and the deliverance* – the two themes run together throughout the Bible, and those with an eye for history will see the pattern amply confirmed again and again.

The wise and the wicked

Verse 2 of Daniel 12 refers to the 'multitudes' who comprise the human race. The prophet describes them as divided into two classes. There are *only* two classes – you are either in one or the other!

First, **the wise**. We learn in verse 3 that they shine like the stars of heaven. Who are they? Why they are those who know and fear God – for it is the fear of the Lord that is the beginning of wisdom. They are people like Lorna Bowden of my childhood missionary background. Such people are remembered, long after the departure of others. When I went to preach at our old home church of Weithaga in Kenya during the 1990s, Lorna Bowden was still remembered from decades earlier. Several generations of Christian workers had lived in her house since the time when I knew her as a boy. But to this day the little stone bungalow with the corrugated iron roof is known by one and all as *Miss Bowden's house.* If such 'stars' as Auntie Lorna endure in the memory of God's people, we can be sure that she – who 'led many to righteousness' – will shine in the firmament of God for ever and ever.

Against the wise are **the wicked**. They occur later in our Scripture passage:

> Many will be purified, made spotless and refined, but the wicked will continue to be wicked. None of the wicked will understand, but those who are wise will understand (Dan. 12:10).

We should not imagine that the wicked cannot change sides in this life; Nebuchadnezzar was one who did! (Dan. 4:37).

At the same time it must be recognised that the coming judgment of God serves to underline the choices that people were making throughout a lifetime. 'Let him who does wrong continue to do wrong; let him who is vile continue to be vile' (Rev. 22:11). It will become apparent, on the day of judgment, who were allotted a place with the wise and who a place with the wicked.

Glorification and judgment

Such a contrast – again, it's one or the other! Bible students should be grateful for verse 2; it provides one of the clearest references in the Old Testament to the glory of everlasting life and the resurrection of God's people. We are going, by God's grace, to rise again. It's there in the Old Testament, and Jesus is the historical guarantee that it is going to happen! Without the Bible revelation before us, we would be completely in the dark about the next life. As intellectual a sage as Xenophanes had said in the sixth century BC, *Guesswork is over all.*

But again at this point there is a separation. The wise will rise to the glorified state of everlasting life; the wicked to everlasting contempt and judgment. You can be best friends, or exact contemporaries – but still be heading towards different destinies. The nineteenth century preacher, D.L. Moody of Chicago, has featured in an earlier chapter. His contemporary in America was a professed agnostic by the name of Robert Ingersoll. Independently of each other, the two men toured America ceaselessly, one preaching Christ, the other promoting unbelief. Both died in the same year, 1899. When Moody died, on December 21, memorial and thanksgiving services were held, and the best of the Sankey hymns reverberated through the land. Ingersoll died on July 21, and – while it is not for us to be his judge – we can only note that by contrast his earlier memorial had included the stark notice, *There will be no singing.* Glorification and judgment; the Bible warns us to look ahead, and to prepare.

The revealed and the hidden

In the last part of Daniel's twelfth chapter, the seer is aware of the presence of a 'man clothed in linen', seemingly identical to the shining figure of chapter 10. If so, then he is the pre-incarnate second Person of the Trinity. Jesus is accompanied by two angelic beings:

> One of them said to the man clothed in linen, who was above the waters of the river, 'How long will it be before these astonishing things are fulfilled?'....
> So I asked, 'My lord, what will the outcome of all this be?' (Dan. 12:6,8).

Two questions are being posed to the Man in shining linen. They amount to:

How long must we wait?
How will it all end?

We might have put it differently. 'Is anything going to change? Is there anything more? *Is that it?'*

The answers to both questions help us in our Christian living today. To the first, *How long?* comes the answer, 'It will be for a time, times and half a time. When the power of the holy people has been finally broken, all these things will be completed' (Dan. 12:7). The three and a half 'years', symbolic of both the oppression and powerful witness of Elijah's time (1 Kings 18:1; cf. James 5:17) is applied in the book of Revelation to the whole of our Christian era. It is an era in which we may *expect* to see the kingdom of God advancing – despite inevitable opposition, and even the ultimate and apparent 'breaking' of the church and its power. It is at 'the time of the end', when things are looking at their worst, that all God's purposes are 'completed', and the Son of Man comes to claim his kingdom in universal power (Dan. 7:13,14).

And to the question of the final outcome, the message is firm and practical: 'Go your way, Daniel, because the words are closed up and sealed until the time of the end' (Dan. 12:9). It amounts to an assurance that the prophet is to receive all that God has revealed, and is to remain humble and patient over what remains sealed (vv. 4,9).

Patience is the name of the game! The divine message to Daniel is, 'Get on with your life and task. You know enough to realise that there is more to what you can see taking place in the present distress'. **'As for you, go your way till the end'** (Dan. 12:13).

Jesus was to say something similar to the apostle Peter, during the post-Resurrection breakfast on the beach. Peter had been commissioned for service, but then asked questions about his colleague John. 'What is that to you?' replied Jesus, *'You must follow me'* (John 21:22).

Is that it? We know enough to recognise that there is more to what is going on than petrol prices, mortgage loans, job losses – and the lurching of nations from crisis to crisis. At the turn of a new millennium, we sense the rise in tension, the crazy books and irrational antics of religious extremists infected by psychic epidemics that sweep our world; the disillusionment when it turns out that nothing much has really changed at all. *Was that it?*

The call is to stand with the Son of Man, who knows the end from the beginning, to identify with God's people in the church and to see this thing through to its completion.

In the Greek epic, *The Iliad,* written by Homer over 700 years before Christ, the war against Troy is vividly described. It's the story of Agamemnon, leader of the combined Greek forces. In it we are given the account of the placing of a sentinel – to keep watch, year after year, for the beacon-blaze signalling that Troy, at last, had been taken. Time rolls by....ten years in all; until one memorable day the strategy of the famous Wooden Horse brings victory. At long last the announcement flares up and is relayed from hill to hill, and reflected in the waves of the Aegean Sea. Then, and only then, as the news arrives, *Troy has fallen,* is the sentinel informed, **'Your duty is done. The long wait is over; you are relieved.'**

Carey Francis was perhaps the greatest educationist that Kenya ever had. I knew him only as Uncle Carey. He was the headmaster of Nairobi's famed Alliance High School. His impact upon the country's leadership was enormous. When he died, hundreds of his former pupils, including members of the Kenya Cabinet, turned out to carry and escort his coffin to the grave, filling it in with their own hands. He once said, 'When I go, I want God to find me with my letters answered, my work up to date, *and me hard at it.*'

**As for you, go your way till the end.
You will rest, and then at the end of the days
you will rise to receive your allotted inheritance**

Christian Focus Publications publishes biblically-accurate books for adults and children. The books in the adult range are published in three imprints.

Christian Heritage contains classic writings from the past.

Christian Focus contains popular works including biographies, commentaries, doctrine, and Christian living.

Mentor focuses on books written at a level suitable for Bible College and seminary students, pastors, and others; the imprint includes commentaries, doctrinal studies, examination of current issues, and church history.

For a free catalogue of all our titles, please write to
Christian Focus Publications,
Geanies House, Fearn,
Ross-shire, IV20 1TW, Great Britain

For details of our titles visit us on our web site
http://www.christianfocus.com

Contents

Introduction

This is BPP Learning Media's AAT Question Bank for *Bookkeeping Controls*. It is part of a suite of ground-breaking resources produced by BPP Learning Media for AAT assessments.

This Question Bank has been written in conjunction with the BPP Course Book, and has been carefully designed to enable students to practise all of the learning outcomes and assessment criteria for the units that make up *Bookkeeping Controls*. It is fully up to date as at May 2019 and reflects both the AAT's qualification specification and the sample assessment provided by the AAT.

This Question Bank contains these key features:

- Tasks corresponding to each chapter of the Course Book. Some tasks are designed for learning purposes, others are of assessment standard

- AAT's AQ2016 practice assessments 1 and 2, and answers for *Bookkeeping Controls* and further BPP practice assessments

The emphasis in all tasks and assessments is on the practical application of the skills acquired.

VAT

You may find tasks throughout this Question Bank that need you to calculate or be aware of a rate of VAT. This is stated at 20% in these examples and questions.

Bookkeeping Controls
Level 2
Foundation Certificate in Accounting
Question Bank

Third edition 2019

ISBN 9781 5097 8168 3

British Library Cataloguing-in-Publication Data
A catalogue record for this book is available from the British Library

Published by

BPP Learning Media Ltd
BPP House, Aldine Place
142-144 Uxbridge Road
London W12 8AA

www.bpp.com/learningmedia

Printed in the United Kingdom

Your learning materials, published by BPP Learning Media Ltd, are printed on paper obtained from traceable sustainable sources.

We are grateful to the AAT for permission to reproduce the practice assessment(s). The answers to the practice assessment(s) have been published by the AAT. All other answers have been prepared by BPP Learning Media Ltd.

©
BPP Learning Media Ltd
2019

Approaching the assessment

When you sit the assessment it is very important that you follow the on screen instructions. This means you need to carefully read the instructions, both on the introduction screens and during specific tasks.

When you access the assessment you should be presented with an introductory screen with information similar to that shown below (taken from the introductory screen from one of the AAT's AQ2016 practice assessments for *Bookkeeping Controls*).

We have provided this **practice assessment** to help you familiarise yourself with our e-assessment environment. It is designed to demonstrate as many of the possible question types you may find in a live assessment. It is not designed to be used on its own to determine whether you are ready for a live assessment.

At the end of this practice assessment you will receive an immediate assessment result.

Assessment information:

You have **1 hour 30 minutes** to complete this practice assessment.

This assessment contains **10 tasks** and you should attempt to complete **every** task.
Each task is independent. You will not need to refer to your answers to previous tasks.
Read every task carefully to make sure you understand what is required.

Where the date is relevant, it is given in the task data.

Both minus signs and brackets can be used to indicate negative numbers **unless** task instructions state otherwise.

You must use a full stop to indicate a decimal point. For example, write 100.57 NOT 100,57 or 100 57

You may use a comma to indicate a number in the thousands, but you don't have to. For example, 10000 and 10,000 are both acceptable.

The tasks in this assessment are set in different business situations where the following apply:

- All businesses use a manual bookkeeping system.
- Double entry takes place in the general ledger. Individual accounts of trade receivables and trade payables are kept in the sales and purchases ledgers as subsidiary accounts.
- The cash book and petty cash book should be treated as part of the double entry system unless the task instructions state otherwise.
- The VAT rate is 20%.

The actual instructions will vary depending on the subject you are studying for. It is very important you read the instructions on the introductory screen and apply them in the assessment. You don't want to lose marks when you know the correct answer just because you have not entered it in the right format.

In general, the rules set out in the AAT practice assessments for the subject you are studying for will apply in the real assessment, but you should carefully read the information on this screen again in the real assessment, just to make sure. This screen may also confirm the VAT rate used if applicable.

A full stop is needed to indicate a decimal point. We would recommend using minus signs to indicate negative numbers and leaving out the comma signs to indicate thousands, as this results in a lower number of key strokes and less margin for error when working under time pressure. Having said that, you can use whatever is easiest for you as long as you operate within the rules set out for your particular assessment.

You have to show competence throughout the assessment and you should therefore complete all of the tasks. Don't leave questions unanswered.

In some assessments, written or complex tasks may be human marked. In this case you are given a blank space or table to enter your answer into. You are told in the assessments which tasks these are (note: there may be none if all answers are marked by the computer).

If these involve calculations, it is a good idea to decide in advance how you are going to lay out your answers to such tasks by practising answering them on a word document, and certainly you should try all such tasks in this Question Bank and in the AAT's environment using the practice assessments.

When asked to fill in tables, or gaps, never leave any blank even if you are unsure of the answer. Fill in your best estimate.

Note that for some assessments where there is a lot of scenario information or tables of data provided (eg tax tables), you may need to access these via 'pop-ups'. Instructions will be provided on how you can bring up the necessary data during the assessment.

Finally, take note of any task specific instructions once you are in the assessment. For example you may be asked to enter a date in a certain format or to enter a number to a certain number of decimal places.

Grading

To achieve the qualification and to be awarded a grade, you must pass all the mandatory unit assessments, all optional unit assessments (where applicable) and the synoptic assessment.

The AAT Level 2 Foundation Certificate in Accounting will be awarded a grade. This grade will be based on performance across the qualification. Unit assessments and synoptic assessments are not individually graded. These assessments are given a mark that is used in calculating the overall grade.

How overall grade is determined

You will be awarded an overall qualification grade (Distinction, Merit, and Pass). If you do not achieve the qualification you will not receive a qualification certificate, and the grade will be shown as unclassified.

The marks of each assessment will be converted into a percentage mark and rounded up or down to the nearest whole number. This percentage mark is then weighted according to the weighting of the unit assessment or synoptic assessment within the qualification. The resulting weighted assessment percentages are combined to arrive at a percentage mark for the whole qualification.

Grade definition	Percentage threshold
Distinction	90–100%
Merit	80–89%
Pass	70–79%
Unclassified	0–69% Or failure to pass one or more assessment/s

Re-sits

Some AAT qualifications such as the AAT Foundation Certificate in Accounting have restrictions in place for how many times you are able to re-sit assessments. Please refer to the AAT website for further details.

You should only be entered for an assessment when you are well prepared and you expect to pass the assessment.

AAT qualifications

The material in this book may support the following AAT qualifications:

AAT Foundation Certificate in Accounting Level 2, AAT Foundation Certificate in Accounting at SCQF Level 5 and AAT Foundation Diploma in Accounting and Business Level 2.

Supplements

From time to time we may need to publish supplementary materials to one of our titles. This can be for a variety of reasons. From a small change in the AAT unit guidance to new legislation coming into effect between editions.

You should check our supplements page regularly for anything that may affect your learning materials. All supplements are available free of charge on our supplements page on our website at:

www.bpp.com/learning-media/about/students

Improving material and removing errors

There is a constant need to update and enhance our study materials in line with both regulatory changes and new insights into the assessments.

From our team of authors BPP appoints a subject expert to update and improve these materials for each new edition.

Their updated draft is subsequently technically checked by another author and from time to time non-technically checked by a proof reader.

We are very keen to remove as many numerical errors and narrative typos as we can but given the volume of detailed information being changed in a short space of time we know that a few errors will sometimes get through our net.

We apologise in advance for any inconvenience that an error might cause. We continue to look for new ways to improve these study materials and would welcome your suggestions. Please feel free to contact our AAT Head of Programme at nisarahmed@bpp.com if you have any suggestions for us.

Question Bank

Chapter 1 Payment methods

Task 1.1

Given below are four cheques received by Southfield Electrical today, 9 January 20X6.

Check each one thoroughly and identify the error on the cheques below, selecting your answer from the picklist.

	Comments	
Cheque from B B Berry Ltd		▼
Cheque from Q Q Stores		▼
Cheque from Dagwell Enterprises		▼
Cheque from Weller Enterprises		▼

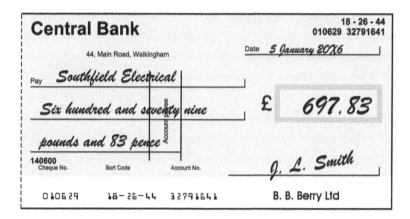

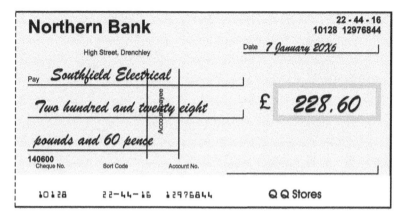

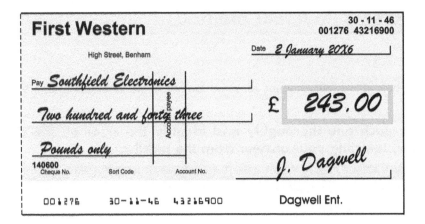

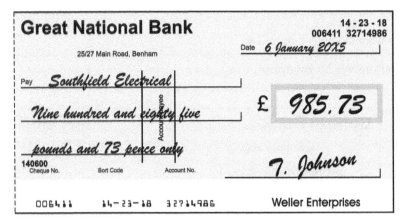

Picklist:

Amount
Date
Payee
Signature

Task 1.2

Frank Limited needs to make several payments to its suppliers. **Select the correct payment method in each case from the picklist provided. You may use the same option more than once.**

Situation	Payment method
Payment to Kim Guitars Ltd for £2,500 for items purchased on credit. The payment is required within 5 days	▼
Payment of £1,000 to Pixie Bass as a deposit on a supply. The payment is required today to release the shipment	▼
Payment of £265,000 to Paz Ltd to secure a new retail unit. Immediate payment is required	▼
Payment to Santiago Strings for £875 to pay an invoice due by the end of the week	▼

Picklist:

BACS Direct Credit
CHAPS
Faster Payment

Task 1.3

Complete the following statements by selecting the relevant banking terms from the picklist.

(a)   A [   ] would be set up to repay a bank loan in equal monthly instalments.

(b)   A [   ] would be set up to make the minimum payment on a credit card by variable amounts each month.

(c)   A bank [   ] would be arranged when short-term borrowing is needed.

Picklist:

direct debit
overdraft
standing order

Task 1.4

Using the picklist, select the most suitable payment method for each of the business expenses.

Situation	Solution
Making regular rent payments	▼
Purchase of office stationery online	▼
Payment of wages to staff	▼
Payment of £2,500 to a supplier after taking 15 days credit	▼
Buying tea bags for the office	▼
Payment of £375 for new tyres for the company van	▼

Picklist:

BACS direct credit
Bank draft
Cash
Debit card
Standing order

Task 1.5

Which TWO of the following items should be checked when a cheque is accepted as payment from customers?

	✓
Funds are available in customer's account	
Issue number	
Words and figures match	
Security number	
Expiry date	
Date is not in the future	

Task 1.6

The director of Parker Flooring Limited has made a number of payments today (2 February 20X6) in respect of materials for the company. **Select the correct impact on the bank account from the picklist below.**

Payment	Impact on the bank account
Cheque written for £550 to Soft Carpets Limited	▼
Debit card to buy diesel for the van £65	▼
Credit card to buy printer cartridges online £30	▼
Payment of a purchase invoice using BACS direct credit to Solvit Limited £1,200	▼
Cheque written for £276 to Wall2Wall Limited	▼
Debit card to buy coffee from the local store of £5.67	▼
Bank draft for £10,000 to purchase a new van	▼

Picklist:

Delayed
Immediate (within 24 hours)

Task 1.7

Given below is a completed cheque. Complete the following statements by selecting from the picklist

Who is the drawee?	▼
Who is the payee?	▼
Who is the drawer?	▼

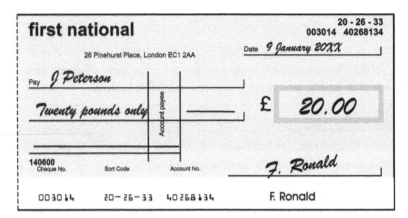

Picklist:

F Ronald
First National
J Peterson

Chapter 2 Bank reconciliations

Task 2.1

Would each of the following transactions appear as a payment in or a payment out on a business's bank statement?

Transaction	Payment out ✓	Payment in ✓
£470.47 paid into the bank		
Standing order of £26.79		
Cheque payment of £157.48		
Interest earned on the bank balance		
BACS payment for wages		

Task 2.2

You are given information about Newmans's receipts during the week ending 27 January. They represent payments by credit customers and receipts for sales to non-credit customers of music, instruments and CDs which were settled by cheque.

Details		Amount £
Tunfield DC	Bank transfer	594.69
Tunshire County Orchestra	Bank transfer	468.29
Sale of music	Cheque	478.90
Tunfield Brass Band	Credit	1,059.72
Sale of instruments	Cheque	752.16
Sale of CDs	Cheque	256.80

You need to update the cash book to reflect the impact of these receipts

(a) **Enter the correct entries from the picklist provided and total the debit side of the cash book given below:**

Cash book – debit side

Date	Details	Bank £
	Bal b/f	379.22
	▼	
	▼	
	▼	
	▼	
	▼	
	▼	
	TOTAL	

Picklist:

Non-credit sales
Tunfield BB
Tunfield DC
Tunshire CO

Given below is the credit side of the cash book for Newmans for the week ending 27 January.

Cash book – credit side

Date	Cheque no	Details	Bank £
27 Jan	003014	Henson Press	329.00
27 Jan	003015	Ely Instr	736.96
27 Jan	003016	Jester Press	144.67
27 Jan	003017	CD Supplies	74.54
27 Jan	003018	Jester Press	44.79
27 Jan	003019	Buser Ltd	273.48
27 Jan	SO	Rates	255.00
27 Jan	DD	Rent	500.00

Given below is the bank statement for Newmans for the week ending 27 January.

STATEMENT

first national
26 Pinehurst Place
London
EC1 2AA

NEWMANS

Account number: 40268134

CURRENT ACCOUNT

Sheet 023

Date		Paid out	Paid in	Balance
20XX				
20 Jan	Balance b/f			379.22 CR
24 Jan	Counter credit – Tunfield		594.69	
	Counter credit – Tunshire Co		468.29	
24 Jan	SO – British Elec	212.00		1,230.20 CR
25 Jan	Counter credit – Tunfield AOS		108.51	1,338.71 CR
26 Jan	Cheque No 003014	329.00		
	Credit		478.90	1,488.61 CR
27 Jan	Cheque No 003017	74.54		
	Cheque No 003015	736.96		
	Credit		1,059.72	
	Credit		752.16	
	SO – TDC	255.00		
	DD – Halpern Properties	500.00		
	Bank interest		3.68	1,737.67 CR

(b) Compare the two sides of the cash book from the information given in part (a) to the bank statement. Note any unmatched items below by selecting items from the picklist below and state whether the item needs including in the cash book or in the bank reconciliation.

Unmatched item	£	Action to be taken
▼		▼
▼		▼
▼		▼
▼		▼
▼		▼
▼		▼
▼		▼

Picklist:

Bank charge
Bank credit
Bank interest received
Cheque 003016
Cheque 003018
Cheque 003019
Include on bank reconciliation
Sales of CDs
Standing order British Elec
Update cash book

(c) **Using the information available from parts (a) and (b) earlier in this task, consider the required amendments to both sides of the cash book using the picklist provided and enter the balance on the cash book as at 27 January.**

Cash book

Date	Details	Bank £	Cheque number	Details	Bank £
	Balance b/f	379.22	003014	Henson Press	329.00
27 Jan	Tunfield DC	594.69	003015	Ely Instr	736.96
27 Jan	Tunshire CO	468.29	003016	Jester Press	144.67
27 Jan	Non-credit sales	478.90	003017	CD Supplies	74.54
27 Jan	Tunfield BB	1,059.72	003018	Jester Press	44.79
27 Jan	Non-credit sales	752.16	003019	Buser Ltd	273.48
27 Jan	Non-credit sales	256.80	SO	Rates	255.00
27 Jan	▼		DD	Rent	500.00
27 Jan	▼			▼	
				▼	
	Total			Total	

Picklist:

Balance b/f
Balance c/d
Bank charges
Bank interest
Standing order
Tunfield AOS
Tunfield DC

13

(d) Identify the **FOUR** reconciling items below to prepare the bank reconciliation statement as at 27 January.

Bank reconciliation statement		£
Balance as per bank statement		
Add:		
	▼	
	▼	
Total to add		
Less:		
	▼	
	▼	
	▼	
Total to subtract		
Balance as per cash book		

Task 2.3

On 28 November The Flower Chain received the following bank statement.

High Street Bank plc				
The Concourse, Badley, B72 5DG				
To: The Flower Chain Account no: 28710191 Date: 25 November				
Statement of Account				
Date	**Details**	**Paid out £**	**Paid in £**	**Balance £**
03 Nov	Balance b/f			9,136 C
07 Nov	Cheque 110870	6,250		2,886 C
17 Nov	Cheque 110872	2,250		636 C
21 Nov	Cheque 110865	3,670		3,034 D
	Direct Debit – Insurance Ensured	500		3,534 D
21 Nov	Counter Credit – BBT Ltd		10,000	6,466 C
24 Nov	Counter credit – Petals Ltd		2,555	9,021 C
	Direct Debit – Rainbow Ltd	88		8,933 C
25 Nov	Cheque 110871	1,164		7,769 C
D = Debit C = Credit				

The cash book as at 28 November is shown below.

Cash book

Date	Details	Bank £	Date	Cheque number	Details	Bank £
01 Nov	Balance b/f	5,466	03 Nov	110870	Roberts & Co	6,250
24 Nov	Bevan & Co	1,822	03 Nov	110871	J Jones	1,164
24 Nov	Plant Pots Ltd	7,998	06 Nov	110872	Lake Walks Ltd	2,250
	▼		10 Nov	110873	PH Supplies	275
	▼		17 Nov	110874	Peters & Co	76
					▼	
					▼	
					▼	
	Total				Total	
	▼					

Picklist:

Balance b/d
Balance c/d
BBT Ltd
Insurance Ensured
Petals Ltd
Peters & Co
Rainbow Ltd

(a) **Match the items on the bank statement against the items in the cash book.**

(b) **Update the cash book as needed using the picklist and entering the cheque or reference details, plus the amount.**

(c) **Total the cash book and clearly show the balance carried down at 28 November AND brought down at 29 November.**

(d) **Using the picklist provided, identify the FOUR transactions that are included in the cash book but missing from the bank statement and complete the bank reconciliation statement as at 28 November.**

Bank reconciliation statement as at 28 November	£
Balance as per bank statement	
Add:	
Total to add	
Less:	
Total to subtract	
Balance as per cash book	

Picklist:

Bevan & Co
Peters & Co
PH Supplies
Plant Pots Ltd

Task 2.4

(a) **Which TWO of the following items reconciling the cash book to the bank statement are referred to as timing differences? Tick the appropriate box in the table below.**

	Timing difference? ✓
Bank charges not recorded in the cash book	
Outstanding lodgements	
Interest charged not recorded in the cash book	
Unpresented cheques	

(b) Your cash book at 31 December shows a bank balance of £565 overdrawn. On comparing this with your bank statement at the same date, you discover the following:

A cheque for £57 drawn by you on 29 December has not yet been presented for payment.

A cheque for £92 from a customer, which was paid into the bank on 24 December, has been dishonoured on 31 December.

The correct cash book balance at 31 December is:

	✓
£714 overdrawn	
£657 overdrawn	
£473 overdrawn	
£530 overdrawn	

(c) The cash book shows a bank balance of £5,675 overdrawn at 31 August. It is subsequently discovered that a standing order for £125 has been entered in the cash book twice, and that a dishonoured cheque for £450 has been debited in the cash book instead of credited.

Select the correct bank balance:

	✓
£5,100 overdrawn	
£6,000 overdrawn	
£6,250 overdrawn	
£6,450 overdrawn	

Task 2.5

(a) Your firm's cash book at 30 April shows a balance at the bank of £2,490. Comparison with the bank statement at the same date reveals the following differences:

Transactions	Amount £
Unpresented cheques	840
Bank charges	50
Receipts not yet credited by the bank	470
Dishonoured cheque from customer	140

Select the correct balance on the cash book at 30 April:

	✓
£1,460	
£2,300	
£2,580	
£3,140	

(b) The bank statement at 31 December 20X1 shows a balance of £1,000. The cash book shows a balance of £750.

Which of the following is the most likely reason for the difference?

	✓
Receipts of £250 recorded in the cash book, but not yet recorded by bank	
Bank charges of £250 shown on the bank statement, not in the cash book	
Standing orders of £250 included on bank statement, not in the cash book	
Cheques issued for £250 recorded in the cash book, but not yet gone through the bank account	

(c) Your firm's cash book at 30 April shows a balance at the bank of £3,526. Comparison with the bank statement at the same date reveals the following differences:

	£
Unpresented cheques	920
Bank interest received not in cash book	150
Uncredited lodgements	270
Dishonoured customer's cheque	310

The correct cash book balance at 30 April is:

£	

Task 2.6

On 26 July Ottaways Ltd received the following bank statement from Ronda Bank as at 23 July.

Assume today's date is 28 July.

<table>
<tr><td colspan="6" align="center">Ronda Bank PLC</td></tr>
<tr><td colspan="6" align="center">Bank Buildings, Flitweck, FT87 1XQ</td></tr>
<tr><td colspan="2">To: Ottaways Ltd</td><td colspan="2">Account No
56235472</td><td colspan="2">23 July</td></tr>
<tr><td colspan="6" align="center">**Bank Statement**</td></tr>
<tr><td>**Date
20XX**</td><td>**Detail**</td><td>**Paid out
£**</td><td>**Paid in
£**</td><td colspan="2">**Balance
£**</td></tr>
<tr><td>03 Jul</td><td>Balance b/f</td><td></td><td></td><td>1,855</td><td>C</td></tr>
<tr><td>03 Jul</td><td>Cheque 126459</td><td>3,283</td><td></td><td>1,428</td><td>D</td></tr>
<tr><td>03 Jul</td><td>Cheque 126460</td><td>1,209</td><td></td><td>2,637</td><td>D</td></tr>
<tr><td>03 Jul</td><td>Cheque 126461</td><td>4,221</td><td></td><td>6,858</td><td>D</td></tr>
<tr><td>04 Jul</td><td>Cheque 126464</td><td>658</td><td></td><td>7,516</td><td>D</td></tr>
<tr><td>09 Jul</td><td>Counter credit
SnipSnap Co</td><td></td><td>8,845</td><td>1,329</td><td>C</td></tr>
<tr><td>11 Jul</td><td>Cheque 126462</td><td>1,117</td><td></td><td>212</td><td>C</td></tr>
<tr><td>11 Jul</td><td>Direct Debit Flit DC</td><td>500</td><td></td><td>288</td><td>D</td></tr>
<tr><td>18 Jul</td><td>Direct Debit Consol
Landlords</td><td>475</td><td></td><td>763</td><td>D</td></tr>
<tr><td>20 Jul</td><td>Bank Charges</td><td>32</td><td></td><td>795</td><td>D</td></tr>
<tr><td>22 Jul</td><td>Interest for month</td><td>103</td><td></td><td>898</td><td>D</td></tr>
<tr><td>23 Jul</td><td>Counter credit</td><td></td><td>5,483</td><td>4,585</td><td>C</td></tr>
<tr><td colspan="6" align="center">D = Debit   C = Credit</td></tr>
</table>

The cash book as at 23 July is shown below.

(a) Match the items on the bank statement against the items in the cash book.

(b) Using the picklist below for the details column, enter any items in the cash book as needed.

(c) Total the cash book and clearly show the balance carried down at 23 July and brought down at 24 July.

(d) Using the picklist below, complete the bank reconciliation statement as at 23 July.

Cash book

Date	Details	Bank £	Date	Cheque number	Details	Bank £
01 Jul	Balance b/f	1,855	01 Jul	126459	Gumpley Co	3,283
20 Jul	Brimfull Ltd	5,483	01 Jul	126460	Warnes Ltd	1,209
21 Jul	Adera Ltd	2,198	01 Jul	126461	Veldt Partners	4,221
22 Jul	Mist Northern	1,004	01 Jul	126462	Pathways	1,117
	▼		02 Jul	126463	Lindstrom Co	846
			02 Jul	126464	Kestrels Training	658
			13 Jul	126465	HGW Ltd	3,200
			13 Jul		Flit DC	500
					▼	
					▼	
					▼	
					▼	
	Total				Total	
	▼					

22

Bank reconciliation statement as at 23 July		£
Balance per bank statement		
Add:		
	▼	
	▼	
Total to add		
Less:		
	▼	
	▼	
Total to subtract		
Balance as per cash book		

Picklist:

Adera Ltd
Balance b/d
Balance c/d
Bank charges
Brimfull Ltd
Consol Landlords
Flit DC
Gumpley Co
HGW Ltd
Interest
Kestrels Training
Lindstrom Co
Mist Northern
Pathways
SnipSnap Co
Veldt Partners
Warnes Ltd

Task 3.1

Assuming they all INCLUDE VAT where relevant, identify the double entry for the following transactions.

Here is a list of the transactions for August 20XX

Transactions	Amount £
Credit purchases	3,390
Credit sales returns	1,860
Payments to credit suppliers	4,590
Receipts from credit customers	5,480
Discounts allowed	400
Discounts received	200

Show the journal entries needed to record the following:

(a) **Purchases**

Account	Amount £	Debit	Credit
▼			
▼			
▼			

(b) **Sales returns**

Account	Amount £	Debit	Credit
▼			
▼			
▼			

(c) **Payments to credit suppliers**

Account	Amount £	Debit	Credit
▼			
▼			

(d) **Receipts from credit customers**

Account	Amount £	Debit	Credit
▼			
▼			

Picklist:

Bank
Discounts allowed
Discounts received
Purchase ledger control
Purchases
Sales ledger control
Sales returns
VAT control a/c

Task 3.2

Your organisation is not registered for VAT. The balance on the sales ledger control account on 1 January was £11,689. The transactions that take place during January are summarised below:

Transactions	Amount £
Credit sales	12,758
Sales returns	1,582
Cash received from trade receivables	11,563
Discounts allowed	738

You are required to write up the sales ledger control account using the picklist below for the month of January.

Sales ledger control

Details	Amount £	Details	Amount £
▼		▼	
▼		▼	
		▼	
		▼	

Picklist:

Balance b/f
Balance c/d
Bank
Discounts allowed
Sales
Sales returns

Task 3.3

Your organisation is not registered for VAT. The opening balance on the purchases ledger control account at 1 January was £8,347. The transactions for the month of January have been summarised below:

Transactions	Amount £
Credit purchases	9,203
Purchases returns	728
Payments to trade payables	8,837
Discounts received	382

You are required to write up the purchases ledger control account for the month of January.

Purchases ledger control

Details	Amount £	Details	Amount £
		Balance b/f	
▼		▼	
▼			
▼			

Picklist:

Balance c/d
Bank
Discounts received
Purchases
Purchases returns

Task 3.4

This is a summary of transactions with credit suppliers during June.

Transactions	Amount £
Balance of trade payables at 1 June	85,299
Goods bought on credit – gross	39,300
Payments made to credit suppliers	33,106
Discounts received	1,000
Goods returned to credit suppliers – gross	275

Prepare a purchases ledger control account from the details shown in the table on the prior page. Show clearly the balance carried down at 30 June AND brought down at 1 July.

Purchases ledger control account

Date	Details	Amount £	Date	Details	Amount £
	▼			Balance b/f	
	▼			▼	
	▼				
	▼				
				▼	

Picklist:

Balance b/d
Balance c/d
Bank
Discounts received
Purchases
Purchases returns

Task 3.5

(a) The sales ledger control account at 1 May had a balance of £31,475. During May, gross sales of £125,000 were made on credit. Receipts from trade receivables amounted to £122,500 and discounts of £550 were allowed. Credit notes of £1,300 gross were issued to customers.

The closing balance on the sales ledger control account at 31 May is:

	✓
£32,125	
£33,975	
£34,725	
£33,225	

(b) Your purchases ledger control account has a balance at 1 October of £34,500 credit. During October, gross credit purchases were £78,400, gross cash purchases were £2,400 and payments made to suppliers, excluding cash purchases, and after deducting settlement discounts of £1,200, were £68,900. Gross purchases returns were £4,700.

The closing balance on the purchases ledger control account was:

	✓
£38,100	
£40,500	
£47,500	
£49,900	

Task 3.6

Sunshine Limited has calculated its VAT for the month of March. It has a VAT control account credit balance of £4,500 brought down on 1 March 20XX.

There are a number of transactions made during the month.

Details	Amount £
VAT on sales	6,000
VAT on sales returns	300
VAT on purchases	2,500
Bank payment made to HMRC	7,000
VAT on purchases returns	250

(a) **Prepare the VAT control account for March 20XX. Show the balance c/d at 31 March 20XX and the balance b/d at 1 April 20XX.**

Details		Amount £	Details		Amount £
▼			Balance b/f		4,500
▼				▼	
▼				▼	
▼					
				▼	

Picklist:

Balance b/d
Balance c/d
Payment to HMRC
VAT on purchases
VAT on purchase returns
VAT on sales
VAT on sales returns

(b) **If VAT of £4,500 was calculated on sales made by Sunshine Limited during April 20XX, and there were no other VAT transactions, what would be the liability to HMRC at 30 April 20XX?**

£ _____

Chapter 4 Preparing and reconciling control accounts

Task 4.1

When reconciling sales ledger and purchases ledger control accounts to the list of balances from the subsidiary ledgers, would the following errors affect the relevant control account, the list of balances or both?

	Control account ✓	List of balances ✓	Both ✓
Invoice entered into the sales day book as £980 instead of £890			
Purchases day book overcast by £1,000			
Discounts allowed of £20 not entered into the cash book (debit side)			
An invoice taken as £340 instead of £440 when being posted to the customer's account			
Incorrect balancing of a memorandum ledger account			
A purchases return not entered into the purchases returns day book			

Task 4.2

James has just completed his first month of trading. James makes sales on credit to four customers and the transactions during his second month of trading were as follows. James is not registered for VAT.

Transactions	Amount £
Sales to H Simms	2,000
Sales to P Good	2,700
Sales to K Mitchell	1,100
Sales to C Brown	3,800
Receipt from H Simms	2,400
Receipts from P Good	3,600
Receipts from K Mitchell	1,100
Receipts from C Brown	4,800

You are required to:

(a) **Using the picklist below, show these transactions in total in the sales ledger control account and in detail in the individual sales ledger accounts. Each of the accounts shows, where appropriate, the opening balance at the start of the second month.**

(b) **Balance the sales ledger control account and the individual sales ledger accounts.**

(c) **Reconcile the list of sales ledger balances to the balance on the control account.**

Sales ledger control account

Details	Amount £	Details	Amount £
Balance b/f	5,000	▼	
▼		▼	
▼			

Sales ledger

H Simms

Details	Amount £	Details	Amount £
Balance b/f	900	▼	
▼		▼	
▼		▼	

P Good

Details	Amount £	Details	Amount £
Balance b/f	1,600	▼	
▼		▼	
▼			

K Mitchell

Details	Amount £	Details	Amount £
▼		▼	

C Brown

Details	Amount £	Details	Amount £
Balance b/f	2,500	▼	
▼		▼	
▼			

Reconciliation of sales ledger balances with the control account balance

	£
H Simms	
P Good	
K Mitchell	
C Brown	
Sales ledger control account	

Picklist:

Balance b/d
Balance c/d
Bank
Sales

Task 4.3

James also buys goods on credit from three suppliers. The transactions with these suppliers in month two are summarised below. James is not registered for VAT.

Transactions	Amount £
Purchase from J Peters	1,600
Purchase from T Sands	2,500
Purchase from L Farmer	3,200

Transactions	Amount £
Payment to J Peters	1,700
Payment to T Sands	3,200
Payment to L Farmer	3,000

BPP
LEARNING MEDIA

You are required to:

(a) Using the picklist below, show these transactions in total in the purchases ledger control account and in detail in the individual purchases ledger accounts. Each of the accounts shows, where appropriate, the opening balance at the start of the second month.

(b) Balance the purchases ledger control account and the individual purchases ledger accounts.

(c) Reconcile the list of purchases ledger balances to the balance on the control account.

Picklist:

Bank
Purchases
Balance b/d
Balance c/d

Purchases ledger control account

Details		Amount £	Details		Amount £
	▼		Balance b/f		2,700
	▼			▼	
				▼	

Purchases ledger

J Peters

Details		Amount £	Details		Amount £
	▼		Balance b/f		300
	▼			▼	
				▼	

T Sands

Details	Amount £	Details	Amount £
		Balance b/f	1,700

L Farmer

Details	Amount £	Details	Amount £
		Balance b/f	700

Reconciliation of purchases ledger balances with control account balance

	£
J Peters	
T Sands	
L Farmer	
Purchases ledger control account	

Task 4.4

The following are the sales ledger transactions for June 20XX

Transactions	Amount £
Items sold on credit	14,500
Returns from customers	700
Receipts from customers	15,600

(a) **You are required to write up the sales ledger control account. Please use the picklist provided:**

Sales ledger control

Details	Amount £	Details	Amount £
Balance b/f	9,450		

Picklist:

Balance b/d
Balance c/d
Bank
Sales on credit
Returns

The following are the balances on the sales ledger.

Details	Amount £
Annabel Limited	3,000
Bahira Limited	1,250
Clara Limited	3,310

(b) **What is the difference between the sales ledger control account and the sales ledger?**

£ [ ]

(c) **Which TWO of the following reasons could explain why there is this difference between the sales ledger control account and the sales ledger?**

Reasons	✓
A cash receipt was incorrectly entered onto the customer's account in the sales ledger	
A sales invoice has been duplicated in the sales ledger	
A sales return credit note has only been recorded in the sales ledger control account	
Discounts have been posted twice in the customer's sales ledger account	

Task 4.5

The following is an extract of the balances on the purchase ledger as at 31 July 20XX.

Transactions	Amount £
Goods purchased on credit during July	8,600
Payments made to credit suppliers in July	9,750
Discounts received	500

The brought forward balance at 1 July 20XX was £12,500.

(a)   Complete the purchase ledger control account using the balances above. Remember to calculate the balance brought down at 1 August 20XX.

Purchase ledger control

Details	Amount £	Details	Amount £
▼		Balance b/f	
▼		▼	
▼			
		▼	

Picklist:

Balance b/d
Balance c/d
Bank
Discounts received
Purchases

The following are the balances on the purchase ledger as at 31 July 20XX:

Purchase ledger

Transactions	Amount £
Cargo Transport Limited	5,400
Utilities Financing Limited	1,200
Airborne Parcels Limited	2,000
LoGist Limited	1,250
Wrap Around Limited	800

(b) **Using the information from the purchase ledger in part (a), complete the purchase ledger account reconciliation in the table below.**

	£
Purchase ledger control account balance as at 31 July 20XX	
Total of the purchase ledger accounts as at 31 July 20XX	
Difference	

(c) **Select the ONE correct possible reason for this difference on the purchase ledger reconciliation.**

Reason	✓
Purchases on credit have been recorded on the debit side of the purchase ledger	
A purchase invoice has been duplicated in the purchase ledger	
Discounts received have been omitted from the purchases ledger but recorded in the purchases ledger control account	
A cash payment to a credit supplier has been recorded in the purchase ledger control account only	

Task 4.6

This is a summary of your business's transactions with credit customers during November.

	£
Balance of trade receivables at 1 November	48,125
Goods sold on credit (gross value)	37,008
Money received from credit customers	28,327
Discounts allowed	240
Goods returned by customers (gross value)	2,316

(a) **Using the picklist provided below, prepare a sales ledger control account from the details shown above. Show clearly the balance carried down at 30 November AND brought down at 1 December.**

Sales ledger control

Date	Details	Amount £	Date	Details	Amount £
	Balance b/f			▼	
	▼			▼	
				▼	
				▼	
	▼				

Picklist:

Balance b/d
Balance c/d
Bank
Discounts allowed
Sales
Sales returns

The following balances were in the sales ledger on 1 December:

Transactions	Amount £
J Hicks Ltd	3,298
Parks and Gardens	4,109
Greener Grass	18,250
TTL Ltd	18,106
Reeves and Wright	10,400

(b) Reconcile the balances shown above with the sales ledger control account balance you have calculated in part (a).

	£
Sales ledger control account balance as at 1 December	
Total of sales ledger accounts as at 1 December	
Difference	

(c) Because of an error in the sales ledger, there is a difference. What might have caused the difference? Tick TWO reasons only.

	✓
VAT has been overstated on an invoice.	
VAT has been understated on an invoice.	
A sales invoice has been entered in the sales ledger twice.	
A sales credit note has been entered in the sales ledger twice.	
A receipt from a customer has been omitted from the sales ledger.	
A receipt from a customer has been entered in the sales ledger twice.	

Task 4.7

The following transactions take place during a three month period (the entity's first trading period)

(a) Calculate the VAT on the balances and complete the table below (round your answers to the nearest pound).

Transactions	Amount £	VAT £
Sales on credit including VAT at 20%	106,800	
Purchases on credit including VAT at 20%	54,000	
Credit notes issued including VAT at 20%	2,820	

(b) **Using the VAT figures calculated above, complete the VAT control account, including the balance brought down at the end of the quarter. Use the picklist provided.**

VAT control

Details	Amount £	Details	Amount £
▼		▼	
▼			
▼			
		▼	

Picklist:

Balance b/d
Balance c/d
Purchases
Sales
Sales returns

(c) **The amount payable to HMRC for the quarter will be**

£ [   ]

....

Task 4.8

At the end of the last VAT period, the VAT account for Fast Fashions showed that a refund was due from HM Revenue & Customs.

(a) **Select ONE reason that would cause a refund to be due to Fast Fashions.**

Reason	
The sales ledger control account shows a difference to the sales ledger account balances	
Sales were less than purchases for the quarter	
There was an underpayment of VAT in the previous quarter	

Sales in June totalled £129,240, all including VAT.

(b) **What is the amount of output VAT on sales?**

£ [   ]

Task 4.9

(a) A supplier sends you a statement showing a balance outstanding of £14,350. Your own records show a balance outstanding of £14,500.

The reason for this difference could be that

	✓
The supplier sent an invoice for £150 which you have not yet received	
The supplier has given you £150 settlement discount which you had not entered in your ledger	
You have paid the supplier £150 which he has not yet accounted for	
You have returned goods worth £150 which the supplier has not yet accounted for	

(b) An invoice for £69 has been recorded in the sales day book as £96.

When the sales ledger reconciliation is prepared, adjustments will be required to:

	✓
The control account only	
The list of balances only	
Both the control account and the list of balances	

At the end of the month, the purchase ledger control account has credit entries amounting to £76,961 and debit balances amounting to £24,500.

The following transactions need to be recorded in the purchase ledger control account:

- Correction of a duplicated supplier's invoice for £4,688
- Standing order payments to suppliers of £1,606

(c) What will be the corrected purchase ledger control account balance brought down after the transactions above have been recorded? Tick the correct entry to show whether this balance will be a debit or a credit.

Amount £	Debit ✓	Credit ✓

Task 4.10

(a) You have been handed an aged receivable analysis which shows a total balance of £109,456.

This amount should reconcile with which TWO of the following?

	✓
The balance on the bank statement	
The balance on the sales ledger control account	
The balance on the purchases ledger control account	
The total of all the purchases ledger balances	
The total of all the sales ledger balances	

(b) Complete the following sentence:

The aged receivable analysis shows:

	✓
How much is owed to suppliers at any point	
Over how many months the outstanding balance owed by each individual credit customer has built up	
The total purchases over the year to date to each credit supplier	

BPP
LEARNING MEDIA

Task 4.11

A credit customer, B B Brand Ltd, has ceased trading, owing Kitchen Kuts £1,560 plus VAT.

(a) **Record the journal entries needed in the general ledger to write off the net amount and the VAT.**

Account name	Amount £	Debit ✓	Credit ✓
▼			
▼			
▼			

Picklist:

Irrecoverable debts
Sales ledger control
VAT control

Kitchen Kuts has the following transactions for the month (all figures include VAT):

- Credit sales of £8,400
- Purchases of £540
- Sales returns of £300

(b) **Record the transactions above in the VAT control account, including the entries for the irrecoverable debt of B B Brand Ltd and the VAT brought down figure for the following month. Use the picklist provided.**

VAT control account

Details	Amount £	Details	Amount £
		Balance b/f	250
▼		▼	
▼			
▼			
▼			
		▼	

Picklist:

Balance b/d
Balance c/d
Irrecoverable debt expense
Purchases
Sales
Sales returns

Task 4.12

A credit customer, ABC Ltd, has ceased trading, owing your firm £240 plus VAT.

Prepare a journal to write off the net amount and VAT in the general ledger.

Journal

Account name	Amount £	Debit ✓	Credit ✓
▼			
▼			
▼			

Picklist:

Irrecoverable debt expense
Sales ledger control
VAT control

Task 4.13

Textile Carpets has a credit customer, Flooring King, who has ceased trading, owing the business £2,370. Textile Carpets is registered for VAT at 20%

Record the journal entries needed in the general ledger to write off the net amount and the VAT.

Account name	Amount £	Debit ✓	Credit ✓
▼			
▼			
▼			

Picklist:

Irrecoverable debt expense
Sales ledger control
VAT control

Chapter 5 The journal

Task 5.1

An organisation has started a new business and a new set of accounts is to be opened. The opening balances for the new business are as follows:

Details	Amount £
Capital	10,000
Furniture and fittings	15,315
Motor vehicles	20,109
Cash at bank	15,000
Purchase ledger control	37,238
Sales ledger control	12,524
Loan from bank	7,000
VAT (owed to HM Revenue & Customs)	8,710

Using the picklist below, prepare a journal to enter these opening balances into the accounts.

Journal

Account name	Debit £	Credit £
▼		
▼		
▼		
▼		
▼		
▼		
▼		
▼		
Totals		

Picklist:

Capital
Cash at bank
Furniture and fittings
Loan from bank
Motor vehicles
Purchases ledger control
Sales ledger control
VAT control (owed to HM Revenue & Customs)

Task 5.2

A new business has already started to trade, though it is not yet registered for VAT, and now wishes to open up its first set of accounts. You are handed the following information:

	£
Bank	300
Petty cash	200
Trade receivables	7,700
Bank loan	9,000
VAT	1,300
Trade creditors	3,400
Van	6,000
Capital	500

Record the journal entries needed in the accounts in the general ledger of the business to deal with the opening entries. Use the picklist below to select your account, write in the amount to be entered and tick the appropriate entry to show whether a debit or a credit.

Account name	Amount £	Debit ✓	Credit ✓
▼			
▼			
▼			
▼			
▼			
▼			
▼			
▼			

Picklist:

Bank
Capital
Loan from bank
Petty cash
Trade creditors
Trade receivables
Van
VAT control

Task 5.3

Kitchen Kuts has started a new business, Kitchen Capers, and a new set of accounts is to be opened. A partially completed journal to record the opening entries is shown below.

Record the journal entries needed in the accounts in the general ledger of Kitchen Capers to deal with the opening entries.

Account name	Amount £	Debit ✓	Credit ✓
Cash	150		
Cash at bank	12,350		
Capital	23,456		
Fixtures and Fittings	2,100		
Trade receivables	3,206		
Loan from bank	10,000		
Motor vehicle	15,650		

Task 5.4

Peter Knight is one of the employees at Short Furniture. The payroll department have calculated his payroll for May as follows.

Details	Amount £
Gross salary	2,200
National Insurance Contributions (Employee)	183
National Insurance Contributions (Employer)	200
Income Tax	256

(a)   Calculate Peter's net salary for the month.

£ [   ]

(b) **Show how all of the elements of Peter's salary including the net salary as shown in part (a) would be entered into the accounting records by using the picklist below and writing up the ledger accounts given.**

Salary expense

Details	Amount £	Details	Amount £
▼			
▼			

Salary control

Details	Amount £	Details	Amount £
▼		▼	
▼		▼	
▼			
▼			

HMRC control

Details	Amount £	Details	Amount £
		▼	
		▼	
		▼	

Bank

Details	Amount £	Details	Amount £
		▼	

Picklist:

Bank
HMRC control
Salary control
Salary expense

Task 5.5

Select the correct recipient of each of the following payroll related costs

Income tax		Employee
NIC (employee)		HMRC
Pension contributions		Pension company
Net salary		Employer

Task 5.6

Georgia Blossom has her monthly salary paid to her on the 28th of the month. She pays into the pension scheme and her employer contributes an additional 4% of her gross salary as pension contributions.

These are the calculations for Georgia's August 20XX salary.

	Amount £
Gross Salary	3,500
Pension contribution by Georgia	200
Income Tax	500
NIC (employee)	180
NIC (employer)	210
Trade union subscription	15

(a)   Calculate the employer's pension contribution

£ _____

(b)   Calculate Georgia's net salary for August

£ _____

(c) **Transfer the pension liability from the salary control account to the pension liability account, using the picklist below.**

Details		Debit £	Credit £
	▼		
	▼		

Picklist:

Pension administrator
Salary control

(d) **Complete the journal for the trade union subscription deduction.**

Details		Debit £	Credit
	▼		
	▼		

Picklist:

Trade union subscription
Salary control

(e) **Complete the journal for the payment of the net salary to Georgia on the 28th.**

Details		Debit £	Credit
	▼		
	▼		

Picklist:

Bank
Salary control

(f) **What is the total monthly cost to the company of employing Georgia?**

£	

Task 6.1

A suspense account has been opened with a balance of £180.

The error has been identified as an entry made in the general ledger from the incorrectly totalled net column in the sales daybook shown below.

Sales daybook

Date 20XX	Details		Invoice number	Total £	VAT £	Net £
29 Sep	F Bacon		2349	768	128	640
30 Sep	J Locke		2350	1,476	246	1,230
30 Sep	D Hume		2351	2,040	340	1,700
	Totals			4,284	714	3,750

(a) **Record the journal entries needed to:**

- **Remove the incorrect entry**
- **Record the correct entry**
- **Remove the suspense account balance**

Do not enter a zero in unused debit or credit column cells.

Journal to remove the incorrect entry

Account name		Debit £	Credit £
	▼		

Picklist:

Sales
Sales ledger control
Sales returns
Suspense
VAT control

Journal to record the correct entry

Account name	Debit £	Credit £
▼		

Picklist:

Sales
Sales ledger control
Sales returns
Suspense
VAT control

Journal to remove the suspense account balance

Account name	Debit £	Credit £
▼		

Picklist:

Sales
Sales ledger control
Sales returns
Suspense
VAT control

Another error has been found in the general ledger. Entries to record cash drawings of £350 has been reversed.

(b)   Record the journal entries needed to:

- **Remove the incorrect entries**
- **Record the correct entries**

Do not enter a zero in unused debit or credit column cells.

Journal to remove the incorrect entries

Account name		Debit £	Credit £
	▼		
	▼		

Picklist:

Bank
Capital
Cash
Drawings

Journal to record the correct entries

Account name		Debit £	Credit £
	▼		
	▼		

Picklist:

Bank
Capital
Cash
Drawings

Task 6.2

A business extracts a trial balance in which the debit column totals £452,409 and the credit column totals £463,490.

What will be the balance on the suspense account? Tick whether this balance will be a debit or a credit.

Account name	Amount £	Debit ✓	Credit ✓
Suspense			

Task 6.3

A business used a suspense account with a credit balance of £124 to balance its initial trial balance.

Correction of which ONE of the following errors will clear the suspense account?

Error	✓
A credit note from a supplier with a net amount of £124 was not entered in the purchases ledger	
Discounts allowed of £124 were only posted to the discounts allowed account	
A cash purchase for £124 was not entered in the purchases account	
An irrecoverable debt write-off of £124 was not entered in the subsidiary ledger	

Task 6.4

A suspense account has been opened with a balance of £54.

The error has been identified as an entry made in the general ledger from the incorrectly totalled VAT column in the purchases daybook shown below.

Purchases daybook

Date 20XX	Details		Invoice number	Total £	VAT £	Net £
31 Dec	I Kant		5521	1,002	167	835
31 Dec	G Hegel		5522	264	44	220
31 Dec	K Marx		5523	1,902	317	1,585
	Totals			3,168	582	2,640

(a) **Record the journal entries needed to:**

- **Remove the incorrect entry**
- **Record the correct entry**
- **Remove the suspense account balance**

Do not enter a zero in unused debit or credit column cells.

Journal to remove the incorrect entry

Account name	Debit £	Credit £
▼		

Picklist:

Purchases
Purchases ledger control
Suspense
VAT control

Journal to record the correct entry

Account name	Debit £	Credit £
▼		

Picklist:

Purchases
Purchases ledger control
Suspense
VAT control

Journal to remove the suspense account balance

Account name	Debit £	Credit £
▼		

Picklist:

Purchases
Purchases ledger control
Suspense
VAT control

Another error has been found in the general ledger. Entries to record cash purchases of £800 have been reversed. (Ignore VAT.)

(b) **Record the journal entries needed to:**

- **Remove the incorrect entries**
- **Record the correct entries**

Do not enter a zero in unused debit or credit column cells.

Journal to remove the incorrect entries

Account name	Debit £	Credit £
▼		
▼		

Picklist:

Bank
Capital
Cash
Purchases

Journal to record the correct entries

Account name	Debit £	Credit £
▼		
▼		

Picklist:

Bank
Capital
Cash
Purchases

Task 6.5

A suspense account has been opened with a balance of £270.

The error has been identified as an entry made in the general ledger from the incorrectly totalled net column in the sales returns daybook shown below.

Sales returns daybook

Date 20XX	Details		Invoice number	Total £	VAT £	Net £
31 Dec	Klein		4839	1,944	324	1,620
31 Dec	Bion		4840	546	91	455
31 Dec	Winnicott		4841	5,604	934	4,670
	Totals			8,094	1,349	6,475

(a) **Record the journal entries needed to:**

- **Remove the incorrect entry**
- **Record the correct entry**
- **Remove the suspense account balance**

Do not enter a zero in unused debit or credit column cells.

Journal to remove the incorrect entry

Account name		Debit £	Credit £
	▼		

Picklist:

Bion
Klein
Sales returns
Sales ledger control
Suspense
VAT control
Winnicott

Journal to record the correct entry

Account name		Debit £	Credit £
▼			

Picklist:

Bion
Klein
Sales returns
Sales ledger control
Suspense
VAT control
Winnicott

Journal to remove the suspense account balance

Account name		Debit £	Credit £
▼			

Picklist:

Bion
Klein
Sales returns
Sales ledger control
Suspense
VAT control
Winnicott

Another error has been found in the general ledger. An entry to record a bank receipt from a credit customer settled by counter credit of £450 has been reversed.

(b)   Record the journal entries needed to:

- **Remove the incorrect entries**
- **Record the correct entries**

Do not enter a zero in unused debit or credit column cells.

Journal to remove the incorrect entries

Account name		Debit £	Credit £
	▼		
	▼		

Picklist:

Bank
Purchases
Purchases ledger control
Sales
Sales ledger control
Suspense
VAT

Journal to record the correct entries

Account name		Debit £	Credit £
	▼		
	▼		

Picklist:

Bank
Purchases
Purchases ledger control
Sales
Sales ledger control
Suspense
VAT

Task 6.6

After extracting an initial trial balance a business finds it has a debit balance of £118 in the suspense account. A number of errors have been noted.

Using the picklists below, record the journal entries needed in the general ledger to reverse the incorrect entries and record the transactions correctly.

(a) **Sales of £500 have been credited to the sales returns account.**

Details		Debit £	Credit £
	▼		
	▼		

Picklist:

Sales returns
Sales

(b) **Entries to record a bank payment of £125 for office expenses have been reversed.**

Details		Debit £	Credit £
	▼		
	▼		
	▼		
	▼		

Picklist

Bank
Office expenses

(c) A bank payment of £299 for purchases (no VAT) has been entered correctly in the purchases column of the cash book but as £29 in the total column.

Details		Debit £	Credit £
	▼		
	▼		
	▼		
	▼		
	▼		

Picklist:

Bank
Purchases
Suspense

(d) Discounts allowed of £388 were only posted to the sales ledger control account in the general ledger.

Details		Debit £	Credit £
	▼		
	▼		
	▼		
	▼		

Picklist:

Discounts allowed
Sales ledger control
Suspense

Task 6.7

On 30 June, a suspense account of a business that is not registered for VAT has a credit balance of £720.

On 1 July, the following errors were discovered:

(i) A bank payment of £225 has been omitted from the rent and rates account.

(ii) An irrecoverable debt expense of £945 has been credited correctly to the sales ledger control account, but debited to both the irrecoverable debt account and the sales account.

(a) **Enter the opening balance in the suspense account below.**

(b) **Make the necessary entries to clear the suspense account using the picklist below.**

Suspense

Date	Details	Amount £	Date	Details	Amount £
	▼			▼	
	▼			▼	

Picklist:

Balance b/f
Bank
Sales

Task 6.8

(a) When posting an invoice received for building maintenance, £980 was entered on the building maintenance expense account instead of the correct amount of £890. In each case, select the correct option from the table below.

What correction should be made to the building maintenance expenses account?

	✓
Debit £90	
Credit £90	
Debit £1,780	
Credit £1,780	

(b) A business receives an invoice from a supplier for £2,800 which is mislaid before any entry has been made, resulting in the transaction being omitted from the books entirely.

This is an

	✓
Error of transposition	
Error of omission	
Error of principle	
Error of commission	

(c) **An error of commission is one where**

	✓
A transaction has not been recorded	
One side of a transaction has been recorded in the wrong account, and that account is of a different class to the correct account	
One side of a transaction has been recorded in the wrong account, and that account is of the same class as the correct account	
A transaction has been recorded using the wrong amount	

(d) **Which ONE of the following is an error of principle?**

	✓
A gas bill credited to the gas account and debited to the bank account	
The purchase of a non-current asset credited to the asset account and debited to the supplier's account	
The purchase of a non-current asset debited to the purchases account and credited to the supplier's account	
The payment of wages debited and credited to the correct accounts, but using the wrong amount	

Task 6.9

(a) **Where a transaction is entered into the correct ledger accounts, but the wrong amount is used, the error is known as an error of**

	✓
Omission	
Original entry	
Commission	
Principle	

(b) When a trial balance was prepared, two ledger accounts were omitted:

Discounts received	£6,150
Discounts allowed	£7,500

A suspense account was opened.

What was the balance on the suspense account?

	✓
Debit £1,350	
Credit £1,350	
Debit £13,650	
Credit £13,650	

(c) **If a purchases return of £48 has been wrongly posted to the debit of the sales returns account, but has been correctly entered in the purchases ledger control account, the total of the trial balance would show**

	✓
The credit side to be £48 more than the debit side	
The debit side to be £48 more than the credit side	
The credit side to be £96 more than the debit side	
The debit side to be £96 more than the credit side	

(d) **Indicate whether preparing a trial balance will reveal the following errors.**

	Yes	No
Omitting both entries for a transaction		
Posting the debit entry for an invoice to an incorrect expense account		
Omitting the debit entry for a transaction		
Posting the debit entry for a transaction as a credit entry		

Task 6.10

Show which of the errors below are, or are not, disclosed by the trial balance.

Error in the general ledger	Error disclosed by the trial balance ✓	Error NOT disclosed by the trial balance ✓
Recording a bank receipt of a cash sale on the debit side of the cash sales account		
Entering an insurance expense in the administration expenses account		
Entering the discounts received account balance on the debit side of the trial balance		
Miscasting the total column of one page of the sales returns day book		
Failing to write up a dishonoured cheque in the cash book		
Recording discount allowed of £15 as £150 in the cash book		

BPP LEARNING MEDIA

Task 6.11

Your organisation's trial balance included a suspense account. All the bookkeeping errors have now been traced and the journal entries shown below have been recorded.

Journal entries

Account name	Debit £	Credit £
Motor vehicles	4,300	
Machinery		4,300
Suspense	750	
Sales ledger control		750
Discounts allowed	209	
Suspense		209

Post the journal entries to the general ledger accounts. Dates are not required but you must complete the 'details' columns accurately.

Discounts allowed

Details	Amount £	Details	Amount £
▼		▼	

Machinery

Details	Amount £	Details	Amount £
▼		▼	

Motor vehicles

Details	Amount £	Details	Amount £
▼		▼	

Sales ledger control

Details	Amount £	Details	Amount £
▼		▼	

Suspense

Details	Amount £	Details	Amount £
▼		Balance b/f	541
▼		▼	

Picklist:

Discounts allowed
Machinery
Motor vehicles
Sales ledger control
Suspense

Task 6.12

Your business extracted an initial trial balance which did not balance, and a suspense account with a debit balance of £6,290 was opened. Journal entries were subsequently prepared to correct the errors that had been found, and clear the suspense account. The list of balances in the initial trial balance, and the journal entries to correct the errors, are shown below.

Journal entries

Account name	Debit £	Credit £
Sales ledger control account	2,875	
Suspense		2,875
Sales ledger control account	2,875	
Suspense		2,875

Account name	Debit £	Credit £
Heat and light		5,172
Suspense	5,172	
Heat and light	5,712	
Suspense		5,712

Taking into account the journal entries, which will clear the suspense account, redraft the trial balance by writing the figures in the debit or credit column.

	Balances extracted on 30 June £	Balances at 1 July Debit £	Credit £
Machinery	82,885		
Computer equipment	41,640		
Insurance	17,520		
Bank (overdraft)	13,252		
Petty cash	240		
Sales ledger control	241,500		
Purchases ledger control	134,686		
VAT (owing to HM Revenue and Customs)	19,920		
Capital	44,826		
Sales	525,092		
Purchases	269,400		
Purchases returns	16,272		
Wages	61,680		
Maintenance expenses	3,283		
Stationery	8,049		
Rent and rates	3,466		

	Balances extracted on 30 June £	Balances at 1 July Debit £	Credit £
Heat and light	5,172		
Telephone	7,596		
Marketing expenses	5,327		
Totals			

Task 6.13

Kitchen Kuts' initial trial balance includes a suspense account with a balance of £100.

The error has been traced to the sales returns day book shown below.

Sales returns day book

Date 20XX	Details	Credit note number	Total £	VAT £	Net £
30 June	Barber Bates Ltd	367	720	120	600
30 June	GTK Ltd	368	4,320	720	3,600
30 June	Peer Prints	369	960	160	800
	Totals		6,000	1,100	5,000

(a) **Identify the error and record the journal entries needed in the general ledger to**

(i) **Remove the incorrect entry**

Account name	Amount £	Debit ✓	Credit ✓
▼			

(ii) Record the correct entry

Account name	Amount £	Debit ✓	Credit ✓
▼			

(iii) Remove the suspense account balance

Account name	Amount £	Debit ✓	Credit ✓
▼			

An entry to record a bank payment of £350 for heat and light has been reversed.

(b) Record the journal entries needed in the general ledger to

(i) Remove the incorrect entries

Account name	Amount £	Debit ✓	Credit ✓
▼			
▼			

(ii) Record the correct entries

Account name	Amount £	Debit ✓	Credit ✓
▼			
▼			

Picklist:

Bank
Heat and light
Suspense
VAT

Answer Bank

Chapter 1

Task 1.1

	Comments
Cheque from B B Berry Ltd	Amount: Words and figures differ, they should match to verify the correct amount payable.
Cheque from Q Q Stores	Signature: Cheque is unsigned. Cheques must be signed by an authorised signatory.
Cheque from Dagwell Enterprises	Payee: Payee name is incorrect – Electronics instead of Electrical
Cheque from Weller Enterprises	Date: Dated 6 January 20X5 instead of 20X6 – this cheque is therefore out of date. Although cheques have no expiry date, generally accepted banking convention is that cheques are not accepted after 6 months. This is due to the possibility of duplication of payment or this being a stolen cheque.

Task 1.2

	Payment method	Comment
Payment to Kim Guitars Ltd for £2500 for items purchased on credit. The payment is required within 5 days	BACS direct credit	No urgency on the payment, so BACS is sufficient
Payment of £1000 to Pixie Bass as a deposit on a supply. The payment is required today to release the shipment	Faster payment	Same day money transfer is required.
Payment of £265,000 to Paz Ltd to secure a new retail unit. Immediate payment is required	CHAPS	A highly secure way of moving large amounts of money
Payment to Santiago Strings for £875 to pay an invoice due by the end of the week	BACS direct credit	No urgency on the payment, so BACS direct credit is sufficient

Task 1.3

(a) A standing order would be set up to repay a bank loan in equal monthly instalments.

(b) A direct debit would be set up to make the minimum payment on a credit card by variable amounts each month.

(c) A bank overdraft would be arranged when short-term borrowing is needed.

Task 1.4

Situation	Solution
Making regular rent payments	Standing order
Purchase of office stationery online	Debit card
Payment of wages to staff	BACS direct credit
Payment of £2500 to a supplier after taking 15 days credit	BACS direct credit
Buying tea bags for the office	Cash
Payment of £375 for new tyres for the company van.	Debit card

A standing order will ensure that regular, same value payments are made on the same day every month to ensure the rent is paid on time without fail.

Buying office stationery online requires payment by a debit (or credit) card.

Payment of wages by BACS Direct Credit ensures that the money is securely sent to the correct recipient. It also reduces the amount of cash which is kept on the business premises.

Payments to supplier after receipt of an invoice are made by BACS. This ensures the correct amount is sent directly to the correct recipient, within the credit terms set. Payment may also be made by cheque, but this is not an option in this scenario.

Teabags and small items for the office are usually purchased using petty cash, due to the small payments required.

The tyres would have required immediate payment at the garage, so the debit card would be the most suitable form of payment as it securely ensures immediate payment.

Task 1.5

	✓
Funds are available in customer's account	
Issue number	
Words and figures match	✓
Security number	
Expiry date	
Date is not in the future	✓

Task 1.6

The director of Parker Flooring Limited has made a number of payments today (2 February 20X6) in respect of materials for the company. Select the correct impact on the bank account

Payment	Impact on the bank account	Comment
Cheque written for £550 to Soft Carpets Limited	Delayed	The money leaves Parker Flooring's account when the cheque is presented at the bank which may be several days after the cheque was issued
Debit card to buy diesel for the van £65	Immediate	Usually reflected in the bank account within a few hours as the debit card draws money from the account
Credit card to buy printer cartridges online £30	Delayed	This will be charged to the credit card account, and the only impact on the bank will be once the monthly payment to the credit card company is made, therefore a delayed impact

Payment	Impact on the bank account	Comment
Payment of a purchase invoice using BACS Direct Credit to Solvit Limited £1200	Immediate	Parker Flooring will see the cash leave their account immediately, although it may take up to three days to be shown in the supplier account. It depends on the banks
Cheque written for £276 to Wall2Wall Limited	Delayed	The money leaves Parker Flooring's account when the cheque is presented at the bank which may be several days
Debit card to buy coffee from the local store of £5.67	Immediate	Usually reflected in the bank account within a few hours as the debit card draws money from the account
Bank draft for £10,000 to purchase a new van	Immediate	Although the bank draft cheque is drawn on the bank's current account, the bank will immediately withdraw the funds from Parker Flooring's account once they authorise the draft

Task 1.7

Who is the drawee?	First National
Who is the payee?	J Peterson
Who is the drawer?	F Ronald

Chapter 2

Task 2.1

Transaction	Payment out ✓	Payment in ✓
£470.47 paid into the bank		✓
Standing order of £26.79	✓	
Cheque payment of £157.48	✓	
Interest earned on the bank balance		✓
BACS payment for wages	✓	

Task 2.2

(a)

Date	Details	Bank £
	Bal b/f	379.22
27 Jan	Tunfield DC	594.69
27 Jan	Tunshire CO	468.29
27 Jan	Non-credit sales	478.90
27 Jan	Tunfield BB	1,059.72
27 Jan	Non-credit sales	752.16
27 Jan	Non-credit sales	256.80
		3,989.78

(b)

Unmatched item		Action to be taken	Explanation
Bank credit	108.51	Update cash book	This must be checked to any supporting documentation such as any remittance advice from Tunfield AOS or the original invoice – when it has been checked the amount should be entered into the cash book
Standing order British Elec	212.00	Update cash book	The standing order schedule should be checked to ensure that this is correct and it should then be entered into the cash book
Bank interest received	3.68	Update cash book	This should be entered into the cash book
Sales of CDs	256.80	Include on bank reconciliation	The £256.80 cash sales of CDs settled by cheque do not appear on the bank statement. This is an outstanding lodgement that will appear in the bank reconciliation statement
Cheque number 003016	144.67	Include on bank reconciliation	Unpresented cheque – will appear in the bank reconciliation statement
Cheque number 003018	44.79	Include on bank reconciliation	Unpresented cheque – will appear in the bank reconciliation statement
Cheque number 003019	273.48	Include on bank reconciliation	Unpresented cheque – will appear in the bank reconciliation statement

(c) **Cash book**

Date	Details	Bank £	Cheque number	Details	Bank £
	Balance b/f	379.22	003014	Henson Press	329.00
27 Jan	Tunfield DC	594.69	003015	Ely Instr	736.96
27 Jan	Tunshire CO	468.29	003016	Jester Press	144.67
27 Jan	Non-credit sales	478.90	003017	CD Supplies	74.54
27 Jan	Tunfield BB	1,059.72	003018	Jester Press	44.79
27 Jan	Non-credit sales	752.16	003019	Buser Ltd	273.48
27 Jan	Non-credit sales	256.80	SO	Rates	255.00
27 Jan	Bank interest	3.68	DD	Rent	500.00
27 Jan	Tunfield AOS	108.51	SO	Standing order British Elec	212.00
				Balance c/d	1,531.53
	Total	4,101.97		Total	4,101.97

(d)

Bank reconciliation statement	£
Balance as per bank statement	1,737.67
Add:	
Non-credit sales	256.80
Total to add	256.80
Less:	
Cheque 003016	144.67
Cheque 003018	44.79
Cheque 003019	273.48
Total to subtract	462.94
Balance as per cash book	1,531.53

Task 2.3

Cash book

Date	Details	Bank £	Date	Cheque no.	Details	Bank £
01 Nov	Balance b/f	5,466	03 Nov	110870	Roberts & Co	6,250
24 Nov	Bevan & Co	1,822	03 Nov	110871	J Jones	1,164
24 Nov	Plant Pots Ltd	7,998	06 Nov	110872	Lake Walks Ltd	2,250
21 Nov	BBT Ltd	10,000	10 Nov	110873	PH Supplies	275
24 Nov	Petals Ltd	2,555	17 Nov	110874	Peters & Co	76
			21 Nov	DD	Insurance Ensured	500
			24 Nov	DD	Rainbow Ltd	88
			28 Nov		Balance c/d	17,238
	Total	27,841			Total	27,841
29 Nov	Balance b/d	17,238				

Note. Cheque number 110865 on the bank statement: the first cheque in the cash book in November is number 110870. As the difference between the opening balances on the bank statement and in the cash book is for the amount of this cheque (£3,670) it is reasonable to assume that cheque 110865 was entered in the cash book in a previous month and would have been a reconciling item in the bank reconciliation in the previous month. This cheque should be ticked to the October bank reconciliation.

Bank reconciliation statement as at 28 November	£
Balance as per bank statement	7,769
Add:	
Bevan & Co	1,822
Plant Pots Ltd	7,998
Total to add	9,820
Less:	
PH Supplies	275
Peters & Co	76
Total to subtract	351
Balance as per cash book	17,238

Task 2.4

(a)

	Timing difference? ✓
Bank charges not recorded in the cash book	
Outstanding lodgements	✓
Interest charged not recorded in the cash book	
Unpresented cheques	✓

(b)

	✓
£714 overdrawn	
£657 overdrawn	✓
£473 overdrawn	
£530 overdrawn	

Working

£(565) o/d - £92 dishonoured cheque = £(657) o/d.

The £57 will not yet have affected the bank account as not been presented at bank yet, hence it does not affect the bank balance as at 31 December.

(c)

	✓
£5,100 overdrawn	
£6,000 overdrawn	
£6,250 overdrawn	
£6,450 overdrawn	✓

Workings

	£	£
Balance b/f		5,675
Reversal – Standing order entered twice	125	
Reversal – Dishonoured cheque entered in error as a debit		450
Correction – Dishonoured cheque		450
Balance c/d (overdraft)	6,450	
	6,575	6,575

Task 2.5

(a)

	✓
£1,460	
£2,300	✓
£2,580	
£3,140	

Workings

	£
Cash book balance	2,490
Adjustment re charges	(50)
Adjustment re dishonoured cheque from customer	(140)
	2,300

(b)

	✓
Receipts of £250 recorded in the cash book, but not yet recorded by bank	
Bank charges of £250 shown on the bank statement, not in the cash book	
Standing orders of £250 included on bank statement, not in the cash book	
Cheques issued for £250 recorded in the cash book, but not yet gone through the bank account	✓

All the other options would give the bank account £250 less than the cash book.

(c) The correct answer is:

£	3,366

Workings

	£
Balance per cash book	3,526
Plus: bank interest received	150
Less: dishonoured cheque	(310)
Amended cash book balance	3,366

Task 2.6

Cash book

Date	Details	Bank £	Date	Cheque number	Details	Bank £
01 Jul	Balance b/f	1,855	01 Jul	126459	Gumpley Co	3,283
20 Jul	Brimfull Ltd	5,483	01 Jul	126460	Warnes Ltd	1,209
21 Jul	Adera Ltd	2,198	01 Jul	126461	Veldt Partners	4,221
22 Jul	Mist Northern	1,004	01 Jul	126462	Pathways	1,117
9 Jul	SnipSnap Co	8,845	02 Jul	126463	Lindstrom Co	846
			02 Jul	126464	Kestrels Training	658
			13 Jul	126465	HGW Ltd	3,200
			13 Jul		Flit DC	500
			18 Jul		Consol Landlords	475
			20 Jul		Bank charges	32
			22 Jul		Interest	103
			23 Jul		Balance c/d	3,741
	Total	19,385			Total	19,385
24 Jul	Balance b/d	3,741				

Bank reconciliation statement as at 23 July	£
Balance per bank statement	4,585
Add:	
Adera Ltd	2,198
Mist Northern	1,004
Total to add	3,202
Less:	
Lindstrom Co	846
HGW Ltd	3,200
Total to subtract	4,046
Balance as per cash book	3,741

Chapter 3

Task 3.1

(a)

Account	Amount £	Debit	Credit
Purchase ledger control	3,390		3,390
VAT control	565	565	
Purchases	2,825	2,825	

(b)

Account	Amount £	Debit	Credit
Sales ledger control	1,860		1,860
VAT control	310	310	
Sales returns	1,550	1,550	

(c)

Account	Amount £	Debit	Credit
Bank	4,590		4,590
Purchase ledger control	4,590	4,590	

(d)

Account	Amount £	Debit	Credit
Bank	5,480	5,480	
Sales ledger control	5,480		5,480

Task 3.2

Sales ledger control

	£		£
Balance b/f	11,689	Sales returns	1,582
Sales	12,758	Bank	11,563
		Discounts allowed	738
		Balance c/d	10,564
	24,447		24,447

Task 3.3

Purchases ledger control

	£		£
Purchases returns	728	Balance b/f	8,347
Bank	8,837	Purchases	9,203
Discounts received	382		
Balance c/d	7,603		
	17,550		17,550

Task 3.4

Purchases ledger control

Date	Details	Amount £	Date	Details	Amount £
30 June	Bank	33,106	1 June	Balance b/f	85,299
30 June	Discounts received	1,000	30 June	Purchases	39,300
30 June	Purchases returns	275			
30 June	Balance c/d	90,218			
		124,599			124,599
			1 July	Balance b/d	90,218

Task 3.5

(a)

	✓
£32,125	✓
£33,975	
£34,725	
£33,225	

Working

	£
Brought forward balance	31,475 (existing outstanding debt)
Sales	125,000
Less receipts	(122,500)
Less credit notes	(1,300)
Less discounts	(550)
Total	32,125

(b)

	✓
£38,100	✓
£40,500	
£47,500	
£49,900	

Working

	£
Opening balance	34,500
Credit purchases	78,400
Discounts received	(1,200)
Payments	(68,900)
Purchases returns	(4,700)
	38,100

....

Task 3.6

(a)

Details	Amount £	Details	Amount £
VAT on purchases	2,500	Balance b/f	4,500
VAT on sales returns	300	VAT on sales	6,000
Payment to HMRC	7,000	VAT on purchase returns	250
Balance c/d	950		
	10,750		10,750
		Balance b/d	950

(b) The answer is

£	5,450

Balance b/d at 31 March 20XX of £950 plus the VAT of £4,500 on sales made during April

Chapter 4

Task 4.1

	Control account ✓	List of balances ✓	Both ✓
Invoice entered into the sales day book as £980 instead of £890			✓
Purchases day book overcast by £1,000	✓		
Discounts allowed of £20 not entered into the cash book (debit side)			✓
An invoice taken as £340 instead of £440 when being posted to the customer's account		✓	
Incorrect balancing of a memorandum ledger account		✓	
A purchases return not entered into the purchases returns day book			✓

Task 4.2

Sales ledger control

Details	Amount £	Details	Amount £
Balance b/f	5,000	Bank (2,400 + 3,600 +1,100 + 4,800)	11,900
Sales (2,000 + 2,700 + 1,100 + 3,800)	9,600	Balance c/d	2,700
	14,600		14,600
Balance b/d	2,700		

Sales ledger

H Simms

Details	Amount £	Details	Amount £
Balance b/f	900	Bank	2,400
Sales	2,000	Balance c/d	500
	2,900		2,900
Balance b/d	500		

P Good

Details	Amount £	Details	Amount £
Balance b/f	1,600	Bank	3,600
Sales	2,700	Balance c/d	700
	4,300		4,300
Balance b/d	700		

K Mitchell

Details	Amount £	Details	Amount £
Sales	1,100	Bank	1,100

C Brown

Details	Amount £	Details	Amount £
Balance b/f	2,500	Bank	4,800
Sales	3,800	Balance c/d	1,500
	6,300		6,300
Balance b/d	1,500		

Reconciliation of sales ledger balances with control account balance

	£
H Simms	500
P Good	700
K Mitchell	–
C Brown	1,500
Sales ledger control account	2,700

Task 4.3

Purchases ledger control

Details	Amount £	Details	Amount £
Bank		Balance b/f	2,700
(1,700 + 3,200 + 3,000)	7,900	Purchases	
Balance c/d	2,100	(1,600 + 2,500 + 3,200)	7,300
	10,000		10,000
		Balance b/d	2,100

Purchases ledger

J Peters

Details	Amount £	Details	Amount £
Bank	1,700	Balance b/f	300
Balance c/d	200	Purchases	1,600
	1,900		1,900
		Balance b/d	200

T Sands

Details	Amount £	Details	Amount £
Bank	3,200	Balance b/f	1,700
Balance c/d	1,000	Purchases	2,500
	4,200		4,200
		Balance b/d	1,000

L Farmer

Details	Amount £	Details	Amount £
Bank	3,000	Balance b/f	700
Balance c/d	900	Purchases	3,200
	3,900		3,900
		Balance b/d	900

Reconciliation of purchases ledger balances with control account balance

	£
J Peters	200
T Sands	1,000
L Farmer	900
Purchases ledger control account	2,100

Task 4.4

(a)

Sales ledger control

Details	Amount £	Details	Amount £
Balance b/f	9,450	Returns	700
Sales on credit	14,500	Bank	15,600
		Balance c/d	7,650
	23,950		23,950
Balance b/d	7,650		

(b) £90 which is the difference between the sales ledger control account balance of £7,650 (balance b/d) and the total balances on the sales ledger (3,000+1,250+3,310 = £7,650)

(c)

Reasons	✓	Explanation
A cash receipt was incorrectly entered onto the customer's account in the sales ledger	✓	As the sales ledger is lower than the sales ledger control account, it is possible that a cash receipt was incorrectly entered onto the customer account.
A sales invoice has been duplicated in the sales ledger		This would increase the sales ledger, so that the sales ledger would be GREATER than the sales ledger control.
A sales return credit note has only been recorded in the sales ledger control account		This would reduce the sales ledger control account, so that the sales ledger would be GREATER than the sales ledger control.
Discounts have been posted twice in the customer's sales ledger account	✓	As the sales ledger is lower than the sales ledger control account, it is possible that discounts have been duplicated on the customer account.

Task 4.5

(a)

Purchase ledger control

Details	Amount £	Details	Amount £
Bank	9,750	Balance b/f	12,500
Discounts received	500	Purchases	8,600
Balance c/d	10,850		
	21,100		21,100
		Balance b/d	10,850

(b)

	£
Purchase ledger control account balance as at 31 July 20XX	10,850
Total of the purchase ledger accounts as at 31 July 20XX	10,650
Difference	200

(c)

Reason	✓	Explanation
Purchases on credit have been recorded on the debit side of the purchase ledger	✓	This would decrease the balance on the purchase ledger, therefore making it less than the control account balance.
A purchase invoice has been duplicated in the purchase ledger		This would increase the balance on the purchase ledger
Discounts received have been omitted from the purchases ledger but recorded in the purchases ledger control account		This makes the balance on the purchase ledger control account lower than that on the purchase ledger
A cash payment to a credit supplier has been booked to the purchase ledger control account only		This makes the balance on the purchase ledger control account lower than that on the purchase ledger

Task 4.6

(a)

Sales ledger control

Date	Details	Amount £	Date	Details	Amount £
01 Nov	Balance b/f	48,125	30 Nov	Bank	28,327
30 Nov	Sales	37,008	30 Nov	Discounts allowed	240
			30 Nov	Sales returns	2,316
			30 Nov	Balance c/d	54,250
		85,133			85,133
01 Dec	Balance b/d	54,250			

(b)

	£
Sales ledger control account balance as at 1 December	54,250
Total of sales ledger accounts as at 1 December	54,163
Difference	87

(c)

	✓
VAT has been overstated on an invoice.	
VAT has been understated on an invoice.	
A sales invoice has been entered in the sales ledger twice.	
A sales credit note has been entered in the sales ledger twice.	✓
A receipt from a customer has been omitted from the sales ledger.	
A receipt from a customer has been entered in the sales ledger twice.	✓

Task 4.7

(a)

Transactions	Amount £	VAT £
Sales on credit including VAT at 20%	106,800	17,800
Purchases on credit including VAT at 20%	54,000	9,000
Credit notes issued including VAT at 20%	2,820	470

(b)

Details	Amount £	Details	Amount £
Sales returns	470	Sales	17,800
Purchases	9,000		
Balance c/d	8,330		
	17,800		17,800
		Balance b/d	8,330

(c) The answer is

£	8,330

. . . .

Task 4.8

(a)

Reason	✓
The sales ledger control account shows a difference to the sales ledger account balances	
Sales were less than purchases for the quarter	✓
There was an underpayment of VAT in the previous quarter	

A difference on the sales ledger control account would have no impact on the VAT due, and an underpayment of VAT in the prior period would not result in a repayment from HMRC.

(b) The correct answer is:

£	21,540

Working

£129,240 × 20/120 = £21,540

··

Task 4.9

(a)

	✓
The supplier sent an invoice for £150 which you have not yet received	
The supplier has given you £150 settlement discount which you had not entered in your ledger	✓
You have paid the supplier £150 which he has not yet accounted for	
You have returned goods worth £150 which the supplier has not yet accounted for	

All other options would lead to a higher balance in the supplier's records.

(b)

	✓
The control account only	
The list of balances only	
Both the control account and the list of balances	✓

(c)

Amount £	Debit ✓	Credit ✓
46,167		✓

Working

	£		£
Debit entries	24,500	Credit entries	76,961
SO Payment	1,606		
Correction (need to remove from PLCA)	4,688		
Balance c/d	46,167		
	76,961		76,961

Once the balance is brought down at the start of the next period, it appears in the credit column

Task 4.10

(a)

	✓
The balance on the bank statement	
The balance on the sales ledger control account	✓
The balance on the purchases ledger control account	
The total of all the purchases ledger balances	
The total of all the sales ledger balances	✓

(b)

	✓
How much is owed to suppliers at any point	
Over how many months the outstanding balance owed by each individual credit customer has built up	✓
The total purchases over the year to date to each credit supplier	

Task 4.11

(a)

Account name	Amount £	Debit ✓	Credit ✓
Irrecoverable debts	1,560	✓	
VAT control	312	✓	
Sales ledger control	1,872		✓

(b)

Details	Amount £	Details	Amount £
		Balance b/f	250
Purchases	90	Sales	1,400
Sales returns	50		
Irrecoverable debt expense	312		
Balance c/d	1,198		
	1,650		1,650
		Balance b/d	1,198

Task 4.12

Journal

Account name	Amount £	Debit ✓	Credit ✓
Irrecoverable debt expense	240	✓	
VAT control(£240 × 20% = £48)	48	✓	
Sales ledger control	288		✓

Task 4.13

Account name	Amount £	Debit ✓	Credit ✓
Irrecoverable debt expense	1,975	✓	
VAT control	395	✓	
Sales ledger control	2,370		✓

Chapter 5

Task 5.1

Journal

Account name	Debit £	Credit £
Capital		10,000
Furniture and fittings	15,315	
Motor vehicles	20,109	
Cash at bank	15,000	
Purchases ledger control		37,238
Sales ledger control	12,524	
Loan from bank		7,000
VAT (owed to HM Revenue & Customs)		8,710
Totals	62,948	62,948

Task 5.2

Account name	Amount £	Debit ✓	Credit ✓
Petty cash	200	✓	
Bank	300	✓	
Capital	500		✓
Van	6,000	✓	
Trade receivables	7,700	✓	
Loan from bank	9,000		✓
VAT control (owed to HM Revenue & Customs)	1,300		✓
Trade creditors	3,400		✓

Task 5.3

Account name	Amount £	Debit ✓	Credit ✓
Cash	150	✓	
Cash at bank	12,350	✓	
Capital	23,456		✓
Fixtures and fittings	2,100	✓	
Trade receivables	3,206	✓	
Loan from bank	10,000		✓
Motor vehicle	15,650	✓	

Task 5.4

(a) The correct answer is:

£	1,761

Working

	£
Gross salary	2,200
Income tax	(256)
Employees' NIC	(183)
Net salary	1,761

(b)

Salary expense

	£		£
Salary control	2,200		
Salary control	200		

Salary control

	£		£
Bank	1,761	Salary expense	2,200
HMRC control	183	Salary expense	200
HMRC control	256		
HMRC control	200		

HMRC control

	£		£
		Salary control	200
		Salary control	256
		Salary control	183

Bank

	£		£
		Salary control	1,761

Task 5.5

Select the correct recipient of each of the following payroll related costs

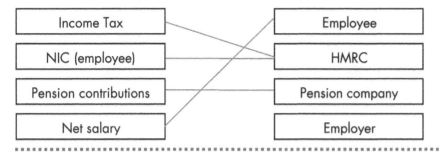

Task 5.6

(a)

£	140

Workings

£3,500 × 0.04

(b)

£	2,605

Workings

Net salary is £2,605 (3,500 – 200 – 500 – 180 – 15)

(c) Journal

Details	Debit £	Credit £
Salary control (200+140)	340	
Pension administrator		340

(d) Journal

Details	Debit £	Credit £
Salary control	15	
Trade union subscription		15

(e) Journal

Details	Debit £	Credit £
Bank		2,605
Salary control	2,605	

(f)

£	3,850

Workings

Gross salary of £3,500 + Employer NIC of £210 + Pension contributions of 4% of gross salary of £140

Task 6.1

(a) **Journal to remove the incorrect entry**

Account name	Debit £	Credit £
Sales	3,750	

Journal to record the correct entry

Account name	Debit £	Credit £
Sales		3,570

Journal to remove the suspense account balance

Account name	Debit £	Credit £
Suspense		180

(b) **Journal to remove the incorrect entries**

Account name	Debit £	Credit £
Drawings	350	
Cash		350

Journal to record the correct entries

Account name	Debit £	Credit £
Drawings	350	
Cash		350

Task 6.2

Account name	Amount £	Debit ✓	Credit ✓
Suspense	11,081	✓	

Task 6.3

Error	✓
A credit note from a supplier with a net amount of £124 was not entered in the purchases ledger	
Discounts allowed of £124 were only posted to the discounts allowed account	✓
A cash purchase for £124 was not entered in the purchases account	
An irrecoverable debt write-off of £124 was not entered in the subsidiary ledger	

The credit note and irrecoverable debt omissions affect only the subsidiary ledgers, so would not cause a suspense account balance. Omitting the cash purchase from the purchases account would lead to a debit balance on the suspense account, not a credit balance. The correction for the discount error is to credit the sales ledger control account and debit suspense, thus clearing the credit balance on the suspense account.

Task 6.4

(a) Journal to remove the incorrect entry

Account name	Debit £	Credit £
VAT control		582

Journal to record the correct entry

Account name	Debit £	Credit £
VAT control	528	

Journal to remove the suspense account balance

Account name	Debit £	Credit £
Suspense	54	

(b)   Journal to remove the incorrect entries

Account name	Debit £	Credit £
Purchases	800	
Cash		800

Journal to record the correct entries

Account name	Debit £	Credit £
Purchases	800	
Cash		800

Task 6.5

(a)   Journal to remove the incorrect entry

Account name	Debit £	Credit £
Sales returns		6,475

Journal to record the correct entry

Account name	Debit £	Credit £
Sales returns	6,745	

Journal to remove the suspense account balance

Account name	Debit £	Credit £
Suspense		270

(b) **Journal to remove the incorrect entries**

Account name	Debit £	Credit £
Bank	450	
Sales ledger control		450

Journal to record the correct entries

Account name	Debit £	Credit £
Bank	450	
Sales ledger control		450

Task 6.6

The journals

(a)

Details	Debit £	Credit £
Sales returns	500	
Sales		500

(b)

Details	Debit £	Credit £
Office expenses	125	
Bank		125
Office expenses	125	
Bank		125

BPP
LEARNING MEDIA

(c)

Details	Debit £	Credit £
Bank	29	
Suspense	270	
Purchases		299
Purchases	299	
Bank		299

(d)

Details	Debit £	Credit £
Sales ledger control	388	
Suspense		388
Discounts allowed	388	
Sales ledger control		388

Task 6.7

Suspense

Date	Details	Amount £	Date	Details	Amount £
01 July	Sales	945	30 June	Balance b/f	720
			01 July	Bank (rent & rates)	225
		945			945

Task 6.8

(a)

	✓
Debit £90	
Credit £90	✓
Debit £1,780	
Credit £1,780	

£890 should have been debited to the expense account. Instead, £980 has been debited. To bring this amount down to £890, the expense account should be credited with £90.

(b)

	✓
Error of transposition	
Error of omission	✓
Error of principle	
Error of commission	

(c)

	✓
A transaction has not been recorded	
One side of a transaction has been recorded in the wrong account, and that account is of a different class to the correct account	
One side of a transaction has been recorded in the wrong account, and that account is of the same class as the correct account	✓
A transaction has been recorded using the wrong amount	

(d)

	✓
A gas bill credited to the gas account and debited to the bank account	
The purchase of a non-current asset credited to the asset account and debited to the supplier's account	
The purchase of a non-current asset debited to the purchases account and credited to the supplier's account	✓
The payment of wages debited and credited to the correct accounts, but using the wrong amount	

Task 6.9

(a)

	✓
Omission	
Original entry	✓
Commission	
Principle	

(b)

	✓
Debit £1,350	✓
Credit £1,350	
Debit £13,650	
Credit £13,650	

Workings

Suspense account

Details	Amount £	Details	Amount £
Opening balance	1,350	Discounts allowed	7,500
Discounts received	6,150		
	7,500		7,500

(c) The correct answer is: The debit side to be £96 more than the credit side

Working

Debits will exceed credits by 2 × £48 = £96

(d)

	Yes	No
Omitting both entries for a transaction		✓
Posting the debit entry for an invoice to an incorrect expense account		✓
Omitting the debit entry for a transaction	✓	
Posting the debit entry for a transaction as a credit entry	✓	

Task 6.10

Error in the general ledger	Error disclosed by the trial balance ✓	Error NOT disclosed by the trial balance ✓
Recording a bank receipt of a cash sale on the debit side of the cash sales account	✓	
Entering an insurance expense in the administration expenses account		✓
Entering the discounts received account balance on the debit side of the trial balance	✓	
Miscasting the total column of one page of the sales returns day book	✓	
Failing to write up a dishonoured cheque in the cash book		✓
Recording discount allowed of £15 as £150 in the cash book		✓

Task 6.11

Discounts allowed

Details	Amount £	Details	Amount £
Suspense	209		

Machinery

Details	Amount £	Details	Amount £
		Motor vehicles	4,300

Motor vehicles

Details	Amount £	Details	Amount £
Machinery	4,300		

Sales ledger control

Details	Amount £	Details	Amount £
		Suspense	750

Suspense

Details	Amount £	Details	Amount £
Sales ledger control	750	Balance b/f	541
		Discounts allowed	209

Task 6.12

Workings to the answer (for information only)

Suspense

Details	Amount £	Details	Amount £
Balance b/f	6,290	Sales ledger control	2,875
Heat and light	5,172	Sales ledger control	2,875
		Heat and light	5,712
	11,462		11,462

Heat & Light

Details	Amount £	Details	Amount £
Balance b/f	5,172	Suspense	5,172
Suspense	5,712	Balance c/d	5,712

Sales ledger control

Details	Amount £	Details	Amount £
Balance b/f	241,500		
Suspense	2,875		
Suspense	2,875	Balance c/d	247,250
	247,250		247,250

Answer

	Balances extracted on 30 June £	Balances at 1 July Debit £	Balances at 1 July Credit £
Machinery	82,885	82,885	
Computer equipment	41,640	41,640	
Insurance	17,520	17,520	
Bank (overdraft)	13,252		13,252
Petty cash	240	240	
Sales ledger control	241,500	247,250	
Purchases ledger control	134,686		134,686
VAT (owing to HM Revenue and Customs)	19,920		19,920
Capital	44,826		44,826
Sales	525,092		525,092
Purchases	269,400	269,400	
Purchases returns	16,272		16,272
Wages	61,680	61,680	
Maintenance expenses	3,283	3,283	
Stationery	8,049	8,049	
Rent and rates	3,466	3,466	

	Balances extracted on 30 June £	Balances at 1 July	
		Debit £	Credit £
Heat and light	5,172	5,712	
Telephone	7,596	7,596	
Marketing expenses	5,327	5,327	
Totals		754,048	754,048

Task 6.13

(a) **(i)**

Account name	Amount £	Debit ✓	Credit ✓
VAT	1,100		✓

(ii)

Account name	Amount £	Debit ✓	Credit ✓
VAT	1,000	✓	

(iii)

Account name	Amount £	Debit ✓	Credit ✓
Suspense	100	✓	

(b) **(i)**

Account name	Amount £	Debit ✓	Credit ✓
Heat and light	350	✓	
Bank	350		✓

(ii)

Account name	Amount £	Debit ✓	Credit ✓
Heat and light	350	✓	
Bank	350		✓

AAT AQ2016 PRACTICE ASSESSMENT 1 BOOKKEEPING CONTROLS

Time allowed: 1 hour 30 minutes

Bookkeeping Controls
AAT practice assessment 1

Task 1 (12 marks)

Organisations use different payment methods.

(a) **Match each situation with the most appropriate payment method below; payment methods may be used more than once.**

(CBT instructions: Click on a box in the left column then on one in the right column to indicate each answer. To remove a line, click on it.)

Situation	Payment method
Making a payment via the internet to purchase office stationery	Standing order
	Cheque
Making a non-automated low value payment in person	Bank draft
	Debit card
Making a payment by post to a credit supplier	CHAPS
	Cash
Making regular payments of regular amounts to the same recipient	

(b) **Show which TWO of the payment methods below will not reduce funds in the payer's bank balance on the date of payment by writing the relevant payment methods from the drop-down list below.**

Payment method
▼
▼

Picklist:

CHAPS
Cheque
Credit card
Direct debit
Standing order

It is important to understand the effect of errors in a bookkeeping system.

(c) **Show whether the errors below will cause an imbalance in the trial balance by writing the appropriate answer against each error. You may use each answer more than once.**

Error	Effect on trial balance	
A cash sale has been recorded in the sales and VAT control accounts only.		▼
The purchase of a new computer has been recorded in the office expenses account. All other entries were correct.		▼
A BACS payment to a credit supplier was debited to the bank account and credited to the purchases ledger control account.		▼
A cash payment of £56 for stationery has been recorded in the cash account as £65. All other entries were correct.		▼

Picklist:

Will cause an imbalance
Will not cause an imbalance

(d) **Show which ONE of the errors below is an error of principle.**

Error	✓
A cash sale has been recorded in the sales and VAT control accounts only.	
The purchase of a new computer has been recorded in the office expenses account. All other entries were correct.	
A BACS payment to a credit supplier was debited to the bank account and credited to the purchases ledger control account.	
A cash payment of £56 for stationery has been recorded in the cash account as £65. All other entries were correct.	

The correction of errors in a bookkeeping system is recorded in the journal.

(e) **Which other transaction from the drop-down list below would be recorded in the journal.**

[_____ ▼]

Picklist:

Interest received from the bank
Irrecoverable debts written off
Prompt payment discounts received
Re-imbursement of petty cash

....

Task 2 (12 marks)

Payroll transactions are recorded using a wages control account.

This is a note from your line manager.

The wages expense for June is £70,560. Other payroll information for the month is shown below.

Income tax and National Insurance amounts are as follows:

- Income tax: £7,125
- Employer's NI: £5,222
- Employees' NI: £4,657

In addition there are voluntary deductions for 42 employees who each pay £15 a month for trade union fees.

Show the journal entries needed to record:

- **The net wages paid to employees**
- **The HM Revenue and Customs liability**
- **The trade union liability**

Journal to record the net wages paid to employees

Account name		Debit £	Credit £
	▼		
	▼		

Picklist:

Bank
Employee's NI
Employer's NI
HM Revenue and Customs
Income tax
Trade union
Wages control
Wages expense

Journal to record the HM Revenue and Customs liability

Account name		Debit £	Credit £
	▼		
	▼		

Picklist:

Bank
Employee's NI
Employer's NI
HM Revenue and Customs
Income tax
Trade union
Wages control
Wages expense

Journal to record the trade union liability

Account name		Debit £	Credit £
	▼		
	▼		

Picklist:

Bank
Employee's NI
Employer's NI
HM Revenue and Customs
Income tax
Trade union
Wages control
Wages expense

Task 3 (10 marks)

This is a customer's account in the sales ledger.

Zoe Daniels

Date 20XX	Details	Amount £	Date 20XX	Details	Amount £
01 Jun	Balance b/f	984	3 Jun	Credit note 98	317
10 Jun	Invoice 812	1,248	15 Jun	Credit note 103	163

The customer has now ceased trading owing the amount outstanding, which includes VAT.

(a) **Record the journal entries needed in the general ledger to write off the net amount and the VAT. Do not enter a zero in unused debit or credit column cells.**

Journal

Account name		Debit £	Credit £
	▼		
	▼		
	▼		

Picklist:

Irrecoverable debts
Purchases
Purchases ledger control
Sales
Sales ledger control
VAT control
Zoe Daniels

A new business has been started and a new set of accounts is to be opened. A partially completed journal to record the opening entries is shown below.

(b) **Complete the journal by showing whether each amount will be a debit or credit entry.**

Journal

Account name	Amount £	Debit ✓	Credit ✓
Cash at bank	1,090		
Capital	5,000		
Computer equipment	6,910		
Loan from bank	3,000		

Task 4 (10 marks)

This is a summary of transactions to be recorded in the VAT control account in June.

(a) **Show whether each transaction will be a debit or a credit entry in the VAT control account.**

Transactions	Amount £	Debit ✓	Credit ✓
VAT owing from HM Revenue and Customs at 1 June	2,055		
VAT total in the sales daybook	5,820		
VAT total in the sales returns daybook	493		
VAT total in the purchases daybook	4,215		
VAT total in the discounts allowed daybook	152		
VAT total in the discounts received daybook	208		
VAT total in the cash book for cash sales	804		
VAT refund received from HM Revenue and Customs	2,055		

At the end of July the VAT control account has debit entries amounting of £7,055 and credit entries amounting to £11,388.

The following transactions have not yet been recorded in the VAT control account.

• VAT total of £380 in the purchases returns daybook
• VAT of £195 on an irrecoverable debt written off.

(b) What will be the balance brought down on the VAT control account after the transactions above have been recorded?

Amount £	Debit ✓	Credit ✓

Task 5 (14 marks)

These are the accounts in the sales ledger at 1 July.

Redlan plc

Details	Amount £	Details	Amount £
Balance b/f	8,927		

Patsy Perry

Details	Amount £	Details	Amount £
		Balance b/f	362

Annal Ltd

Details	Amount £	Details	Amount £
Balance b/f	14,066		

Samson and Dyer

Details	Amount £	Details	Amount £
Balance b/f	21,932		

(a) What is the total of the balances in the sales ledger on 1 July?

£

The balance at the sales ledger control account on 1 July is £43,108.

(b) **What is the difference between the balance of the sales ledger control account and the total of the balances in the sales ledger you calculated in (a)?**

£ [   ]

(c) **Which TWO of the reasons below could explain the difference you calculated in (b)?**

Reasons	✓
Goods returned were entered twice in a customer's account in the sales ledger.	
Discounts allowed were not entered in the sales ledger control account.	
Goods sold were entered twice in a customers' account in the sales ledger.	
Goods returned were not entered in the sales ledger control account.	
Irrecoverable debts written off were entered twice in the sales ledger control account.	
A cheque received was entered twice in a customer's account in the sales ledger.	

This is a summary of transactions with credit suppliers during July.

Transactions	Amount £
Balance of payables at 1 July 20XX	38,677
Payments made by cheque	29,512
Goods purchased	32,619
Goods returned	4,037

(d) **Record these transactions in the purchases ledger control account and show the balance carried down.**

Purchases ledger control

Details	Amount £	Details	Amount £
▼		▼	
▼		▼	
▼		▼	
▼		▼	
▼		▼	
▼		▼	

Picklist:

Balance b/d
Balance c/d
Bank
Discounts allowed
Discounts received
Purchases
Purchases returns
Sales
Sales returns

Task 6 (10 marks)

The bank statement and cash book for May are shown below.

Check the bank statement against the cash book and enter:

- **Any transactions into the cash book as needed**

- **The cash book balance carried down at 31 May and brought down at 1 June**

Bank statement

Date 20XX	Details	Paid out £	Paid in £	Balance £
01 May	Balance b/f			1,466 C
02 May	Bank interest		29	1,495 C
05 May	Cheque 011382	707		788 C
06 May	Cheque 011365	698		90 C
15 May	Counter credit		5,415	5,505 C
17 May	Khan and Wade – BACS		854	6,359 C
19 May	Cheque 011385	2,240		4,119 C
21 May	Cheque 011384	1,627		2,492 C
25 May	PQ Partners – SO	3,500		1,008 D
26 May	Counter credit		1,316	308 C
29 May	Cheque 011387	289		19 C

Cash book

Date 20XX	Details	Bank £	Date 20XX	Cheque number	Details	Bank £
1 May	Balance b/f	768	1 May	011382	Cully and Ball	707
15 May	Ballo plc	5,415	4 May	011383	Gaye Green	622
26 May	Heidi Chin	1,316	6 May	011384	KBC Ltd	1,627
	▼		10 May	011385	Farr traders	2,240
	▼		12 May	011386	Robson Ltd	525
	▼		16 May	011387	Lindy Lee	289
					▼	
	▼				▼	

Picklist:

Balance b/d
Balance c/d
Ballo plc
Bank interest
Cheque 011365
Counter credit
Cully and Ball
Farr Traders
Gaye Green
Heidi Chin
KBC Ltd
Khan and Wade
Lindy Lee
PQ Partners
Robson Ltd

Task 7 (14 marks)

Leyla Ltd's bank statement for July showed an opening balance of £3,518 and a closing balance of £5,342.

The cash book below has been checked against the bank statement and the two highlighted items have been identified as unmatched. A bank reconciliation statement has been partially completed.

Cash book

Date 20XX	Details	Bank £	Date 20XX	Cheque number	Details	Bank £
1 Jul	Balance b/f	3,921	1 Jul	018470	Benning Ltd	1,446
3 Jul	L G Landlords	1,882	5 Jul	018471	Janssen Joiners	1,108
9 Jul	Elson plc	987	11 Jul	018472	Crownley and Co	397
12 Jul	HLB Interiors	3,704	19 Jul		Brentley Ltd	2,492
17 Jul	Fielding Ltd	2,225	21 Jul	018473	L G Landlords	187
22 Jul	O'Leary Ltd	854	27 Jul		PTP Ltd	906

(a) **Complete the bank reconciliation statement as at 31 July.**

Bank reconciliation statement	£
Balance as per bank statement	
Outstanding lodgements	
L G Landlords	
Unpresented cheques	
L G Landlords	
Balance as per cash book	

(b) **Check that the bank reconciliation statement in (a) has been correctly completed by calculating:**

- **the balance carried down in the cash book**
- **the total of the bank columns in the cash book after the balance carried down has been recorded.**

Balance carried down £	Bank column totals £

This is the bank statement and cash book for a different organisation.

Bank statement

Date 20XX	Details	Paid out £	Paid in £	Balance £
01 Jul	Balance b/f			3,418 C
01 Jul	Bank charges	87		3,331 C
01 Jul	Willmott Wares		1,118	4,449 C
08 Jul	Cheque 047422	902		3,547 C
08 Jul	Cheque 047416	1,384		2,163 C
11 Jul	Dawson Products	5,790		3,627 D
12 Jul	Counter credit		4,621	994 C

Date 20XX	Details	Paid out £	Paid in £	Balance £
14 Jul	VMB Ltd	1,392		398 D
17 Jul	Counter credit		1,665	1,267 C
22 Jul	Forman Ltd	118		1,149 C
25 Jul	Ranson plc	404		745 C
29 Jul	Cheque 047424	551		194 C
29 Jul	Lee Ray		779	973 C
31 Jul	Cheque 047425	385		588 C

D = Debit C = Credit

Cash book

Date 20XX	Details	Bank £	Date 20XX	Cheque number	Details	Bank £
1 Jul	Balance b/f	3,152	2 Jul	047422	Court and Cox	902
12 Jul	Shatif Designs	4,621	4 Jul	047423	LMR plc	349
14 Jul	King Cranes	388	10 Jul	047424	D L Stationers	551
17 Jul	Portman plc	1,665	14 Jul		VMB Ltd	1,392
29 Jul	Lee Ray	779	17 Jul	047425	MDC Ltd	385
			25 Jul		Ranson plc	404

You are preparing to produce a bank reconciliation statement at 31 July, starting with the balance taken from the bank statement.

(c) **Identify which TWO transactions have caused the difference in the opening balances.**

Transaction		Transaction		Transaction	
Bank charges	☐	Forman Ltd	☐	Portman plc	☐
Cheque 047416	☐	King Cranes	☐	Ranson plc	☐
Court and Cox	☐	Lee Ray	☐	Shatif Designs	☐
D L Stationers	☐	LMR plc	☐	VMB Ltd	☐
Dawson Products	☐	MDC Ltd	☐	Willmott Wares	☐

(d) **Identify the details and amount of ONE outstanding lodgement that should be entered into the bank reconciliation statement and show whether the amount should be added or subtracted.**

Details	Amount £	Add	Subtract
▼		☐	☐

Picklist:

Bank charges
Cheque 047416
Counter credit
Court and Cox
D L Stationers
Dawson Products
Forman Ltd
King Cranes
Lee Ray
LMR plc
MDC Ltd
Portman plc
Ranson plc
Shatif Designs
VMB Ltd
Willmott Wares

(e) **Identify the details and amount of ONE unpresented cheque that should be entered into the bank reconciliation statement and show whether the amount should be added or subtracted.**

Details	Amount £	Add	Subtract
▼		☐	☐

Picklist:

Bank charges
Cheque 047416
Counter credit
Court and Cox
D L Stationers
Dawson Products
Forman Ltd
King Cranes
Lee Ray
LMR plc
MDC Ltd
Portman plc
Ranson plc
Shatif Designs
VMB Ltd
Willmott Wares

Task 8 (14 marks)

A suspense account has been opened with a balance of £180.

The error has been identified as an entry made in the general ledger from the incorrectly totalled net column in the sales daybook shown below.

Sales day book

Date 20XX	Details		Invoice number	Total £	VAT £	Net £
30 Jul	SM Barber		1170	528	88	440
30 Jul	Pastel Prints		1171	1,230	205	1,025
30 Jul	Hyffe Ltd		1172	936	156	780
	Totals			2,694	449	2,425

(a) Record the journal entries needed to:

- **Remove the incorrect entry**
- **Record the correct entry**
- **Remove the suspense account balance**

Do not enter a zero in unused debit or credit column cells.

Journal to remove the incorrect entry

Account name		Debit £	Credit £
▼			

Picklist:

Sales
Sales ledger control
Sales returns
Suspense
VAT control

Journal to record the correct entry

Account name		Debit £	Credit £
▼			

Picklist:

Sales
Sales ledger control
Sales returns
Suspense
VAT control

Journal to remove the suspense account balance

Account name		Debit £	Credit £
▼			

Picklist:

Sales
Sales ledger control
Sales returns
Suspense
VAT control

Another error has been found in the general ledger. Entries to record cash drawings of £425 have been reversed.

(b) Record the journal entries needed to:

- **Remove the incorrect entries**
- **Record the correct entries**

Do not enter a zero in unused debit or credit column cells.

Journal to remove the incorrect entries

Account name		Debit £	Credit £
	▼		
	▼		

Picklist:

Bank
Capital
Cash
Drawings

Journal to record the correct entries

Account name		Debit £	Credit £
	▼		
	▼		

Picklist:

Bank
Capital
Cash
Drawings

Task 9 (10 marks)

The journal entries below have been prepared to correct an error.

Journal

Account name	Debit £	Credit £
Office furniture	1,476	
Suspense		1,476
Suspense	1,764	
Office furniture		1,764

Record the journal entries in the general ledger accounts below and show the balance carried down in the office furniture account.

Office furniture

Details	Amount £	Details	Amount £
Balance b/f	8,363	▼	
Bank	611	▼	
▼		▼	
▼		▼	
▼		▼	

Picklist:

Balance b/d
Balance c/d
Bank
Office furniture
Suspense

Suspense

Details	Amount £	Details	Amount £
▼		Balance b/d	288
▼		▼	
▼		▼	
	1,764		1,764

Picklist:

Balance b/d
Balance c/d
Bank
Office furniture
Suspense

Task 10 (14 marks)

On 30 September a trial balance was extracted and did not balance. The debit column totalled £199,601 and the credit column totalled £200,827.

(a) **What entry is needed in the suspense account to balance the trial balance?**

Do not enter a zero in the unused column cell.

Account names	Debit £	Credit £
Suspense		

The journal entries to correct all the bookkeeping errors, and a list of balances as they appear in the trial balance, are shown below.

Journal

Account name	Debit ✓	Credit ✓
Office expenses	241	
Bank		241
Office expenses	241	
Bank		241

Account name	Debit ✓	Credit ✓
Fixtures and fittings	1,569	
Suspense		1,569
Suspense	343	
Rent received		343

(b) **Complete the table below to show:**

- **The balance of each account after the journal entries have been recorded**
- **Whether each balance will be a debit or credit entry in the trial balance, by ticking the appropriate column**

List of balances

Account name	Original balance £	New balance £	Debit ✓	Credit ✓
Office expense	1,967			
Bank (overdraft)	1,076			
Fixtures and fittings	12,334			
Rent received	602			

On 31 October a partially prepared trial balance had debit balances totalling £210,678 and credit balances totalling £208,911. The accounts below have not yet been entered into the trial balance.

(c) **Complete the table below to show whether each balance will be a debit or credit entry in the trial balance.**

Account names	Balance £	Debit ✓	Credit ✓
VAT control (owing to HM Revenue and Customs)	12,053		
Sales returns	4,671		
Drawing	5,615		

(d) **What will be the totals of each column of the trial balance after the balances in (c) have been entered?**

Account name	Debit £	Credit £
Totals		

AAT AQ2016 PRACTICE ASSESSMENT 1
BOOKKEEPING CONTROLS

ANSWERS

Bookkeeping Controls
AAT practice assessment 1

Task 1 (12 marks)

(a) Match each situation with the most appropriate payment method below; payment methods may be used more than once.

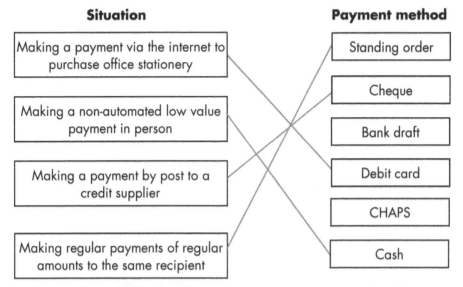

Situation	Payment method
Making a payment via the internet to purchase office stationery	Standing order
	Cheque
Making a non-automated low value payment in person	Bank draft
	Debit card
Making a payment by post to a credit supplier	CHAPS
Making regular payments of regular amounts to the same recipient	Cash

(b) Show which **TWO** of the payment methods below will not reduce funds in the payer's bank balance on the date of payment by writing the relevant payment methods from the drop-down list below.

Payment method
Credit card
Cheque

(c) **Show whether the errors below will cause an imbalance in the trial balance by writing the appropriate answer against each error. You may use each answer more than once.**

Error	Effect on trial balance
A cash sale has been recorded in the sales and VAT control accounts only.	Will cause an imbalance
The purchase of a new computer has been recorded in the office expenses account. All other entries were correct.	Will not cause an imbalance
A BACS payment to a credit supplier was debited to the bank account and credited to the purchases ledger control account.	Will not cause an imbalance
A cash payment of £56 for stationery has been recorded in the cash account as £65. All other entries were correct.	Will cause an imbalance

(d) **Show which ONE of the errors below is an error of principle.**

Error	✓
A cash sale has been recorded in the sales and VAT control accounts only.	
The purchase of a new computer has been recorded in the office expenses account. All other entries were correct.	✓
A BACS payment to a credit supplier was debited to the bank account and credited to the purchases ledger control account.	
A cash payment of £56 for stationery has been recorded in the cash account as £65. All other entries were correct.	

The correction of errors in a bookkeeping system is recorded in the journal.

(e) **Select one other transaction that is recorded in the journal.**

Irrecoverable debts written off

Task 2 (12 marks)

Show the journal entries needed to record:

- **The net wages paid to employees**
- **The HM Revenue and Customs liability**
- **The trade union liability**

Journal to record the net wages paid to employees

Account name	Debit £	Credit £
Wages control	52,926	
Bank		52,926

Journal to record the HM Revenue and Customs liability

Account name	Debit £	Credit £
Wages control	17,004	
HM Revenue and Customs		17,004

Journal to record the trade union liability

Account name	Debit £	Credit £
Wages control	630	
Trade union		630

Task 3 (10 marks)

(a) **Record the journal entries needed in the general ledger to write off the net amount and the VAT. Do not enter a zero in unused debit or credit column cells.**

Journal

Account name	Debit £	Credit £
Irrecoverable debts	1,460	
VAT control	292	
Sales ledger control		1,752

(b) **Complete the journal by showing whether each amount will be a debit or credit entry.**

Journal

Account name	Amount £	Debit ✓	Credit ✓
Cash at bank	1,090	✓	
Capital	5,000		✓
Computer equipment	6,910	✓	
Loan from bank	3,000		✓

Task 4 (10 marks)

(a) **Show whether each transaction will be a debit or a credit entry in the VAT control account.**

Account name	Amount £	Debit ✓	Credit ✓
VAT owing from HM Revenue and Customs at 1 June	2,055	✓	
VAT total in the sales daybook	5,820		✓
VAT total in the sales returns daybook	493	✓	
VAT total in the purchases daybook	4,215	✓	
VAT total in the discounts allowed daybook	152	✓	
VAT total in the discounts received daybook	208		✓
VAT total in the cash book for cash sales	804		✓
VAT refund received from HM Revenue and Customs	2,055		✓

(b) **What will be the balance brought down on the VAT control account after the transactions above have been recorded?**

Amount £	Debit ✓	Credit ✓
4,518		✓

Task 5 (14 marks)

(a) **What is the total of the balances in the sales ledger on 1 July?**

£	44,563

(b) **What is the difference between the balance of the sales ledger control account and the total of the balances in the sales ledger you calculated in (a)?**

£	1,455

(c) **Which TWO of the reasons below could explain the difference you calculated in (b)?**

Reasons	✓
Goods returned were entered twice in a customer's account in the sales ledger.	
Discounts allowed were not entered in the sales ledger control account.	
Goods sold were entered twice in a customers' account in the sales ledger.	✓
Goods returned were not entered in the sales ledger control account.	
Irrecoverable debts written off were entered twice in the sales ledger control account.	✓
A cheque received was entered twice in a customer's account in the sales ledger.	

(d) Record these transactions in the purchases ledger control account and show the balance carried down.

Purchases ledger control

Details	Amount £	Details	Amount £
Bank	29,512	Balance b/d	38,677
Purchases returns	4,037	Purchases	32,619
Balance c/d	37,747		
	71,296		71,296

Task 6 (10 marks)

Check the bank statement against the cash book and enter:
- **Any transactions into the cash book as needed**
- **The cash book balance carried down at 31 May and brought down at 1 June**

Cash book

Date 20XX	Details	Bank £	Date 20XX	Cheque number	Details	Bank £
1 May	Balance b/f	768	1 May	011382	Cully and Ball	70
15 May	Ballo plc	5,415	4 May	011383	Gaye Green	62
26 May	Heidi Chin	1,316	6 May	011384	KBC Ltd	1,62
2 May	Bank interest	29	10 May	011385	Farr traders	2,24
17 May	Khan and Wade	854	12 May	011386	Robson Ltd	52
31 May	Balance c/d	1,128	16 May	011387	Lindy Lee	28
			25 May		PQ Partners	3,50
		9,510				9,51
			1 Jun		Balance b/d	1,12

Task 7 (14 marks)

(a) **Complete the bank reconciliation statement as at 31 July.**

Bank reconciliation statement	£
Balance as per bank statement	5,342
Outstanding lodgements	
L G Landlords	1,882
Unpresented cheques	
L G Landlords	187
Balance as per cash book	**7,037**

(b) **Check that the bank reconciliation statement in (a) has been completed correctly by calculating:**

- **the balance carried down in the cash book**
- **the total of the bank columns in the cash book after the balance carried down has been recorded.**

Balance carried down £	Bank column totals £
7,037	13,573

(c) **Identify which TWO transactions have caused the difference in the opening balances.**

Transaction		Transaction		Transaction	
Bank charges	☐	Forman Ltd	☐	Portman plc	☐
Cheque 047416	☑	King Cranes	☐	Ranson plc	☐
Court and Cox	☐	Lee Ray	☐	Shatif Designs	☐
D L Stationers	☐	LMR plc	☐	VMB Ltd	☐
Dawson Products	☐	MDC Ltd	☐	Willmott Wares	☑

(d) Identify the details and amount of ONE outstanding lodgement that should be entered into the bank reconciliation statement and show whether the amount should be added or subtracted.

Details	Amount £	Add	Subtract
King Cranes	388	✓	☐

(e) Identify the details and amount of ONE unpresented cheque that should be entered into the bank reconciliation statement and show whether the amount should be added or subtracted.

Details	Amount £	Add	Subtract
LMR plc	349	☐	✓

Task 8 (14 marks)

(a) Record the journal entries needed to:

- Remove the incorrect entry
- Record the correct entry
- Remove the suspense account balance

Do not enter a zero in unused debit or credit column cells.

Journal to remove the incorrect entry

Account name	Debit £	Credit £
Sales	2,425	

Journal to record the correct entry

Account name	Debit £	Credit £
Sales		2,245

Journal to remove the suspense account balance

Account name	Debit £	Credit £
Suspense		180

(b) **Record the journal entries needed to:**

- **Remove the incorrect entries**
- **Record the correct entries**

Do not enter a zero in unused debit or credit column cells.

Journal to remove the incorrect entries

Account name	Debit £	Credit £
Drawings	425	
Cash		425

Journal to record the correct entries

Account name	Debit £	Credit £
Drawings	425	
Cash		425

Task 9 (10 marks)

Record the journal entries in the general ledger accounts below and show the balance carried down in the office furniture account.

Office furniture

Details	Amount £	Details	Amount £
Balance b/f	8,363	Suspense	1,764
Bank	611	Balance c/d	8,686
Suspense	1,476		
	10,450		10,450

Suspense

Details	Amount £	Details	Amount £
Office furniture	1,764	Balance b/d	288
		Office furniture	1,476
	1,764		1,764

Task 10 (14 marks)

(a) **What entry is needed in the suspense account to balance the trial balance?**

Do not enter a zero in the unused column cell.

Account names	Debit £	Credit £
Suspense	1,226	

(b) **Complete the table below to show:**

- **The balance of each account after the journal entries have been recorded**
- **Whether each balance will be a debit or credit entry in the trial balance, by ticking the appropriate column**

List of balances

Account names	Original balance £	New balance £	Debit in trial balance ✓	Credit in trial balance ✓
Office expense	1,967	2,449	✓	
Bank (overdraft)	1,076	1,558		✓
Fixtures and fittings	12,334	13,903	✓	
Rent received	602	945		✓

(c) **Complete the table below to show whether each balance will be a debit or credit entry in the trial balance.**

Account names	Balance £	Debit in trial balance ✓	Credit in trial balance ✓
VAT control (owing to HM Revenue and Customs)	12,053		✓
Sales returns	4,671	✓	
Drawing	5,615	✓	

(d) **What will be the totals of each column of the trial balance after the balances in (c) have been entered?**

Account name	Debit £	Credit £
Totals	220,964	220,964

AAT AQ2016 PRACTICE ASSESSMENT 2
BOOKKEEPING CONTROLS

You are advised to attempt practice assessment 2 online from the AAT website. This will ensure you are prepared for how the assessment will be presented on the AAT's system when you attempt the real assessment. Please access the assessment using the address below:

https://www.aat.org.uk/training/study-support/search

BPP PRACTICE ASSESSMENT 1
BOOKKEEPING CONTROLS

Time allowed: 1 hour 30 minutes

PRACTICE ASSESSMENT 1

Bookkeeping Controls
BPP practice assessment 1

This assessment contains **10 tasks** and you should attempt to complete **every** task.

Each task is independent. You will not need to refer to your answers to previous tasks.

Read every task carefully to make sure you understand what is required.

Where the date is relevant, it is given in the task data.

Both minus signs and brackets can be used to indicate negative numbers **unless** task instructions say otherwise.

You must use a full stop to indicate a decimal point. For example, write 100.57 **not** 100,57 **or** 100 57.

You may use a comma to indicate a number in the thousands, but you don't have to. For example, 10000 and 10,000 are both OK.

Other indicators are not compatible with the computer-marked system.

You are employed by the business, Russell Hardware, as a bookkeeper.

- Russell Hardware uses a manual accounting system.

- Double entry takes place in the general ledger. Individual accounts of trade receivables and trade payables are kept in the sales and purchases ledgers as subsidiary accounts.

- The cash book and petty cash book should be treated as part of the double entry system unless the task instructions state otherwise.

- The VAT rate is 20%.

Task 1 (12 marks)

(a) **Match each situation with the most appropriate payment method.**

(CBT instructions: Click on a box in the left column then on one in the right column to indicate each answer. To remove a line, click on it.)

Situation

Making a payment via the internet to purchase office supplies

Making a non-automated low value payment in person

Making a payment to a supplier by post

Making regular payments of set amounts to the same recipient

Payment method

Standing order

Cheque

Bank draft

Debit card

CHAPS

Cash

(b) **Show which TWO of the payment methods below will reduce funds in the payer's bank balance on the date of payment, by ticking the appropriate boxes.**

Payment method	Reduce funds on the date of payment ✓
Credit card	
Direct debit	
Cash	
CHAPS	
Cheque	

(c) Show which TWO of the errors below will cause an imbalance in the trial balance by ticking the appropriate boxes

Error	Imbalance in the trial balance ✓
The purchase of new desks for the office has been recorded in the office expenses account. All other entries were correct	
A cash payment of £64 for stationery has been recorded in the cash account as £46. All other entries were correct	
Recording a credit note from a supplier on the debit side of the purchases ledger control account and the debit side of the purchase returns account	
Recording a purchase from a credit supplier for £5,000 as £500 in both the purchases and the purchase ledger account (no VAT)	

(d) Show which ONE error is an error of principle, by selecting the appropriate box in the table below.

Error	Error of principle ✓
The purchase of a new computer has been recorded in the office expenses account. All other entries were correct	
A cash sale has been recorded in the sales and VAT control accounts only	
A cash payment of £64 for stationery has been recorded in the cash account as £46. All other entries were correct	
A BACS payment to a credit supplier was debited to the bank account and credited to the purchases ledger control account	

The correction of errors in a bookkeeping system is recorded in the journal.

(e) **Select one other transaction that is recorded in the journal.**

Statements	✓
Prompt payment discounts received	
Interest received from the bank	
Irrecoverable debts written off	
Re-imbursement of petty cash	

Task 2 (12 marks)

Russell Hardware pays its employees by BACS direct credit transfer every month and maintains a wages control account.

A summary of last month's payroll transactions is shown below:

Item	£
Gross wages	7,450
Employees' NI	682
Income tax	1,204
Trade union subscriptions	90
Employer's NI	809

Record the journal entries needed in the general ledger to:

(a) **Record the net wages paid to the employees**

Account name	Debit £	Credit £
▼		
▼		

(b) **Record the HM Revenue and Customs liability**

Account name	Debit £	Credit £
▼		
▼		

(c)   Record the trade union liability

Account name		Debit £	Credit £
	▼		
	▼		

Picklist:

Bank
Employees' NI
Employer's NI
HM Revenue and Customs
Income tax
Trade union subscription
Wages control
Wages expense

Task 3 (10 marks)

This is a customer's account in the sales ledger.

Bryson Construction

Date 20XX	Details	Amount £	Date 20XX	Details	Amount £
01 Jan	Balance b/f	450	4 Jan	Credit note 45	35
15 Jan	Invoice 951	785	17 Jan	Credit note 46	210

The customer has now ceased trading owing the amount outstanding which includes VAT.

(a)   Record the journal entries needed in the general ledger to write off the net amount and the VAT.

Account name		Debit £	Credit £
	▼		
	▼		
	▼		

Picklist:

Irrecoverable debt expense
Sales ledger control
VAT control

A new business has been started and a new set of accounts are to be opened. A partially completed journal to record the opening entries is shown below.

(b) **Complete the journal by ticking either the debit or credit column.**

Account name	Amount £	Debit ✓	Credit ✓
Cash at bank	2,400		
Capital	6,000		
Loan from bank	1,200		
Computer equipment	4,800		

Task 4 (10 marks)

This is a summary of transactions to be recorded in the VAT control account in April.

(a) **Show whether each transaction will be a debit or a credit entry in the VAT control account by ticking the relevant box in the debit or credit column**

Details	Amount £	Debit ✓	Credit ✓
VAT owing from HM Revenue and Customs at 1 April	1,604		
VAT total in the sales daybook	4,750		
VAT total in the sales returns daybook	320		
VAT total in the purchases daybook	3,710		
VAT total in the discounts allowed daybook	780		

Details	Amount £	Debit ✓	Credit ✓
VAT total in the discounts received daybook	150		
VAT total in the cash book for cash purchases	840		
VAT refund received from HM Revenue and Customs	1,604		

At the end of July the VAT control account has debit entries amount to £6,410 and credit entries amount to £10,900.

The following transactions have not yet been recorded in the VAT control account:

- VAT total of £395 in the purchases returns daybook
- VAT of £225 on an irrecoverable debt written off

(b) What will be the balance brought down on the VAT control account after the transactions above have been recorded?

Amount £	Debit ✓	Credit ✓

Task 5 (14 marks)

These are the accounts in the sales ledger at 1 October.

Charlotte Ltd

Details	Amount £	Details	Amount £
Balance b/f	8,700		

Anne plc

Details	Amount £	Details	Amount £
Balance b/f	21,500		

Emily & Co

Details	Amount £	Details	Amount £
		Balance b/f	450

Haworths

Details	Amount £	Details	Amoun £
Balance b/f	11,200		

(a) **What is the total of the balances in the sales ledger on 1 October?**

£ [   ]

The balance of the sales ledger control account on 1 October is £41,590.

(b) **What is the difference between the balance of the sales ledger control account and the total of the balances in the sales ledger you calculated in (a)?**

£ [   ]

(c) **Which TWO of the reasons below could explain the difference you calculated in (b)? Tick the relevant options in the table below.**

Reasons	✓
Goods returned may have been entered in the customer's account in the sales ledger twice	
Discounts allowed were entered in the sales ledger control account only	
Goods returned were omitted from the sales ledger control account	
Goods sold were entered twice in a customer's account in the sales ledger	
A cheque received was entered in the sales ledger control account twice	

This is a summary of transactions with credit suppliers during May 20XX.

Transactions	Amount £
Balance of payables at 1 May 20XX	27,500
Payments made by cheque	23,200
Goods purchased	13,800
Goods returned	6,800

(d) **Record these transactions in the purchases ledger control account and show the balance carried down.**

Purchases ledger control

Details	Amount £	Details	Amount £
▼		▼	
▼		▼	
▼			

Picklist:

Balance b/f
Balance c/d
Bank
Discount received
Purchases
Purchases returns

Task 6 (10 marks)

The bank statement and cash book for December are shown below

Required

Check the bank statement against the cash book and enter:

- **Any transactions into the cash book as needed**
- **The cash book balance carried down at 23 December and brought down at 24 December**

Enter dates in the format "XX Dec".

Bank statement

Date 20XX	Details	Paid out £	Paid in £	Balance £
01 Dec	Balance b/f			5,230 C
05 Dec	Counter credit Percival Ltd		8,560	13,790 C
10 Dec	Cheque 04256	400		13,390 C
13 Dec	Cheque 04257	690		12,700 C
14 Dec	Direct Debit Greenville DC	750		11,950 C
16 Dec	Cheque 04258	2,754		9,196 C
20 Dec	Counter credit: Bardier Bricks		5,500	14,696 C
21 Dec	Direct Debit Triggers Ltd	325		14,371 C
22 Dec	Cheque No 04260	850		13,521 C
23 Dec	Bank charges	25		13,496 C
23 Dec	Bank interest		15	13,511 C

D = Debit C = Credit

Cash book

Date 20XX	Details	Bank £	Date 20XX	Cheque number	Details	Bank £
01 Dec	Balance b/f	5,230	01 Dec	04256	Jacksons Ltd	400
20 Dec	Bardier Bricks Ltd	5,500	01 Dec	04257	Ristov & co	690
21 Dec	Darlingfords	4,650	07 Dec	04258	ARP Ltd	2,754
22 Dec	Scotts	3,755	08 Dec	04259	Tolkens	1,450
	▼		15 Dec	04260	Loose Chips Co	850
	▼		22 Dec	04261	SM Griggs	312
					▼	
					▼	
					▼	
					▼	
	▼				▼	

Picklist:

ARP Ltd
Balance b/d
Balance c/d
Bank charges
Bank interest
Bardier Bricks
Darlingfords
Greenville DC
Jacksons Ltd
Loose chips Ltd
Percival Ltd
Ristov & Co
Scotts
SM Griggs
Tolkens
Triggers Ltd

Task 7 (14 marks)

Below is the bank statement for March.

Date 20XX	Details	Paid out £	Paid in £	Balance £
01 Mar	Balance b/f			3,460 C
05 Mar	Cheque 1165	465		2,995 C
12 Mar	Cheque 1167	7,200		4,205 D
15 Mar	GreenBee		9,460	5,255 C
16 Mar	Cheque 1166	533		4,722 C
23 Mar	Port Cookers		7,000	11,722 C
24 Mar	Cheque No 1169	2,400		9,322 C
26 Mar	Bank charges	25		9,297 C
28 Mar	Bank interest		27	9,324 C

D = Debit C = Credit

Bank reconciliation statement

(a)   Cash book

Date 20XX	Details	Bank £	Date 20XX	Cheque number	Details	Bank £
01 Mar	Balance b/f	3,460	02 Mar	1165	Bobbin & Co	465
10 Mar	GreenBee	9,460	03 Mar	1166	Freddies Ltd	533
14 Mar	Port Cookers	7,000	07 Mar	1167	Irons	7,200
21 Mar	Kitchen Co	3,452	05 Mar	1168	Jerry & Co	2,500
23 Mar	Nigella's	2,468	15 Mar	1169	P Smith	2,400
26 Mar	Bank interest	27	23 Mar	1170	J Frost	362
	▼		28 Mar		Bank charges	25
					▼	
	▼				▼	

Picklist:

Balance b/d
Balance c/d

The cash book and bank reconciliation statement for March have not been finalised.

Identify the four transactions that are included in the cash book but are missing from the bank statement and complete the bank reconciliation statement as at 31 March.

Note. Do not make any entries in the shaded boxes.

Bank reconciliation statement		£
Balance per bank statement		
Add:		
	▼	
	▼	
Total to add		
Less:		
	▼	
	▼	
Total to subtract		
Balance as per cash book		

Picklist:

Balance b/d
Balance c/d
Bank charges
Bank interest
Bobbin & Co
Freddies Ltd
GreenBee
Irons
J Frost
Jerry & Co
Kitchen Co
Nigella's
P Smith
Port Cookers

(b) Refer to the cash book in (a) and check that the bank statement has been correctly reconciled by calculating:

- **The balance carried down**
- **The total of each of the bank columns after the balance carried down has been recorded**

Balance carried down £	Bank column totals £

Task 8 (14 marks)

A suspense account has been opened with a balance of £118.

The error has been identified as an entry made in the general ledger from the incorrectly totalled net column in the sales day book, as shown below.

Sales day book

Date 20XX	Details	Invoice number	Total £	VAT £	Net £
31 Oct	Drury Ltd	144	288	48	240
31 Oct	Davenport	145	1,740	290	1,450
31 Oct	Williams & Co	146	3,174	529	2,645
	Totals		5,202	867	4,453

(a) **Record the journal entries needed to:**

- **Remove the incorrect entry**
- **Record the correct entry**
- **Remove the suspense account balance**

Journal to remove the incorrect entry

Account name	Amount £	Debit ✓	Credit ✓
▼			

Journal to record the correct entry

Account name	Amount £	Debit ✓	Credit ✓
▼			

Journal to remove the suspense account balance

Account name	Amount £	Debit ✓	Credit ✓
▼			

Picklist:

Davenport
Drury Ltd
Sales
Sales ledger control
Suspense
VAT
Williams & Co

Another error has been found in the general ledger. Entries to record cash drawings of £550 have been reversed.

(b) **Record the journal entries needed to:**

- **Remove the incorrect entry**
- **Record the correct entries**

Do not enter a zero in unused debit or credit column cells.

Journal to remove the incorrect entries

Account name	Amount £	Debit ✓	Credit ✓
▼			
▼			

Picklist:

Bank
Capital
Cash
Drawings

181

Journal to record the correct entry

Account name		Amount £	Debit ✓	Credit ✓
	▼			
	▼			

Picklist:

Bank
Capital
Cash
Drawings

Task 9 (10 marks)

The journal entries below have been prepared to correct an error.

Journal

Account name	Debit £	Credit £
Heat & Light	1,650	
Suspense		1,650
Suspense	1,560	
Heat & Light		1,560

Post the journal entries in the general ledger accounts below and show the balance carried down in the heat and light account.

Heat & Light

Details	Amount £	Details		Amount £
Balance b/f	4,760		▼	
▼			▼	

Suspense

Details	Amount £	Details	Amount £
Balance b/f	90	▼	
▼		▼	

Picklist:

Balance b/f
Balance c/d
Heat & Light
Suspense

Task 10 (14 marks)

On 28 February a trial balance was extracted and did not balance. The debit column totaled £448,100 and the credit column totaled £450,100.

(a) **What entry would be made in the suspense account to balance the trial balance? Select whether this would be a debit or a credit.**

Account name	Amount £	Debit ✓	Credit ✓
Suspense			

The journal entries to correct all the bookkeeping errors, and a list of balances as they appear in the trial balance, are shown below

Account name	Debit ✓	Credit ✓
Suspense	200	
Bank		200
Heat & Light	200	
Bank		200

Account name	Debit ✓	Credit ✓
Rent paid	2,500	
Suspense		2,500
Suspense	300	
Advertising		300

(b) **Complete the table below to show:**

- **The balance of each account after the journal entries have been recorded**
- **Whether each balance will be a debit or credit entry in the trial balance**

List of balances

Account name	Original balance £	New balance £	Debit ✓	Credit ✓
Heat & Light	800			
Bank (debit)	4,500			
Advertising	960			
Rent paid	6,500			

On 30 April a partially prepared trial balance had debit balances totalling £171,600 and credit balances totalling £168,200. The accounts below have not yet been entered into the trial balance.

(c) **Complete the table below to show whether each balance will be a debit or credit entry in the trial balance.**

Account name	Balance £	Debit ✓	Credit ✓
VAT control (owing to HM Revenue and Customs)	2,800		
Loan	9,000		
Computer equipment	8,400		

(d) **What will be the totals of each column of the trial balance after the balances in (c) have been entered?**

Account name	Debit £	Credit £
Totals		

BPP PRACTICE ASSESSMENT 1
BOOKKEEPING CONTROLS

ANSWERS

Bookkeeping Controls
BPP practice assessment 1

Task 1 (12 marks)

(a)

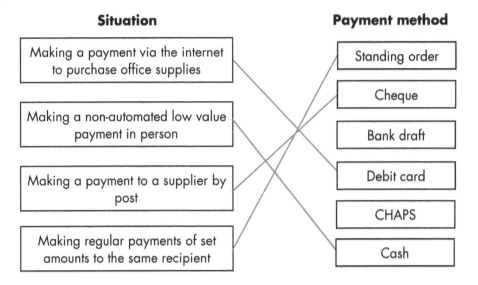

Situation	Payment method
Making a payment via the internet to purchase office supplies	Standing order
	Cheque
Making a non-automated low value payment in person	Bank draft
	Debit card
Making a payment to a supplier by post	CHAPS
Making regular payments of set amounts to the same recipient	Cash

(b)

Payment method	Reduce funds on the date of payment ✓
Credit card	
Direct debit	✓
Cash	
CHAPS	✓
Cheque	

(c)

Error	Imbalance in the trial balance ✓
The purchase of new desks for the office has been recorded in the office expenses account. All other entries were correct	
A cash payment of £64 for stationery has been recorded in the cash account as £46. All other entries were correct	✓
Recording a credit note from a supplier on the debit side of the purchases ledger control account and the debit side of the purchase returns account.	✓
Recording a purchase from a credit supplier for £5,000 as £500 in both the purchases and the purchase ledger account (no VAT)	

Errors one and four will not show an imbalance in the trial balance as equal debits and credits have been posted, but not to the correct accounts. These will not be detected in the trial balance

Error two has shown an imbalance as the debits and credits do not match, so the trial balance will show the error.

Error three has two debit entries, therefore, there will be an imbalance in the trial balance.

(d)

Error	Error of principle ✓
The purchase of a new computer has been recorded in the office expenses account. All other entries were correct	✓
A cash sale has been recorded in the sales and VAT control accounts only	
A cash payment of £64 for stationery has been recorded in the cash account as £46. All other entries were correct	
A BACS payment to a credit supplier was debited to the bank account and credited to the purchases ledger control account	

An error of principle occurs where the bookkeeper enters a transaction in the wrong type of account. Only error one is posted to the incorrect account, the others are incorrect postings to the correct accounts (such as the payment to the supplier being posted as a credit, whereas it should have been a debit posting).

(e)

Statements	✓
Prompt payment discounts received	
Interest received from the bank	
Irrecoverable debts written off	✓
Re-imbursement of petty cash	

Task 2 (12 marks)

(a)   Journal to record the net wages paid to the employees

Account name	Debit £	Credit £
Wages control	5,474	
Bank		5,474

(b)   Journal to record the HM Revenue and Customs liability

Account name	Debit £	Credit £
Wages control	2,695	
HMRC		2,695

(c)   Journal to record the trade union liability

Account name	Debit £	Credit £
Wages control	90	
Trade union subscription		90

Task 3 (10 marks)

(a)

Account name	Debit £	Credit £
Irrecoverable debt expense	825	
Sales ledger control		990
VAT control	165	

(b)

Account name	Amount £	Debit ✓	Credit ✓
Cash at bank	2,400	✓	
Capital	6,000		✓
Loan from bank	1,200		✓
Computer equipment	4,800	✓	

Task 4 (10 marks)

(a)

Details	Amount £	Debit ✓	Credit ✓
VAT owing from HM Revenue and Customs at 1 April	1,604	✓	
VAT total in the sales daybook	4,750		✓
VAT total in the sales returns daybook	320	✓	
VAT total in the purchases daybook	3,710	✓	
VAT total in the discounts allowed daybook	780	✓	
VAT total in the discounts received daybook	150		✓

Details	Amount £	Debit ✓	Credit ✓
VAT total in the cash book for cash purchases	840	✓	
VAT refund received from HM Revenue and Customs	1,604		✓

(b)

Amount £	Debit ✓	Credit ✓
4,660		✓

The requirement asks for the balance b/d. This is on the opposite side to the balance c/d and completes the double entry.

Task 5 (14 marks)

(a)

£	40,950

(b)

£	640

(c)

Reasons	✓
Goods returned may have been entered in the customer's account in the sales ledger twice	✓
Discounts allowed were entered in the sales ledger control account only	
Goods returned were omitted from the sales ledger control account.	✓
Goods sold were entered twice in a customer's account in the sales ledger.	
A cheque received was entered in the sales ledger control account twice	

(d)

Purchases ledger control

Details	Amount £	Details	Amount £
Bank	23,200	Balance b/f	27,500
Purchases returns	6,800	Purchases	13,800
Balance c/d	11,300		
	41,300		41,300

Task 6 (10 marks)

Cash book

Date 20XX	Details	Bank £	Date 20XX	Cheque number	Details	Bank £
01 Dec	Balance b/f	5,230	01 Dec	04256	Jacksons Ltd	400
20 Dec	Bardier Bricks Ltd	5,500	01 Dec	04257	Ristov & co	690
21 Dec	Darlingfords	4,650	07 Dec	04258	ARP Ltd	2,754
22 Dec	Scotts	3,755	08 Dec	04259	Tolkens	1,450
05 Dec	**Percival Ltd**	**8,560**	15 Dec	04260	Loose Chips Co	850
23 Dec	**Bank interest**	**15**	22 Dec	04261	SM Griggs	312
			23 Dec		**Bank charges**	**25**
			14 Dec	**DD**	**Greenville DC**	**750**
			21 Dec	**DD**	**Triggers Ltd**	**325**
					Balance c/d	**20,154**
		27,710				27,710
	Balance b/d	**20,154**				

In order to reconcile the adjusted cash book with the bank statement via the bank reconciliation statement, the first step is to review both documents and identify the items which are already entered in the cash book and have cleared the bank statement.

Cash book

The opening balances of the cash book and bank statement are the same, meaning there are no entries relating to a prior period reconciliation.

After the crossing-off exercise, note that the bank statement had three payments that need to be recorded in the cash book (£25, £750 and £325) and two deposits (£8,560 and £15). Remember that withdrawals are a credit in the cash book and deposits are a debit.

To balance off the cash book both the debt and credit sides are totalled. The debit column is higher, so that total is put at the bottom of BOTH columns. The balancing figure on the credit side of £20,154 becomes the balance c/d. It is brought down on the opposite side of the account (the debit side), ready for the start of the new period.

Task 7 (14 marks)

(a) Cash book

Date 20XX	Details	Bank £	Date 20XX	Cheque number	Details	Bank £
01 Mar	Balance b/f	3,460	02 Mar	1165	Bobbin & Co	465
10 Mar	GreenBee	9,460	03 Mar	1166	Freddies Ltd	533
14 Mar	Port Cookers	7,000	07 Mar	1167	Irons	7,200
21 Mar	Kitchen Co	3,452	05 Mar	1168	Jerry & Co	2,500
23 Mar	Nigella's	2,468	15 Mar	1169	P Smith	2,400
26 Mar	Bank interest	27	23 Mar	1170	J Frost	362
			28 Mar		Bank charges	25
			31 Mar		**Balance c/d**	**12,382**
		25,867				**25,867**
1 Apr	Balance b/d	12,382				

Bank reconciliation statement	£
Balance per bank statement	9,324
Add:	
Nigella's	2,468
Kitchen Co	3,452
Total to add	5,920
Less:	
Jerry & Co	2,500
J Frost	362
Total to subtract	2,862
Balance as per cash book	12,382

(b)

Balance carried down £	Bank column totals £
12,382	25,867

··

Task 8 (14 marks)

(a)

Account name	Amount £	Debit ✓	Credit ✓
Sales	4,453	✓	

Account name	Amount £	Debit ✓	Credit ✓
Sales	4,335		✓

Account name	Amount £	Debit ✓	Credit ✓
Suspense	118		✓

(b)

Account name	Amount £	Debit ✓	Credit ✓
Drawings	550	✓	
Cash	550		✓

Account name	Amount £	Debit ✓	Credit ✓
Drawings	550	✓	
Cash	550		✓

Task 9 (10 marks)

Heat & Light

Details	Amount £	Details	Amount £
Balance b/f	4,760	Suspense	1,560
Suspense	1,650	Balance c/d	4,850
	6,410		6,410

Suspense

Details	Amount £	Details	Amount £
Balance b/f	90	Heat & Light	1,650
Heat & Light	1,560	Balance c/d	
	1,650		1,650

Task 10 (14 marks)

(a)

Account name	Amount £	Debit ✓	Credit ✓
Suspense	2,000	✓	

(b)

Account name	Original balance £	New balance £	Debit ✓	Credit ✓
Heat & Light	800	1,000	✓	
Bank (debit)	4,500	4,100	✓	
Advertising	960	660	✓	
Rent paid	6,500	9,000	✓	

(c)

Account name	Balance £	Debit ✓	Credit ✓
VAT control (owing to HM Revenue and Customs)	2,800		✓
Loan	9,000		✓
Computer equipment	8,400	✓	

(d)

Account name	Debit £	Credit £
Totals	180,000	180,000

BPP PRACTICE ASSESSMENT 2
BOOKKEEPING CONTROLS

Time allowed: 1 hour 30 minutes

Bookkeeping Controls
BPP practice assessment 2

This assessment contains **10 tasks** and you should attempt to complete **every** task.

Each task is independent. You will not need to refer to your answers to previous tasks.

Read every task carefully to make sure you understand what is required.

Where the date is relevant, it is given in the task data.

Both minus signs and brackets can be used to indicate negative numbers **unless** task instructions say otherwise.

You must use a full stop to indicate a decimal point. For example, write 100.57 **not** 100,57 **or** 100 57.

You may use a comma to indicate a number in the thousands, but you don't have to. For example, 10000 and 10,000 are both OK.

Other indicators are not compatible with the computer-marked system.

You are employed by the business, Jones & Co, as a bookkeeper.

- Jones & Co uses a manual accounting system.

- Double entry takes place in the general ledger. Individual accounts of trade receivables and trade payables are kept in the sales and purchases ledgers as subsidiary accounts.

- The cash book and petty cash book should be treated as part of the double entry system unless the task instructions state otherwise.

- The VAT rate is 20%.

Task 1 (12 marks)

(a) Identify the effect the different payment methods have on the bank balance.

Payment method	Reduce funds on the date of payment ✓	Reduce funds at a later date ✓
Credit card		
Cash withdrawal from the bank account		
BACS direct credit		
Cheque		
CHAPS		

(b) Select the most appropriate method of payment for the following transactions

Situation	Payment method
Payment of an invoice to a supplier where goods were purchased on credit. The payment is due today and is for £1,300	▼
Purchasing tea and coffee supplies for the office from the local supermarket	▼
Ordering new printer paper online	▼
Payment of local business rates on a monthly basis for the same value each month (£250)	▼
Payment of legal fees to the company's solicitor for general business advice (£550)	▼

Picklist:

Cash
CHAPS
Cheque
Debit card
Direct Debit
Faster payment

(c) **Show which of the errors below are, or are not, disclosed by the trial balance.**

Error in the general ledger	Error disclosed by the trial balance ✓	Error NOT disclosed by the trial balance ✓
Making a transposition error in the debit entry from the journal in the general ledger but not in the credit entry		
Recording a sale to a customer for £75 cash (no VAT) as £57 in both the cash account and the sales account		
Recording a payment for a cash purchase (no VAT) in the trade payables column of the cash book		
Recording a discount allowed to a customer on the debit side of the discount allowed account and the debit side of the sales ledger control account		
Recording a payment to a supplier on the credit side of the supplier's purchases ledger account		
Recording a sales return by debiting the sales ledger control account and crediting the sales returns account		

One of the errors in (c) above can be classified as an error of reversal of entries.

(d) **Show which error is an error of reversal of entries.**

Error in the general ledger	✓
Making a transposition error in the debit entry from the journal in the general ledger but not in the credit entry	
Recording a sale to a customer for £75 cash (no VAT) as £57 in both the cash account and the sales account	
Recording a payment for a cash purchase (no VAT) in the trade payables column of the cash book	
Recording discount allowed to a customer on the debit side of the discount allowed account and the debit side of the sales ledger control account	
Recording a payment to a supplier on the credit side of the supplier's purchases ledger account	
Recording a sales return by debiting the sales ledger control account and crediting the sales returns account	

Task 2 (10 marks)

This is a summary of transactions to be recorded in the VAT control account in March.

(a) **Show whether each transaction will be a debit or a credit entry in the VAT control account.**

Details	Amount £	Debit ✓	Credit ✓
VAT owing to HM Revenue and Customs at 1 March	2,300		
VAT total in the sales daybook	5,320		
VAT total in the sales returns daybook	410		
VAT total in the purchases daybook	3,100		
VAT total in the discounts allowed daybook	250		
VAT total in the discounts received daybook	170		

Details	Amount £	Debit ✓	Credit ✓
VAT total in the cash book for cash sales	900		
VAT payment sent to HM Revenue and Customs	2,300		

(b) **What is the VAT balance at 31 March?**

Amount £	Debit ✓	Credit ✓

(c) **One of Jones & Co's customers, Jenson Ltd, has ceased trading owing the company £500 plus VAT. Record the journal entries needed in the general ledger to write off the net amount and the VAT.**

Account name	Amount £	Debit ✓	Credit ✓
▼			
▼			
▼			

Picklist:

Irrecoverable debts
Jenson Ltd
Jones & Co
Purchases
Purchases ledger control
Sales
Sales ledger control
VAT control

Task 3 (10 marks)

The following is an extract from Jones & Co's books of prime entry.

Sales day book

Details	Gross £	VAT £	Net £
Q1	64,260	10,710	53,550

Purchases day book

	Gross £	VAT £	Net £
Q1	19,530	3,255	16,275

Sales returns day book

Details	Gross £	VAT £	Net £
Q1	3,360	560	2,800

Purchase returns day book

	Gross £	VAT £	Net £
Q1	1,302	217	1,085

There were also cash sales made of £1,008 (including VAT) during the quarter

(a) What will be the entries in the VAT control account to record the VAT transactions in the quarter?

VAT control

Details	Amount £	Details	Amount £
▼		▼	
▼		▼	
▼		▼	

Picklist:

Cash book
Cash sales
Purchases
Purchases day book
Purchases returns
Purchases returns day book
Sales
Sales day book
Sales returns
Sales returns day book
VAT control

(b) **The VAT return must now be completed. What is the balance owing to or from HM Revenue and Customs for the period?**

Amount £	Amount due from HMRC ✓	Amount owed to HMRC ✓

(c) **Which of the following TWO statements are true**

Statement	✓
The VAT control account is used to establish any balance due to or reclaimable from HMRC	
Payments to HMRC in respect of VAT owed are debited to the cash book and credited to the VAT control account	
The balance b/d on the VAT control account is the amount owed to (credit balance) or refundable by (debit balance) HMRC	
A return on sales (where VAT is charged) increases the VAT liability in the VAT control account	

Task 4 (14 marks)

These are the accounts in the sales ledger at 1 January.

Sukhi Ltd

Details	Amount £	Details	Amount £
Balance b/f	1,560		

Ayesha plc

Details	Amount £	Details	Amount £
Balance b/f	4,790		

Sinead & Co

Details	Amount £	Details	Amount £
		Balance b/f	890

Iona's Pebbles Limited

Details	Amount £	Details	Amount £
		Balance b/f	7,250

(a) **What is the total of the balances in the sales ledger on 1 January?**

£ [ ]

The balance of the sales ledger control account on 1 January is £12,600.

(b) **What is the difference between the balance of the sales ledger control account and the total of the balances in the sales ledger you calculated in (a)?**

£ [ ]

(c) **Which ONE of the reasons below could explain the difference you calculated in (b) by ticking the appropriate answer in the table below?**

Reasons	✓
A payment from a customer was allocated against the wrong customer	
Discounts allowed were not entered in the sales ledger control account	
Goods sold were entered twice in the sales ledger control account	
Goods returned were omitted from the sales ledger.	

(d) Another error is found on the purchase ledger account, whereby the invoice for electricity was found to be recorded in the rent account. Select the type of error that has occurred by ticking the appropriate box in the table below.

Error	✓
Error of principle	
Unequal amounts error	
Error of omission	
Error of commission	

Task 5 (12 marks)

Jones & Co pays its employees by BACS direct credit transfer every month and maintains a wages control account.

A summary of September's payroll transactions is shown below:

Item	£
Gross wages	10,645
Employees' NI	1,230
Income tax	1,945
Employees' pension contributions	320
Employer's NI	1,450

Record the journal entries needed in the general ledger to:

(a) Journal to record the net wages paid to the employees

Account name		Debit £	Credit £
	▼		
	▼		

(b) **Journal to record the HM Revenue and Customs liability**

Account name		Debit £	Credit £
	▼		
	▼		

Picklist:

Bank
HMRC control account
Wages control account
Wages expense account

Employees contribute to their pension through their salary. For those employees who make these payments, the company contributes a further 6% of their gross wages.

Assuming all employees contribute to their pension, what is the amount that the company will be contributing in September? Record your answers in the journals below.

(c) **Record the employee's pension contributions in the journal below**

Account name		Debit £	Credit £
	▼		
	▼		

(d) **Record the employer's pension contributions in the journal below (round your answer to the nearest pound)**

Account name		Debit £	Credit £
	▼		
	▼		

(e) **Transfer the employer's pension contributions (calculated in part (d)) to the Pension administrator control account**

Account name		Debit £	Credit £
	▼		
	▼		

Picklist:

Bank
Employees' NI
Employer's NI
HMRC control account
Income tax
Pension administrator control account
Trade union subs
Wages control account
Wages expense account

Task 6 (14 marks)

Scriven Trading's trial balance was extracted and did not balance. The debit column of the trial balance totalled £139,406 and the credit column totalled £137,200.

(a) **What entry would be made in the suspense account to balance the trial balance?**

Account name	Amount £	Debit ✓	Credit ✓
Suspense			

In the following month Scriven Trading's initial trial balance includes a suspense account with a balance of £90.

The error has now been identified as arising from an incorrectly totalled net column in the sales day book shown below.

Sales day book

Date 20XX	Details	Invoice number	Total £	VAT £	Net £
30 Jul	Brancaster & Co	456	600	100	500
30 Jul	Norfolk Ales	457	570	95	475
30 Jul	Cley Cookery	458	816	136	680
	Totals		1,986	331	1,565

(b) Record the journal entry needed in the general ledger to remove the incorrect entry made from the sales day book.

Account name	Amount £	Debit ✓	Credit ✓
▾			

(c) Record the journal entry needed in the general ledger to record the correct entry that should have been made from the sales day book.

Account name	Amount £	Debit ✓	Credit ✓
▾			

(d) Record the journal entry needed in the general ledger to remove the suspense account balance arising from the error in the sales day book.

Account name	Amount £	Debit ✓	Credit ✓
▾			

Picklist:

Balance b/f
Balance c/d
Sales
Suspense
Total
Trade receivables
VAT control

Task 7 (10 marks)

The journal entries below have been prepared to correct an error.

Journal

Account name	Debit £	Credit £
Office expenses	2,455	
Suspense		2,455
Suspense	2,540	
Office expenses		2,540

Post the journal entries in the general ledger accounts below and show the balance carried down in the office expenses account.

Office expenses

Details	Amount £	Details	Amount £
Balance b/f	6,720	▼	
▼		▼	
▼			

Suspense

Details	Amount £	Details	Amount £
		Balance b/f	85
▼		▼	

Picklist:

Balance b/f
Balance c/d
Office expenses
Suspense

Task 8 (14 marks)

On 30 June Jones & Co extracted an initial trial balance which did not balance, and a suspense account with a debit balance of £1,690 was opened. On 1 July journal entries were prepared to correct the errors that had been found, and clear the suspense account. The list of balances in the initial trial balance, and the journal entries to correct the errors, are shown below.

Journal entries

Account name	Debit £	Credit £
Furniture and fittings		8,690
Suspense	8,690	
Furniture and fittings	9,680	
Suspense		9,680

Account name	Debit £	Credit £
Sales returns	350	
Suspense		350
Sales returns	350	
Suspense		350

Taking into account the journal entries, which will clear the suspense account, re-draft the trial balance by writing the figures in the debit or credit column. Do not enter your figures with decimal places in this task and do not enter a zero in the empty column.

	Balances extracted on 30 June £	Balances at 1 July	
		Debit £	Credit £
Machinery	15,240		
Furniture and fittings	8,690		
Inventory	11,765		
Bank (overdraft)	5,127		

	Balances extracted on 30 June £	Balances at 1 July	
		Debit £	Credit £
Petty cash	100		
Sales ledger control	72,536		
Purchases ledger control	11,928		
VAT (owing to HM Revenue and Customs)	2,094		
Capital	80,000		
Sales	98,162		
Purchases	39,278		
Purchases returns	4,120		
Wages	22,855		
Sales returns	110		
Administration expenses	10,287		
Rent and rates	12,745		
Marketing expenses	3,289		
Irrecoverable debts	1,275		
Maintenance	1,571		
Totals			

Task 9 (10 marks)

The bank statement and cash book for May are shown below

Required

Check the bank statement against the cash book and enter:

- **Any transactions into the cash book as needed**
- **The cash book balance carried down at 31 May and brought down at 1 June.**

Enter dates in the format "XX Dec".

Bank statement

Date 20XX	Details	Paid out £	Paid in £	Balance £
01 May	Balance b/f			900 D
02 May	Counter credit		4,250	3,350 C
02 May	Cheque 00793	250		3,100 C
05 May	Cheque 00795	1,300		1,800 C
08 May	Direct debit: PinkGreen Ltd	200		1,600 C
12 May	Direct debit: Maple Leaf & Co	425		1,175 C
18 May	Counter credit		6,400	7,575 C
21 May	Counter credit		2,475	10,050 C
22 May	Bank interest		15	10,065 C
23 May	Bank charges	30		10,035 C
30 May	Direct debit: Oak Insurance	130		9,905 C

D = Debit C = Credit

(a) Cash book

Date 20XX	Details	Bank £	Date 20XX	Cheque number	Details	Bank £
02 May	Parks & Co	4,250	01 May		Balance bf	900
18 May	Flower Bulb Co	6,400	01 May	00793	Greenways	250
20 May	Mowaway ltd	2,475	01 May	00794	Blossom & co	2,100
	▼		01 May	00795	White Pines	1,300
					▼	
					▼	
					▼	
					▼	
					▼	
	▼				▼	

Picklist:

Balance b/d
Balance c/d
Bank charges
Bank interest
Blossom & co
Greenways
Maple Leaf & Co
Mowaway Ltd
Oak insurance
PinkGreen Ltd
White Pines

(b) Calculate the difference between the bank statement and the cash book balance as at 31 May.

	£
Balance on the bank statement as at 31 May	
Balance on the cash book as at 31 May	
Difference	

(c) **Which of the following items would need to be entered into the bank reconciliation in order for the bank statement and the cash book to balance at 31 May.**

	£
Cheque to Blossom & Co for £2,100	
Bank interest of £15	
Credit from Mowaway Ltd of £2,475	

Task 10 (14 marks)

Below is the bank statement dated 30 April

Date 20XX	Details	Paid out £	Paid in £	Balance £
01 Apr	Balance b/f			450 C
02 Apr	Counter credit		7,125	7,575 C
02 Apr	Bank charges	45		7,530 C
05 Apr	Cheque 0077	1,260		6,270C
10 Apr	Counter credit		435	6,705 C
15 Apr	Direct debit	2,700		4,005C
22 Apr	Counter credit		2,330	6,335 C
28 Apr	L Barlow (payroll payment)	1,200		5,135 C
28 Apr	J Lowenstein (payroll payment)	845		4,290 C

D = Debit C = Credit

Required

(a) **Complete the missing entries for the cash book below.**

(b) **On 30 April 20XX, a further three cheques were raised to pay suppliers. Ensure that the cash book has been updated for these transactions. Put the cash book totals in and ensure the balance carried down has been calculated.**

Details	Amount £
LTC Limited 0078	3,400
Gaffney & Co 0079	950
Bubble Corp 0080	245

Cash book

Date 20XX	Details	Bank £	Date 20XX	Cheque number	Details	Bank £
01 Apr	Balance b/d	450	01 Apr	0077	Joyful Ltd	1,260
02 Apr	Scrape & Co	7,125	15 Apr	DD	Rent	2,700
10 Apr	Eric & Sons Ltd	435				
22 Apr	B Fay	2,330				
30 Apr	Bake Sale plc	1,450				

Picklist:

Balance b/d
Balance c/d
Bank charges
Bank interest

Bubble Corp
Gaffney & Co
Joyful Ltd
LTC Limited
Payroll
Rent

(c) **Complete the bank reconciliation identifying the reconciling items**

Bank reconciliation statement		£
Balance per bank statement		
Add:		
	▼	
Total to add		
Less:		
	▼	
	▼	
	▼	
Total to subtract		
Balance as per cash book		

Picklist:

Bake Sale plc
Balance b/d
Balance c/d
Bank charges
Bank interest
Bubble Corp
Eric & Sons
Gaffney & Co
Joyful Ltd
LTC Limited
Payroll
Rent
Scrape & Co

BPP PRACTICE ASSESSMENT 2
BOOKKEEPING CONTROLS

ANSWERS

Bookkeeping Controls
BPP practice assessment 2

Task 1 (12 marks)

(a)

Payment method	Reduce funds on the date of payment ✓	Reduce funds at a later date ✓
Credit card		✓
Cash withdrawal from the bank account	✓	
BACS direct credit	✓	
Cheque		✓
CHAPS	✓	

The credit card statement will be affected in the first instance, so the current account will not be affected until the credit statement is paid at a later date. Cash is withdrawn from the bank account immediately. The BACS direct credit leaves the payer's account immediately and is usually received within 24 hours by the payee. Cheques affect the bank account when the payee presents them, which may take several days or weeks. CHAPS has an immediate effect on the bank account once it has been processed by the payer.

(b)

Situation	Payment method
Payment of an invoice to a supplier where goods were purchased on credit. The payment is due today and is for £1,300	Faster payment
Purchasing tea and coffee supplies for the office from the local supermarket	Cash
Ordering new printer paper online	Debit card
Payment of local business rates on a monthly basis for the same value each month (£250)	Direct Debit
Payment of legal fees to the company's solicitor for general business advice (£550)	Debit card

The final option in the table could be paid by cheque, but many businesses use debit cards for smaller payments. A debit card is relevant here as it is quick and suitable for smaller monetary transactions.

(c)

Error in the general ledger	Error disclosed by the trial balance ✓	Error NOT disclosed by the trial balance ✓
Making a transposition error in the debit entry from the journal in the general ledger but not in the credit entry	✓	
Recording a sale to a customer for £75 cash (no VAT) as £57 in both the cash account and the sales account		✓
Recording a payment for a cash purchase (no VAT) in the trade payables column of the cash book		✓
Recording a discount allowed to a customer on the debit side of the discount allowed account and the debit side of the sales ledger control account	✓	
Recording a payment to a supplier on the credit side of the supplier's purchases ledger account		✓
Recording a sales return by debiting the sales ledger control account and crediting the sales returns account		✓

(d)

Error in the general ledger	✓
Making a transposition error in the debit entry from the journal in the general ledger but not in the credit entry	
Recording a sale to a customer for £75 cash (no VAT) as £57 in both the cash account and the sales account	
Recording a payment for a cash purchase (no VAT) in the trade payables column of the cash book	
Recording discount allowed to a customer on the debit side of the discount allowed account and the debit side of the sales ledger control account	
Recording a payment to a supplier on the credit side of the supplier's purchases ledger account	
Recording a sales return by debiting the sales ledger control account and crediting the sales returns account	✓

Task 2 (10 marks)

(a)

Details	Amount £	Debit ✓	Credit ✓
VAT owing to HM Revenue and Customs at 1 March	2,300		✓
VAT total in the sales daybook	5,320		✓
VAT total in the sales returns daybook	410	✓	
VAT total in the purchases daybook	3,100	✓	
VAT total in the discounts allowed daybook	250	✓	
VAT total in the discounts received daybook	170		✓
VAT total in the cash book for cash sales	900		✓
VAT payment sent to HM Revenue and Customs	2,300	✓	

(b)

Amount £	Debit ✓	Credit ✓
2,630		✓

(c)

Account name	Amount £	Debit ✓	Credit ✓
Irrecoverable debts	500	✓	
VAT control	100	✓	
Sales ledger control	600		✓

Task 3 (10 marks)

(a)

VAT control

Details	Amount £	Details	Amount £
Sales returns	560	Sales	10,710
Purchases	3,255	Purchases returns	217
		Cash sales	168

(b) The answer is Jones and Co owe HMRC £7,280 (this is the carried down figure as seen in the workings below)

Working:

Details	Amount £	Details	Amount £
Sales returns	560	Sales	10,710
Purchases	3,255	Purchases returns	217
		Cash sales	168
Balance c/d	**7,280**		
	11,095		11,095
		Balance b/d	**7,280**

(c)

Statement	✓
The VAT control account is used to establish any balance due to or reclaimable from HMRC	✓
Payments to HMRC in respect of VAT owed are debited to the cash book and credited to the VAT control account	
The balance b/d on the VAT control account is the amount owed to (credit balance) or refundable by (debit balance) HMRC	✓
A return on sales (where VAT is charged) increases the VAT liability in the VAT control account	

Task 4 (14 marks)

(a)

£	12,710

(b)

£	110

(c)

Reasons	✓
A payment from a customer was allocated against the wrong customer	
Discounts allowed were not entered in the sales ledger control account	
Goods sold were entered twice in the sales ledger control account	
Goods returned were omitted from the sales ledger.	✓

(d)

Error	✓
Error of principle	
Unequal amounts error	
Error of omission	
Error of commission	✓

Error of commission is where the item has been recorded in the right type of account (in this case, that of the Statement of Profit and Loss) but the wrong account has been used (in this case rent instead of electricity). It is not an error of principle (it would have had to been recorded onto the Statement of Financial Position, the wrong type of account). The amounts are equal (therefore not an error of unequal amounts). The item has been recorded therefore it is not an error of omission.

Task 5 (12 marks)

(a)

Account name	Debit £	Credit £
Wages control account	7,150	
Bank		7,150

(b)

Account name	Debit £	Credit £
Wages control account	4,625	
HMRC control account		4,625

(c)

Account name	Debit £	Credit £
Wages control account	320	
Pension administrator control account		320

(d)

Account name	Debit £	Credit £
Wages expense account	639	
Wages control account		639

(e)

Account name	Debit £	Credit £
Wages control account	639	
Pension administrator control account		639

Task 6 (14 marks)

(a)

Account name	Amount £	Debit ✓	Credit ✓
Suspense	2,206		✓

(b)

Account name	Amount £	Debit ✓	Credit ✓
Sales	1,565	✓	

(c)

Account name	Amount £	Debit ✓	Credit ✓
Sales	1,655		✓

(d)

Account name	Amount £	Debit ✓	Credit ✓
Suspense	90	✓	

Task 7 (10 marks)

Office expenses

Details	Amount £	Details	Amount £
Balance b/f	6,720	Suspense	2,540
Suspense	2,455	Balance c/d	6,635
	9,175		9,175

Suspense

Details	Amount £	Details	Amount £
		Balance b/f	85
Office expenses	2,540	Office expenses	2,455
	2,540		2,540

Task 8 (14 marks)

	Balances extracted on 30 June £	Balances at 1 July Debit £	Credit £
Machinery	15,240	15,240	
Furniture and fittings	8,690	9,680	
Inventory	11,765	11,765	
Bank (overdraft)	5,127		5,127
Petty cash	100	100	
Sales ledger control	72,536	72,536	
Purchases ledger control	11,928		11,928
VAT (owing to HM Revenue and Customs)	2,094		2,094
Capital	80,000		80,000
Sales	98,162		98,162
Purchases	39,278	39,278	
Purchases returns	4,120		4,120
Wages	22,855	22,855	
Sales returns	110	810	
Administration expenses	10,287	10,287	
Rent and rates	12,745	12,745	
Marketing expenses	3,289	3,289	
Irrecoverable debts	1,275	1,275	
Maintenance	1,571	1,571	
Totals		201,431	201,431

Task 9 (10 marks)

Bank statement

Date 20XX	Details	Paid out £	Paid in £	Balance £
01 May	Balance b/f			900 D
02 May	Counter credit		4,250	3,350 C
02 May	Cheque 00793	250		3,100 C
05 May	Cheque 00795	1,300		1,800 C
08 May	Direct debit: PinkGreen Ltd	200		1,600 C
12 May	Direct debit: Maple Leaf & Co	425		1,175 C
18 May	Counter credit		6,400	7,575 C
21 May	Counter credit		2,475	10,050 C
22 May	Bank interest		15	10,065 C
23 May	Bank charges	30		10,035 C
30 May	Direct debit: Oak Insurance	130		9,905 C

D = Debit C = Credit

(a) Cash book

Date 20XX	Details	Bank £	Date 20XX	Cheque number	Details	Bank £
02 May	Parks & Co	4,250	01 May		Balance bf	900
18 May	Flower Bulb Co	6,400	01 May	00793	Greenways	250
20 May	Mowaway ltd	2,475	01 May	00794	Blossom & co	2,100
22 May	Bank interest	15	01 May	00795	White Pines	1,300
			08 May	DD	PinkGreen Ltd	200
			12 May	DD	Maple Leaf & Co	425
			23 May		Bank charges	30
			30 May	DD	Oak Insurance	130
			31 May		Balance c/d	7,805
		13,140				13,140
1 Jun	Balance b/d	7,805				

(b)

	£
Balance on the bank statement as at 31 May	9,905
Balance on the cash book as at 31 May	7,805
Difference	2,100

(c)

	£
Cheque to Blossom & Co for £2,100	✓
Bank interest of £15	
Credit from Mowaway Ltd of £2,475	

Task 10 (14 marks)

Cash book

(a) and (b)

Date 20XX	Details	Bank £	Date 20XX	Cheque number	Details	Bank £
01 Apr	Balance b/d	450	01 Apr	0077	Joyful Ltd	1,260
02 Apr	Scrape & Co	7,125	15 Apr	DD	Rent	2,700
10 Apr	Eric & Sons Ltd	435	**02 Apr**		**Bank charges**	**45**
22 Apr	B Fay	2,330	**28 Apr**		**Payroll**	**1,200**
30 Apr	Bake Sale plc	1,450	**28 Apr**		**Payroll**	**845**
			30 Apr	0078	**LTC Limited**	**3,400**
			30 Apr	0079	**Gaffney & Co**	**950**
			30 Apr	0080	**Bubble Corp**	**245**
			30 Apr		**Balance c/d**	**1,145**
		11,790				**11,790**
	Balance b/d	**1,145**				

(c)

Bank reconciliation statement	£
Balance per bank statement	4,290
Add:	
Bake Sale plc	1,450
Total to add	1,450
Less:	
LTC Limited	3,400
Gaffney & Co	950
Bubble Corp	245
Total to subtract	4,595
Balance as per cash book	1,145

BPP PRACTICE ASSESSMENT 3
BOOKKEEPING CONTROLS

Time allowed: 1 hour 30 minutes

PRACTICE ASSESSMENT 3

Bookkeeping Controls
BPP practice assessment 3

This assessment contains **10 tasks** and you should attempt to complete **every** task.

Each task is independent. You will not need to refer to your answers to previous tasks.

Read every task carefully to make sure you understand what is required.

Where the date is relevant, it is given in the task data.

Both minus signs and brackets can be used to indicate negative numbers **unless** task instructions say otherwise.

You must use a full stop to indicate a decimal point. For example, write 100.57 **not** 100,57 **or** 100 57.

You may use a comma to indicate a number in the thousands, but you don't have to. For example, 10000 and 10,000 are both OK.

Other indicators are not compatible with the computer-marked system.

You are employed by the business, Pratesh Supplies Limited, as a bookkeeper.

- Pratesh Supplies Limited uses a manual accounting system.

- Double entry takes place in the general ledger. Individual accounts of trade receivables and trade payables are kept in the sales and purchases ledgers as subsidiary accounts.

- The cash book and petty cash book should be treated as part of the double entry system unless the task instructions state otherwise.

- The VAT rate is 20%.

Task 1 (12 marks)

(a) Identify the effect the different payment methods have on the bank balance. Please tick the appropriate box in each case.

Payment method	Reduce funds on the date of payment ✓	Reduce funds at a later date ✓
Credit card		
Bank draft		
Cheque		
CHAPS		
Direct Debit		

(b) Select the most appropriate method of payment for the following transactions from the picklist below

Situation	Payment method
Purchase of a new computer from Laptops Limited, which is an online discount supplier	
Invoice payment to a supplier who requires immediate payment today for £2,400	
Payment of the payroll for the month of March to employees	
Payment of rent on a new office on a monthly basis (£2,450)	
Purchase of a new warehouse for the business (£125,000)	

Picklist:

BACS direct credit
Cash
CHAPS
Cheque
Credit card
Direct Debit
Faster payment
Standing order

(c) **Select which TWO of the following statements are correct by ticking the appropriate option**

Error	✓
When a payment is made using a credit card, the money leaves the bank account immediately	
Standing orders are regular payments set up by the payer	
A bank draft can be cancelled by the payer after it has been issued	
Money leaves the payer's bank account immediately upon issuance of a bank draft	

(d) **Show which error is an error of original entry by ticking the appropriate option**

Error in the general ledger	✓
Writing in the balance on the office stationery account incorrectly	
Recording a purchase from a credit supplier for £5,000 (no VAT) as £500 in both the purchases and the purchases ledger control accounts	
Recording a receipt from a credit customer in the cash sales account	
Recording a credit note from a supplier on the debit side of the purchases ledger control account and the debit side of the purchases returns account	

Task 2 (10 marks)

Show whether the errors below will cause an imbalance in the trial balance by ticking the appropriate column.

Error in the general ledger	Error disclosed by the trial balance ✓	Error NOT disclosed by the trial balance ✓
For a cash sale of £340 (no VAT), recording the amount as £34 in the cash book		
Recording £50 discount received on the credit side of PLCA and the debit side of the discount received account		
Recording a purchase from a supplier for £180 including VAT as £180 in the PLCA and purchases accounts and £30 in the VAT account		
Making a transposition error when transferring a balance from the ledger account to the trial balance		
Recording a payment from a credit customer for £200 in the debit side of the sales ledger account		

Task 3 (10 marks)

The following is an extract from the bank statement for March. The two staff members are paid on the closest working day to the 15th of each month.

The cash book and bank reconciliation statement for March have not been finalised.

Required

(a) **Complete the cash book for any missing entries during March, including the balance brought down at 1 April 20XX**

Date 20XX	Details	Paid out £	Paid in £	Balance £
01 Mar	Balance b/f			7,250 C
02 Mar	Cheque 820	4,450		2,800 C
02 Mar	Cheque 821	2,100		700 C
09 Mar	Counter credit: Jeffersons & Co		750	1,450 C
12 Mar	Direct debit: Carter insurance	990		460 C
13 Mar	K Brown	1,800		1,340 D
13 Mar	J Patel	1,600		2,940 D
22 Mar	Counter credit: Clinton & Clinton		9,250	6,310 C
28 Mar	Bank charges	100		6,210 C

D = Debit   C = Credit

The cash book as at 31 March is shown below:

Cash book

Date 20XX	Details	Bank £	Date 20XX	Cheque number	Details	Bank £
01 Mar	Balance b/f	7,250	01 Mar	820	Nixon Ltd	4,450
02 Mar	Jeffersons & Co	750	01 Mar	821	Roosevelts	2,100
22 Mar	Clinton & Clinton	9,250	02 Mar	822	GWB LLP	1,750
30 Mar	Garfield & Son	1,450			▼	
30 Mar	Adams	4,600			▼	
					▼	
					▼	
					▼	
	▼					

Picklist:

Adams
Balance b/d
Balance c/d
Bank charges
Bank interest
Carter insurance
Clinton & Clinton
Garfield & Son
GWB LLP
J Patel
Jeffersons & Co
K Brown
Nixon Ltd
Roosevelts

(b) Complete the bank reconciliation statement as at 31 March.

Note. Do not make any entries in the shaded boxes.

Bank reconciliation statement as at 31 March 20XX	£
Balance per bank statement	
Add:	
▼	
▼	
Total to add	
Less:	
▼	
▼	
Total to subtract	
Balance as per cash book	

Picklist:

Adams
Balance b/d
Balance c/d
Bank charges
Bank interest
Clinton & Clinton
Garfield & Son
GWB LLP
Jeffersons & Co
J Patel
K Brown
Nixon Ltd
Roosevelts

(c) Refer to the cash book in (a) and check that the bank statement has been correctly reconciled by calculating:

- **The balance carried down**

- **The total of each of the bank columns after the balance carried down has been recorded.**

Balance carried down £	Bank column totals £

··

Task 4 (10 marks)

This is a customer's account in the sales ledger.

Worcester Building Co

Date 20XX	Details	Amount £	Date 20XX	Details	Amount £
01 Jan	Invoice 482	1,400	15 Jan	Payment	1,350
15 Feb	Invoice 495	785	22 Feb	Credit Note 24	509
22 Mar	Invoice 522	250			

(a) **Calculate the amount outstanding by Worcester Building Co as at 31 March**

The customer has now ceased trading as of 15 April owing the amount outstanding which **includes** VAT. Enter your answer in the box provided

£ [   ]

(b) **Record the journal entries needed in the general ledger to write off the net amount and the VAT as at 30 April. Use the picklist provided.**

Account name		Amount £	Debit ✓	Credit ✓
	▼			
	▼			
	▼			

Picklist:

Irrecoverable debts
Sales ledger control
VAT control

242

(c) **In the next quarter, the VAT control account has debit entries amounting to £4,690 and credit entries amounting to £3,460**

The following transactions have not yet been recorded in the VAT control account:

- VAT total of £600 in the purchases daybook

- VAT of £180 on an irrecoverable debt written off

- Payment made to HMRC of £1,200 in respect of VAT payable for the previous quarter

Complete the VAT control account below, including the balance c/d at the end of the month

VAT Control

Account name	Amount £	Account name	Credit ✓
▼		Balance b/f	
▼		▼	
▼		▼	
▼			

Picklist:

Balance c/d
Bank
Irrecoverable debt
Purchases
Sales
Sales ledger control

Task 5 (12 marks)

Pratesh Supplies Limited pays its employees by BACS direct credit transfer every month and maintains a wages control account.

A summary of last month's payroll transactions is shown below:

Item	£
Gross wages	10,260
Employees' NI	925
Income tax	2,335
Employees' pension contributions	780
Employer's pension contribution	900
Employer's NI	1,300

Record the journal entries needed in the general ledger to:

(a)   Journal to record wages expense

Account name		Debit £	Credit £
	▼		
	▼		

(b)   Journal to record the HM Revenue and Customs liability

Account name		Debit £	Credit £
	▼		
	▼		

(c)   Journal to record the pension administrator liability

Account name		Debit £	Credit £
	▼		
	▼		

Picklist:

Bank
Employees' NI
Employer's NI
HM Revenue and Customs
Income tax
Net wages
Pension administrator
Wages control
Wages expense

Task 6 (14 marks)

This is a summary of transactions with customers during the month of August.

(a) **Show whether each entry will be a debit or credit in the sales ledger control account in the general ledger.**

Sales ledger control account

Details	Amount £	Debit ✓	Credit ✓
Balance of receivables at 1 August	15,100		
Goods sold on credit	28,375		
Payments received from credit customers	16,450		
Discounts allowed	425		
Goods returned by credit customers	900		

(b) **What will be the balance brought down on 1 September on the above account?**

£

(c) The following debit balances were in the sales ledger on 31 August.

	£
Kendrick plc	7,300
Askwith Ltd	4,680
Raston Permanent Ltd	5,461
Biomass plc	1,400
Nistral plc	2,009
Larkmead & Co	4,650

Complete the following table to reconcile the balances shown above with the sales ledger control account balance you have calculated in part (b).

	£
Sales ledger control account balance as at 31 August	
Total of sales ledger accounts as at 31 August	
Difference	

(d) What may have caused the difference you calculated in part (c)?

	✓
Goods returned may have been omitted from the sales ledger	
Discounts allowed may have been omitted from the sales ledger	
Goods returned may have been entered in the sales ledger twice	
Sales invoices may have been entered in the sales ledger twice	

It is important to reconcile the sales ledger control account on a regular basis.

(e) **Which ONE of the following statements is true?**

	✓
Reconciliation of the sales ledger control account assures managers that the amount showing as outstanding from customers is correct.	
Reconciliation of the sales ledger control account assures managers that the amount showing as outstanding to suppliers is correct.	
Reconciliation of the sales ledger control account will show if a purchases invoice has been omitted from the purchases ledger.	
Reconciliation of the sales ledger control account will show if a sales invoice has been omitted from the purchases ledger.	

Task 7 (14 marks)

A credit purchase return of £1,170 has been entered in the accounting records as £1,710. (Ignore VAT.)

(a) **Using the picklist below, record the journal entries needed in the general ledger to remove the incorrect entry.**

Account name	Amount £	Debit ✓	Credit ✓
▼			
▼			

(b) **Record the journal entries needed in the general ledger to record the correct entry.**

Account name	Amount £	Debit ✓	Credit ✓
▼			
▼			

Picklist:

Bank
Cash
Purchases ledger control
Purchases returns

Purchases returns day book
Suspense
Trade payables

(c) **Show ONE reason for producing the trial balance.**

	✓
To detect fraud	
To check that double entry has been performed correctly	
To comply with the statutory requirement	
To save time	

Task 8 (14 marks)

The bank statement and cash book for June are shown below

Required

(a) **Check the bank statement against the cash book and enter:**

- **Any transactions into the cash book as needed using the picklist provided**
- **The cash book balance carried down at 10 June**

Enter dates in the format "XX Jun".

Bank statement

Date 20XX	Details	Paid out £	Paid in £	Balance £
01 Jun	Balance b/f			1,250 C
02 Jun	Counter credit: Jonas Limited		5,000	6,250 C
02 Jun	Direct Debit: Waterville DC	250		6,000 C
03 Jun	Direct debit: Ocksan CC	300		5,700 C
03 Jun	Counter credit: Nadia & Co		3,250	8,950 C
03 Jun	Cheque 0123	2,500		6,450 C
06 Jun	Cheque 0125	750		5,700 C
07 Jun	Direct debit: Billymots Insurance	125		5,575 C
09 Jun	Bank interest		10	5,585 C
09 Jun	Bank charges	26		5,559 C
10 Jun	Counter credit: Jakir Ltd		850	6,409 C

D = Debit C = Credit

Cash book

Date 20XX	Details	Bank £	Date 20XX	Cheque number	Details	Bank £
01 Jun	Balance b/f	1,250	01 Jun	0123	Freddo Ltd	2,500
02 Jun	Jonas Limited	5,000	01 Jun	0124	Quicksand	1,200
03 Jun	Nadia & Co	3,250	01 Jun	0125	New & Co	750
10 Jun	Brilliant Ltd	4,500	01 Jun	0126	Wilmers	650
	▼		02 Jun	DD	Waterville DC	250
	▼				▼	
					▼	
					▼	
					▼	

Picklist:

Balance c/d
Bank charges
Bank interest
Billymots Insurance
Jakir Ltd
Nadia & Co
Ocksan CC
Waterville DC

(b) **Once the cash book has been updated, identify which of the following would be reconciling items on the bank reconciliation at 10 June. Make your selection by ticking the appropriate option(s).**

Reconciling Item	✓
Quicksand £1,200	
Wilmers £650	
Bank interest £10	
Brilliant Ltd £4,500	
Jakir Ltd £850	

Task 9 (10 marks)

On 30 June Pratesh Supplies extracted an initial trial balance which did not balance, and a suspense account with a credit balance of £420 was opened. On 1 July journal entries were prepared to correct the errors that had been found, and clear the suspense account. The journal entries to correct the errors, and the list of balances in the initial trial balance, are shown below.

Journal entries

Account name	Debit £	Credit £
Purchases ledger control		507
Suspense	507	
Purchases ledger control		507
Suspense	507	

Account name	Debit £	Credit £
Heat and light		1,056
Suspense	1,056	
Heat and light	1,650	
Suspense		1,650

Taking into account the journal entries, which will clear the suspense account, re-draft the trial balance by writing the figures in the debit or credit column. Do not enter your figures with decimal places in this task and do not enter a zero in the empty column.

	Balances extracted on 30 June £	Balances at 1 July	
		Debit £	Credit £
Motor vehicles	13,920		
Furniture and fittings	9,208		
Inventory	10,129		
Cash at bank	673		
Petty cash	250		
Sales ledger control	7,832		
Purchases ledger control	4,292		
VAT (owing to HM Revenue and Customs)	1,029		
Capital	10,000		
Sales	89,125		
Purchases	35,268		
Purchases returns	1,092		
Wages	18,279		
Marketing expenses	1,290		
Office expenses	3,287		

	Balances extracted on 30 June £	Balances at 1 July Debit £	Credit £
Rent and rates	2,819		
Heat and light	1,056		
Irrecoverable debts	127		
Motor expenses	1,820		
Totals			

Task 10 (14 marks)

On 28 February a trial balance was extracted and did not balance. The debit column totaled £245,100 and the credit column totaled £244,535.

(a) **What entry would be made in the suspense account to balance the trial balance?**

Account name	Amount £	Debit ✓	Credit ✓
Suspense			

The journal entries to correct all the bookkeeping errors, and a list of balances as they appear in the trial balance, are shown below

Account name	Debit ✓	Credit ✓
Suspense	1,200	
Bank		1,200
Advertising	1,200	
Bank		1,200

Account name	Debit ✓	Credit ✓
Office supplies	785	
Suspense		785
Suspense	150	
Bank interest		150

(b) **Complete the table below to show:**

- the balance of each account after the journal entries have been recorded
- whether each balance will be a debit or credit entry in the trial balance.

List of balances

Account name	Original balance £	New balance £	Debit ✓	Credit ✓
Office supplies	800			
Bank (debit)	4,500			
Advertising	1,960			
Bank interest received	450			

On 30 April a partially prepared trial balance for Pratesh Supplies new subsidiary company, Tarka Limited, had debit balances totalling £172,600 and credit balances totalling £168,400. The accounts below have not yet been entered into the trial balance.

(c)   Complete the table below to show whether each balance will be a debit or credit entry in the trial balance.

Account name	Balance £	Debit ✓	Credit ✓
Bank Loan	4,600		
VAT control (owed to HMRC)	3,496		
Fixed assets, fixtures & fitting	2,000		
Rent paid	1,896		

(d)   What will be the totals of each column of the trial balance after the balances in (c) have been entered?

Account name	Debit ✓	Credit ✓
Totals		

BPP PRACTICE ASSESSMENT 3
BOOKKEEPING CONTROLS

ANSWERS

Bookkeeping Controls
BPP practice assessment 3

Task 1 (12 marks)

(a)

Payment method	Reduce funds on the date of payment ✓	Reduce funds at a later date ✓
Credit card		✓
Bank draft	✓	
Cheque		✓
CHAPS	✓	
Direct Debit	✓	

(b)

Situation	Payment method
Purchase of a new computer from Laptops Limited, which is an online discount supplier	Credit card
Invoice payment to a supplier who requires immediate payment today for £2,400	Faster payment
Payment of the payroll for the month of March to employees	BACS direct credit
Payment of rent on a new office on a monthly basis (£2,450)	Standing order
Purchase of a new warehouse for the business (£125,000)	CHAPS

(c)

Error	✓
When a payment is made using a credit card, the money leaves the bank account immediately	
Standing orders are regular payments set up by the payer	✓
A bank draft can be cancelled by the payer after it has been issued	
Money leaves the payer's bank account immediately upon issuance of a bank draft	✓

(d)

Error in the general ledger	✓
Writing in the balance on the office stationery account incorrectly	
Recording a purchase from a credit supplier for £5,000 (no VAT) as £500 in both the purchases and the purchases ledger control accounts	✓
Recording a receipt from a credit customer in the cash sales account	
Recording a credit note from a supplier on the debit side of the purchases ledger control account and the debit side of the purchases returns account	

Task 2 (10 marks)

Error in the general ledger	Error disclosed by the trial balance ✓	Error NOT disclosed by the trial balance ✓
For a cash sale of £340 (no VAT), recording the amount as £34 in the cash book		✓
Recording £50 discount received on the credit side of PLCA and the debit side of the discount received account		✓
Recording a purchase from a supplier for £180 including VAT as £180 in the PLCA and purchases accounts and £30 in the VAT account	✓	
Making a transposition error when transferring a balance from the ledger account to the trial balance	✓	
Recording a payment from a credit customer for £200 in the debit side of the sales ledger account		✓

Task 3 (10 marks)

(a)

Date 20XX	Details	Bank £	Date 20XX	Cheque number	Details	Bank £
01 Mar	Balance b/f	7,250	01 Mar	820	Nixon Ltd	4,450
02 Mar	Jeffersons & Co	750	01 Mar	821	Roosevelts	2,100
22 Mar	Clinton & Clinton	9,250	02 Mar	822	GWB LLP	1,750
30 Mar	Garfield & Son	1,450	12 Mar	DD	Carter insurance	990
30 Mar	Adams	4,600	13 Mar	Payroll	K Brown	1,800
			13 Mar	Payroll	J Patel	1,600
			22 Mar		Bank charges	100
			31 Mar		Balance c/d	10,510
		23,300				23,300
1 Apr	Balance b/d	10,510				

(b)

Bank reconciliation statement	£
Balance per bank statement	6,210
Add:	
Garfield & Son	1,450
Adams	4,600
Total to add	6,050
Less:	
GWB LLP	1,750
Total to subtract	1,750
Balance as per cash book	10,510

(c)

Balance carried down £	Bank column totals £
10,510	23,300

Task 4 (10 marks)

(a) The answer is £576 (1,400 + 785 + 250 −1,350 − 509)

(b)

Account name	Amount £	Debit ✓	Credit ✓
Irrecoverable debts	480	✓	
VAT control	96	✓	
Sales ledger control	576		✓

(c)

Account name	Amount £	Account name	Credit ✓
Purchases	4,690	Balance b/f	1,200
Purchases	600	Sales	3,460
Irrecoverable debt	180	Balance c/d	2,010
Bank	1,200		
	6,670		6,670

Task 5 (12 marks)

(a)

Account name	Debit £	Credit £
Wages expense (900 + 10,260 + 1,300)	12,460	
Wages control		12,460

(b)

Account name	Debit £	Credit £
Wages control (2,335 + 925 + 1,300)	4,560	
HM Revenue and Customs		4,560

(c)

Account name	Debit £	Credit £
Wages control (900 + 780)	1,680	
Pension administrator		1,680

Task 6 (14 marks)

(a) **Sales ledger control account**

Details	Amount £	Debit ✓	Credit ✓
Balance of receivables at 1 August	15,100	✓	
Goods sold on credit	28,375	✓	
Payments received from credit customers	16,450		✓
Discounts allowed	425		✓
Goods returned by credit customers	900		✓

(b)

£	25,700

(c)

	£
Sales ledger control account balance as at 31 August	25,700
Total of sales ledger accounts as at 31 August	25,500
Difference	200

(d) The correct answer is: Goods returned may have been entered in the sales ledger twice

(e) The correct answer is: Reconciliation of the sales ledger control account assures managers that the amount showing as outstanding from customers is correct

Task 7 (14 marks)

(a)

Account name	Amount £	Debit ✓	Credit ✓
Purchases returns	1,710	✓	
Purchases ledger control	1,710		✓

(b)

Account name	Amount £	Debit ✓	Credit ✓
Purchases ledger control	1,170	✓	
Purchases returns	1,170		✓

(c)

	✓
To detect fraud	
To check that double entry has been performed correctly	✓
To comply with the statutory requirement	
To save time	

Task 8 (14 marks)

(a)

Date 20XX	Details	Bank £	Date 20XX	Cheque number	Details	Bank £
01 Jun	Balance b/f	1,250	01 Jun	0123	Freddo Ltd	2,50
02 Jun	Jonas Limited	5,000	01 Jun	0124	Quicksand	1,20
03 Jun	Nadia & Co	3,250	01 Jun	0125	New & Co	75
10 Jun	Brilliant Ltd	4,500	01 Jun	0126	Wilmers	65
09 Jun	Bank interest	10	02 Jun	DD	Waterville DC	25
10 Jun	Jakir Ltd	850	03 Jun	DD	Ocksan CC	30
			07 Jun	DD	Billymots Insurance	12
			09 Jun		Bank charges	2
			10 Jun		Balance c/d	9,05
		14,860				14,86

(b)

Reconciling Item	✓
Quicksand £1,200	✓
Wilmers £650	✓
Bank interest £10	
Brilliant Ltd £4,500	✓
Jakir Ltd £850	

Task 9 (10 marks)

	Balances extracted on 30 June £	Balances at 1 July Debit £	Balances at 1 July Credit £
Motor vehicles	13,920	13,920	
Furniture and fittings	9,208	9,208	
Inventory	10,129	10,129	
Cash at bank	673	673	
Petty cash	250	250	
Sales ledger control	7,832	7,832	
Purchases ledger control	4,292		5,306
VAT (owing to HM Revenue and Customs)	1,029		1,029
Capital	10,000		10,000
Sales	89,125		89,125
Purchases	35,268	35,268	
Purchases returns	1,092		1,092
Wages	18,279	18,279	
Marketing expenses	1,290	1,290	
Office expenses	3,287	3,287	
Rent and rates	2,819	2,819	
Heat and light	1,056	1,650	
Irrecoverable debts	127	127	
Motor expenses	1,820	1,820	
Totals		106,552	106,552

Task 10 (14 marks)

(a)

Account name	Amount £	Debit ✓	Credit ✓
Suspense	565		✓

(b)

Account name	Original balance £	New balance £	Debit ✓	Credit ✓
Office supplies	800	1,585	✓	
Bank (debit)	4,500	2,100	✓	
Advertising	1,960	3,160	✓	
Bank interest received	450	600		✓

(c)

Account name	Balance £	Debit ✓	Credit ✓
Bank Loan	4,600		✓
VAT control (owed to HMRC)	3,496		✓
Fixed assets, fixtures & fitting	2,000	✓	
Rent paid	1,896	✓	

(d)

Account name	Debit ✓	Credit ✓
Totals	176,496	176,496

Notes

Notes

Notes

Notes

Notes

Notes

```
LEARNING CENTRE
WINDSOR FOREST COLLEGES GROUP
HIGH STREET
EGHAM
SURREY
TW20 9DR
```